DAN HEISMAN

THE IMPROVING
CHESS THINKER

Second Edition
Revised and Expanded

MONGOOSE
Press

Publisher: Mongoose Press
1005 Boylston Street, Suite 324
Newton Highlands, MA 02461
info@mongoosepress.com
www.MongoosePress.com

ISBN 978-1-936277-48-3
Library of Congress Control Number: 2009926552

Distributed to the trade by National Book Network
custserv@nbnbooks.com, 800-462-6420
For all other sales inquiries please contact the publisher.

Editor: Jorge Amador
Cover Design: Kaloyan Nachev
Layout: Andrey Elkov
Printed in the United States of America

Second Edition
0 9 8 7 6 5 4 3 2 1

Dedication

To Dr. Adriaan de Groot, who I was amazed to learn had only passed away just before publication of the first edition of this book! Because Dr. de Groot performed his experiments years before I was born, I had assumed that he had passed away some time ago. But he performed his pioneering work at the age of 23 and lived into his 90s. Thanks for the legacy. I hope I have carried it forward in a worthy manner, at least in some tiny way.

Acknowledgements

I would like to thank my publisher, Mongoose Press, for giving me the incentive to get this material into the public's hands. I would also like to thank Howard Goldowsky for putting me in touch with Mongoose and for Howard's help with the manuscript. I would like to thank my first editor, Dr. Alexey Root, and the proofreader, NM Jonathan Hilton. Similarly, thanks to second edition editor Jorge Amador, who also provided guidance and feedback for all the work for this new edition, and second-edition proofreaders Troy Duncan and FM Rodion Rubenchik. I thank all the players who, over a period of more than forty years, participated in the exercises contained in this work — and the many more whose exercises were not included. Thanks to Hanon Russell, and now Mark Donlan, for allowing me to express my thoughts on chess instruction at the leading online magazine, Chess Café, via my *Novice Nook* column. Finally, I would like to thank IM Jeremy Silman, who gave me permission to include material from my *Thinking Cap* column, which I had written for his website.

Table of Contents

Preface to the First Edition

The Improving Chess Thinker owes its origins to two previous books:

* *Thought and Choice in Chess,* by Dr. Adriaan de Groot
* *Silman's Complete Endgame Course,* by IM Jeremy Silman

De Groot's work, because I duplicated his experiment requiring subjects to "think out loud" to find the best move in chess positions; and Silman's, because the layout of this book is similar to his, with each of the middle chapters devoted to protocols (the transcripts of "think out loud" exercises) provided by players one class higher than in the previous chapter. The strong acceptance and approval of this format encouraged me to seek out a publisher and make this book a reality.

A third book, *Inside the Chess Mind* by GM Jacob Aagaard, consists almost entirely of protocols. However, *Inside the Chess Mind* differs from *The Improving Chess Thinker* in several ways – the former primarily covers grandmaster- and international master-level players with little additional comment.

The Improving Chess Thinker fills in the gaps by including players of all strengths below grandmaster. It also contains instructive comments and additional chapters on the thought process.

Finally, a tip of the hat to one of my earlier books, *The Improving Annotator,* whose title helped me to decide on *The Improving Chess Thinker.*

Preface to the Second Edition

This edition is a major upgrade. Here's an overview of the most significant changes. We have:

- Added protocols to all the class (rating under 2000) chapters but significantly boosted the "Expert and Above" chapter with numerous additional protocols by players in the 2000-2500 range, for a total of almost one hundred protocols;

- Added the chapter "The Most Common Thought Process Mistakes," which provides discussion and examples of these errors;

- Added a short chapter providing additional humorous and interesting stories about giving lessons and using the de Groot exercise;

- Made corrections and numerous additions to the material from the first edition;

- Expanded the Glossary to include more terms used within the book;

- Expanded Chapter 13, changed the title, and included a section about finding positions suitable for giving de Groot exercises, with an additional half-dozen sample positions; and

- Moved Chapter 9, "Thought Process Basics," to after the protocols. It was formerly Chapter 2.

The net result is a more extensive examination of the typical thinking processes of players below grandmaster level, and the lessons that can be learned from them. I believe that this work represents the most extensive compilation of examples illustrating how players think at all levels from beginner up to 2500, and hope that the reader will find it entertaining, instructional, and valuable from a historical viewpoint.

Introduction

I enjoy performing chess research in the following two areas:

1) How do players learn and improve?
2) How do players think during a game?

These two questions may seem to be only remotely related, but they have many aspects in common.

When someone is taught to play baseball, they don't primarily learn about innings, outs, and bases. Instead, they are taught how to bat, throw, catch, and run the bases. But when players learn chess, the only things they are usually taught — even by competent beginner's books — are the basic rules such as checkmate and draws, and how to move the pieces. Then they are taught more and more about what the pieces can do. A few principles like "Get all your pieces into the game," "At the start of the game try to control the center," "For your first move, push a pawn two squares in the center," "Castle your king early," or "Knight on the rim your future is dim" are thrown in for good measure.

But chess is a thinking game, and few beginners are taught *how to think* to find their move. No wonder everyone learns their "chess thought process" in a non-systematic way that quickly leads to bad thinking habits. A thought process represents all the generic "steps" or sequences of logic that go through the player's mind during both his move and his opponent's move. A thought *process* does *not* include the *content* of what is being thought.

For example, systematically searching for threats after an opponent's move is part of a process, but deciding where to put a bishop in a particular position is content.

Beginners are first taught basics such as how to differentiate the queen and the king, how each piece moves, and that the players alternate making moves. It is not effective to immediately thereafter attempt to teach a thought process via suggestions such as, "The first thing you do is examine your opponent's move to see its effect on the position..." Beginners need time to assimilate basic concepts before attempting to implement higher-level ideas.

However, it is also true that *never* to teach someone the basics of the thinking process can lead to bad habits and, consequently, to unnecessarily chaotic mental habits. Some aspects of the thought process are common among good chessplayers and can be taught relatively early in a player's development.

I have explored this phenomenon in many places, notably online via my columns *Novice Nook* at Chess Café and *The Thinking Cap* at IM Jeremy Silman's website; in blogs and articles for Chess.com; and with books such as *Everyone's Second Chess Book, A Guide to Chess Improvement,* and *Looking for Trouble.*

The Improving Chess Thinker explores the results of "think out loud" exercises performed by subjects of differing levels of ability. These exercises are based on those performed by the first serious researcher into the chess thought process, Dr. Adriaan de Groot.

In the late 1930's, Dr. de Groot, a Dutch professional psychologist and chess master, recorded the thought processes of dozens of players at all levels (mostly stronger players). His purpose was to investigate scientifically how chessplayers really think. Players were given a position and asked to find a move while at the same time verbalizing everything they were thinking. Each subject's verbalization was recorded and transcribed; these transcriptions were called *protocols.*

Dr. de Groot analyzed dozens of protocols and published his results. His publication was a doctoral-type thesis that was eventually translated into English as the book *Thought and Choice in Chess* (1965; reprinted in 2008 by the Amsterdam Academic Archive). *Thought and Choice in Chess* is not so much a "chess book" as it is a psychology book about chess.

With the 1938 AVRO tournament nearby, Dr. de Groot garnered some of the best players of the day to participate in his experiment: Alexander Alekhine, Reuben Fine, Dr. Max Euwe, Paul Keres, and right on down the line to a few class players. Most of the protocols were by players of at least master strength. Dr. de Groot wanted to find out how players arrived at a move in a typical tournament setting. He did *not* show them "White/Black to Play and Win" positions, since the thought process for problems is much different:

- In "play and win" problems, the solver is not just looking for the best move: he is required to find a move that leads to a forced win in all variations. If he doesn't find a forced win with one candidate, he tries another. When solving these problems, one doesn't give up until a solution is found, because it is given that there is one!

- In normal positions, such as those found in tournament games and most de Groot exercises, one should attempt to find the best move possible *in the available time*. Weak players often play more quickly than they should; for strong players, the opposite problem is often the case. Since *proving* the best move on each move throughout the game often takes more time than the clock allows, subjects should use time management and practical alterations of their maximal thought process to find a move in a reasonable amount of time.

Therefore Dr. de Groot selected interesting positions from some of his games and asked the players to come up with a move in a reasonable amount of time, as if they were playing an important tournament game. He chose "rich" positions that would be interesting and would help to differentiate the abilities of the various subjects. Dr. de Groot used dozens of positions, but most of his work was centered around three, which he labeled Positions "A," "B," and "C."

As a result of this fascinating experiment, Dr. de Groot was the first to prove that, contrary to popular belief, grandmasters do *not* think deeper than strong club players — say, those at United States Chess Federation (USCF) "expert" level, rated between 2000-2199. What separates grandmasters from experts is not just the incisiveness of their analysis — they analyze much more accurately and efficiently — but also the *number of positions they already know how to play*. Dr. de Groot speculated that grandmasters know how to play roughly 100,000+ positions, while masters know only 10,000+. It is much easier to know something than to figure it out. I might add that grandmasters are also much better at *evaluating* positions than are experts, enabling them to choose better moves even when their actual move-by-move analysis is similar to that of lesser players.

Thought and Choice in Chess is a tough but fascinating read. I persevered enough to plow my way through it in the late 1960s. Afterwards, I began recording the thought processes of some local players. I remember doing this in college, but I believe I began while in high school.

Today I use de Groot's exercise as a tool in my full-time profession as a chess instructor. Thus I have been administering his thinking process "protocol" exercise for some 45 years! I hope it is not considered immodest to say that I undoubtedly have given the "de Groot exercise" to many more players than did Dr. de Groot!

To administer the exercise, I primarily used the same positions that Dr. de Groot gives in his book. Immediately after the exercise, I debrief the student and usually read him what Dr. Max Euwe or others thought about the same position. I then compare the student's thought process to that of the former world champion's.

Many of my students have expressed the "eye-opener" effect of doing the de Groot exercise, hearing my feedback, and comparing their processes to that of Dr. Euwe or others. If I repeat the exercise with the same student, I use different positions, occasionally ones from my own games.

Now for a little background on how the exercise positions were chosen. There are two types of positions with regard to the type of thought process best used to find a move: *analytical* and *non-analytical:*

- Analytical positions are identified by the clash of the two forces, and require the well-known "if I go there, then he has to go there" thinking process. These usually involve the kind of analysis trees found in *Thought and Choice in Chess* or in Alexander Kotov's *Think Like a Grandmaster.*

- Non-analytical positions usually lack tactical opportunities and are more positional in nature. These are found in the early opening or sometimes in closed or locked positions, and contain little direct clash of the armies. A non-analytical thought process relies on a player's application of principles and less on analysis, and thus requires more judgment. Non-analytical positions can be considered *judgmental.*

This book, like de Groot's and Aagaard's, is heavily biased toward analytical positions. Analytical positions are both much more conducive to objective play and usually more critical. Analytical positions are easier (and, in a sense, more fun) to study because one examines specific moves and the evaluations of the resultant positions. In contrast, in non-analytical positions, one relies on the general principles of strategic play. That is not to say that non-analytical positions are not important. However, at least at most lower levels of play, playing analytical positions well is the key to winning most games.

Chapter Overview

The first chapter describes the de Groot exercise. The several chapters that follow (2 though 8) each contain about a dozen representative protocols made by players in a particular rating class, starting with Class F (below 1000) and working up to Expert (above 2000) and Master (above 2200).

Each protocol includes the identification of the protocol position, the subject's rating, his age ("adult" if 18 or over), and the estimated total time taken. Subjects with Internet Chess Club (ICC) standard ratings are rated approximately 150 rating points above their USCF equivalents. So a subject with an ICC rating of 1500 is about 1350 USCF. All ratings are USCF unless otherwise noted.

To make the information more interesting and instructive, comments are added after each protocol, such as what was done correctly or incorrectly, or what could be learned from studying the player's thought process.

The end of each "class" chapter features a summary of thought process aspects characteristic of that level. Also highlighted are suggestions that would help a player progress to the next class level. For example, the section on C players (1400-1599 USCF) contrasts the thought processes of C players with those of players in the 1600-1799 (Class B) range.

The latter chapters, beginning with Chapter 9, "Thought Process Basics," contain additional instructional material on the thought process, including a separate chapter on time management and lessons I have learned from administering the de Groot exercise. They conclude with Chapter 14, "Additional Exercise and Lesson Tales."

Appendix A contains Dr. Max Euwe's protocol (recorded transcript) of the "de Groot A" position, plus some observations. Appendix B contains computer-aided analysis of each exercise position.

How to Use This Book

This book can be used in multiple ways:

- As a text supporting psychologists, demonstrating how chessplayers think at various levels;

- As a "chess book" showing players how the thought process works in practice. This includes aspects such as which approaches are effective and which are not, how much time players use in determining a move, how much effort is spent on various tasks such as identifying candidate moves, and so on;

- As a manual for improving one's chess thinking process. This can be accomplished by doing any or all of the following:

  o The protocols in the book are for the six positions found in Chapter 1. Before reading the rest of the book, take each of the six positions and carefully choose which move you would play, taking no longer than you would in an important slow event. That way you can compare the moves you chose and the thought process you used to choose them with the players' protocols throughout the book;

  o Read the chapter (2 through 8) representing your rating class. Then read the chapters one and two classes above your level to see what knowledge, process, and logic is applied by superior players to arrive at their move;

  o Focus on the sections of the book which address the thought process and its cousin, time management, found primarily in Chapters 9-13;

  o Skim the protocols and focus on the comments after each and on the summaries for each section. Much of the instructional value in the book is contained in these comments;

  o Learn from the general principles involving the thought process. These principles are placed in *italics* outside the protocols.

Tip: Because there are only six protocol positions, it would be repetitious if we provided a diagram of one of these six positions before every protocol. Therefore, if you are reading a protocol and want to see the *starting* position, bookmark the protocol positions in Chapter 1 or make a separate copy of these positions to keep them handy. To minimize this concern, most protocols include a diagram of a key analysis position.

Chapter 1

The Exercise

The de Groot experiment allows a researcher to determine how chessplayers find their moves during competitive play. This is clearly different from how a player solves a puzzle. In a puzzle, the solution is guaranteed. Thus a player can adopt the attitude that, "If this attempt does not solve the puzzle, then I will try something else. The solution has to be there."

In the de Groot exercise, the players (or subjects of the experiment) are asked to find moves just as they would in a tournament game. During a game there is no guarantee that there is anything good to find, such as a mate or the win of material. The position may contain no clear ideas or candidate moves that lead to winning or even drawn positions. In many practical positions there is no "best" move — there may be several almost equally good alternatives.

Thus a researcher performing the de Groot exercise is interested in how players find their moves when the goals are open-ended and a clearly best move may or may not exist. For the chessplayer, performing the exercise and learning from its results can have enormous practical benefits.

Since chess is a mental sport — a thinking game — the process used to find a move is of importance not only in examining the source of the player's current strength, but also in determining his future possibilities for improvement. If a player has a poor process for move selection, then his ability to increase his playing strength is impaired, even if his other chess skills and knowledge improve. An exercise that can diagnose a player's process and expose him to a superior player's process is a beneficial tool for both instruction and psychological study.

In *Thought and Choice in Chess,* de Groot relied on one position for many of his conclusions. He also included two other "primary" positions and a few supplemental ones as well. In giving this exercise to hundreds of my students, friends, and acquaintances, I also utilized mostly de Groot's first position, which he labeled "de Groot A." But I also occasionally used the other two primary de Groot exercises ("de Groot B" and "de Groot C") as well as a few of my own.

The following six diagrams are the ones discussed in this book. The first three are from de Groot's book; "de Groot Shafritz" is from one of my games; and the final two were from my students' games.

If you have not looked ahead and attempted to play the positions, I suggest you now set aside some time and decide which move you would play in each of the following six positions, assuming a 40/2 (40 moves in 2 hours) time control and sufficient time on your clock. If you want to make note of how you came to your conclusions and the salient points behind the move you selected, that can be additionally helpful.

de Groot A: White to play

de Groot B: Black to play

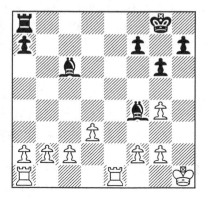

de Groot C: Black to play

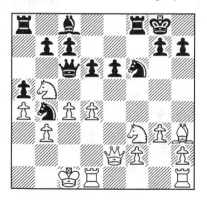

de Groot Shafritz: White to play

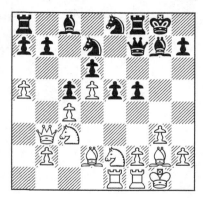

de Groot Zyme: White to play

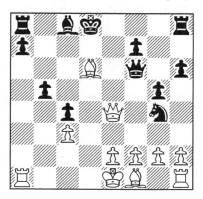

de Groot Ernie: White to play

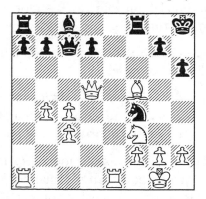

All of the above positions are at least somewhat analytical. Among the six, the de Groot Shafritz is the most "quiet" but it still depends partly on analysis. The most frequently used position, de Groot A, requires analysis primarily. Thus the bias in this book is toward the analytical thought process. While it is possible to do a de Groot exercise with a purely non-analytical position, it is not as instructive. So I always choose a position requiring at least some analysis.

The best ways for a student to improve his thinking process in *non-analytical* positions are the "traditional" best ways to improve chess judgment: extensive experience in slow games, reviewing one's games with stronger players, reading annotated master games, learning principles and how to apply them, and so on. My archived *Novice Nook* columns at www.chesscafe. com deal with the best ways to implement these traditional learning methods.

Instructions for the de Groot Exercise

Before participating in the exercise, each subject was given the following instructions:

- Pretend you are playing at the World Open, with the time limit 40 moves in two hours;

- Your game is important but not necessarily the final round when you are playing for big money;

- You have plenty of time left on your clock — more than an hour, but certainly not an unlimited time;

- Don't do more or less analysis than you would in the above situation; i.e. don't "show off" for the exercise;

- This is not a "play and win" problem. This is supposed to be an interesting position from a real game, and so to look for a "winning" (as opposed to "best") move may be a futile effort;

- Use stream-of-consciousness verbalization. Try to say everything you think; don't think quietly and then summarize. This is important because I can only help you based on what you say; if you think something and don't say it, I have to assume you did not think it; and

- Use algebraic notation. That is, don't say, "I will take that pawn." Instead say "♘xd5."

Live subjects were given a clock to time their move and instructed to make their move and hit the clock when finished. For Internet and/or over-the-phone students, I recorded the starting and ending times so that I could calculate their total thinking times. These subjects were instructed to conclude by stating their move choice and then saying, "Push Clock!" to indicate that they were finished.

During a student's verbalization, I tried to restrict my comments and interruptions to the following:

- "Please speak up – I can't hear you;" and

- "You are not saying anything. I cannot use the exercise to help you improve if you don't articulate what you are thinking."

As happened with Dr. de Groot, I occasionally had to remind a subject that the clock was running and they had used significant time. I usually did not do this until 30 minutes or more had elapsed.

Although the purpose of the exercise was to see how players found a move under "real" conditions, I let each subject know that there were two reasons why their verbalization would take much longer than it would to make an identical move at the World Open:

- No one can think out loud as quickly or as efficiently as they can in silence; and

- Unlike a real game, players were given the position "cold" and needed time to get acclimated – to figure out the material count, the threats, etc.

I estimate that these two factors caused roughly a 2:1 ratio in the length of time it would take to make a move, so if a player were to take 7 minutes for the same move at the World Open, it would take about 14 minutes to do it as a de Groot exercise. Therefore, subjects were advised to divide by two to roughly estimate their equivalent over-the-board thinking times. All times given in the book are the actual times.

Although some of my earliest protocols were tape-recorded, all the protocols in this book were recorded manually. This necessitated taking some shortcuts – whenever a subject said something irrelevant or redundant, it was usually ignored. For example, if a player said, "I can play knight takes the queen's pawn. That's capturing the pawn in the center. Let's see what that capture does. I am threatening to win a knight and go ahead a piece," then I might have written, "I can play ♘xd5 to win a center pawn. Let's see – I am threatening to win a knight and go ahead a piece," or something similar.

The exception was a student on the Internet Chess Club who was hard of hearing and, by necessity, typed his thoughts. That made his protocols (A-1 and A-2 in Chapter 7) different and interesting, so they were included in this book.

Just as the subject can't talk as fast as he can think, I can't write as fast as they talk! There was no budget to hire a professional stenographer. I strongly believe that for the hundreds of protocols transcribed I retained the essence of what the subject intended. But if a researcher is trying to find how many times a player stuttered or used passive tense, these protocols will be quite useless since they are certainly not verbatim. However, I do believe that the "shortened" protocols presented in the book in no way detract from its chess utility.

Chapters 2-8 present samples of actual protocols by ascending rating class. Each chapter represents a rating class and contains protocols of players who were in that class at the time of the exercise. Analysis diagrams are provided for instructional purposes and as an aid to reader visualization of the protocol (not that visualizing an entire protocol is suggested or necessary).

Occasionally, multiple protocols are presented for the same subject, each utilizing a different position. For ease of reading, multiple exercises by a single subject are placed consecutively in the chapter representing his lowest (initial) rating.

There are two types of comments interspersed in the middle of the protocol:

- Parentheses indicate outside actions or comments that reflect the action *of the player,* such as "(silent)" if he paused for a long time;

- Brackets represent my thoughts at the time. Since I did not interrupt my students (with the two exceptions noted above), these comments were not verbalized but were often used during the post-exercise review. My use of "[*sic*]" usually means that the subject is making a clear mistake in analysis or visualization. The use of "[!]"indicates that the subject has made a comment that is very insightful for their level of ability; finally noticed an important point or move that should have been noticed earlier; or committed a surprising error considering the player's previous comments or his level of play. A frequent note is "[no eval]," meaning that the subject did not try to evaluate which side stood better, by how much, and why.

After each protocol, there is a discussion of the interesting aspects of that protocol. These aspects may include typical problems for the protocol, identification of key steps that were lacking (such as counting material or doing an evaluation), and/or good points that others at that level may lack. The summary at the end of each chapter identifies common strengths and weaknesses at that level, and discusses thought process improvements that could be made by those players to get to the next level.

The post-protocol discussion usually does not emphasize mistakes in the subject's analysis — everyone makes mistakes in their analysis. Instead, the emphasis is on discussing the pros and cons of the subject's *process* for their analysis. However, instructive mistakes in analysis may still be included in the discussion.

Post-Exercise Review

After each exercise, I reviewed the most instructive points with the student, including both things they did well and particular areas to note for improvement. There is a good correlation between the comments found after the protocols and these review sessions with the student, though some parts of the post-exercise reviews were omitted to avoid repetition.

The review of the exercise often took longer than the exercise itself. It was not uncommon for a de Groot exercise plus the review to take more than a normally scheduled lesson of one hour. During the review we would discuss the student's process — looking to see whether he or she ever evaluated the exercise position, looked for possible opponent threats, took a reasonable amount of time compared to the criticality of the position, and was thorough and systematic in their analysis — and covered any other issue that was particularly striking or instructive.

As part of the review, I usually read Dr. Euwe's instructive protocol (de Groot A), especially if the student had analyzed the same position (see Appendix A). Before reading Dr. Euwe, I have found it very helpful to make the following suggestion:

"You don't have to follow all of Dr. Euwe's analysis, which can be quite rigorous. I want you to concentrate upon following his process — how he was able to find his move; what logic he used."

I also took questions from the student, e.g. if they were curious about the "truth" of the position (see Appendix B), desired analytical reasons why their moves were not best, wished to pinpoint ways to improve their process-es, or wondered why Dr. Euwe approached the problem the way he did.

For example, at the end of Dr. Euwe's protocol he concludes with con-ditional comments like, "Probably some more accidents will happen" and "Much is still up in the air," so I often ask my student:

"Why would a world champion make a bunch of statements about not being sure about the move and then immediately make it without resolving those issues?"

The instructive answer is that Euwe, like all good players, *is not as interested in predicting the future or figuring out whether his move wins as he is in proving that he has found the best move he can*. Once he does that, his work is over. If you asked Euwe whether or not his move was winning, he might have answered, "Maybe; we will know in a move or two." So once he found that his move was better than any other, he made it and, efficiently, left the rest of the analysis for later.

If the student showed interest in reading additional high-level protocols, I usually referred him to GM Aagaard's book *Inside the Chess Mind*.

After completing this review, one of my students (now a lawyer in New York) exclaimed, "That was the best lesson I ever had! I wish that all my lessons could be so helpful." I replied, "Yes, unfortunately there is only one 'first' time for doing a de Groot exercise. But most everyone finds the exer-cise rewarding and instructive."

Often I would conclude my review this way: "After this exercise, I don't expect you to think like Dr. Euwe — I just want to take you one step in the right direction on your journey. Next time you have an analytical position, you can approach it just a little bit more like he did. It's as if you wanted to go to the moon but you did not know which direction to go — it's still far away, but at least now your small steps are in the right direction."

Exercise Tales

When you give the same exercise several hundred times, there are bound to be a few humorous or interesting anecdotes. Here are two:

Soon after I purchased *Thought and Choice in Chess,* I took out my reel-to-reel tape recorder and asked my friend, USCF Expert Jerry Kolker, to do the "de Groot A" exercise. Jerry statically evaluated the position as clearly better for White. However, once he started selecting candidate moves and analyzing them, he could not find a continuation that matched his static evaluation. That is, he could not find a candidate move which would lead to a position where White was ahead as much as he thought White should be. At this point he could have done one of three things:

1. Realized that his static evaluation was too high, and lowered his expectations. To justify this conclusion, he should find a reason why he over-evaluated White's position;

2. Realized that he hadn't found the best move, and played a less-than-optimal move because his clock was running and it wouldn't be worth the extra time to try and find the better move; or

3. Kept searching until he found a move which matched his static evaluation.

Well, since Jerry was not playing a real game with a clock, he certainly didn't do #2! Instead, he stated that he was convinced that his static evaluation was correct and that he just hadn't found the right continuation yet. He said, "There must be a better move!" He continued to search until, *mirabile dictu,* he finally found the continuation that made him satisfied. And, according to de Groot and future computer analysis, it was the right move! (See Appendix B.)

What is the moral of Jerry's tale? Your static evaluation can set your expectation for your search. If you are losing, you should not expect to find a move that wins. If you are better by a certain amount, then you should be able to find a move that results in your position being better by about that same amount.

Another time I had an adult student who complained that he did not know how to play slowly. He felt he played too fast because that was all he could do. There was nothing more for him to think about. I told him that I should be able to help him. When slow chess is played correctly, it generally takes time to find the best move one can. If grandmasters are given more time, they use it.

For the de Groot exercise, I gave that student the usual instructions, including, "Pretend you are at the World Open – don't do more or less analysis than you really would do in a game there." The idea is that you don't want to show off for the exercise. I can't help diagnose your thought process and make you a better player if you are not using the same thought process you would use in a real game.

I assumed that, armed with this instruction, my "fast" student would, indeed, play quickly. Then I could help him figure out what else he should be thinking about and help him slow down appropriately. My student began the exercise. However, instead of rapidly making a move, he became the "Energizer Bunny" of thinking! He kept going, and going, and going. After 35 minutes it was clear that he was not even close to coming to a decision! So I interrupted him and asked,

"Are you sure taking this long is what you would really do on each move in a tournament game?" He answered,

"Of course not!"

So much for the instruction about taking the de Groot exercise just as if you were in a real game. It turned out this student did, after all, know how to take his time on a move...

For more Exercise Tales, see Chapter 14.

Chapter 2

Class F and Below

This chapter includes players rated below 1000 USCF, or roughly below 1150 Internet Chess Club (ICC) standard.

This beginning level is composed primarily of youngsters or adults who have just started playing. Their thought processes (especially youngsters') are usually way too fast, quite superficial, and rarely systematic, and they contain little regard for safety.

For each protocol, I list the de Groot position (for example, de Groot A, de Groot B, de Groot C, etc.; see Chapter 1 for those positions); the age of the subject; the subject's rating; and the time the subject spent to choose his move.

Comments in parentheses indicate outside actions or comments that reflect the action of the player, such as (silent) if he paused for a long time. Comments in brackets are my thoughts. My frequent use of [*sic*] means that the subject is making a clear mistake in analysis or visualization. In contrast, [!] indicates that the player has made a comment that is either very insightful for their level of ability or a surprising error. A frequent note is [no eval], meaning that the subject did not try to evaluate which side stood better, by how much, and why.

Protocol F-1 (de Groot A; adult; 750; 13 minutes):
1.♗h6 [no eval]. 1.♘d7 no good. 1.♘xf7. 1.♖fe1 doesn't help. 1.♗h6 to attack rook. 1.♘xd5 he can just recapture and get his rook open. 1.♗xd5: no, that doesn't work. 1.♘d7 attacks the rook but then 1...♘xd7 2.♗xe7 ♘xe7. The knight on e5 is safe. 1.♕a5 does not make much sense [?]. Hmm. 1.♘d7 then 1...♘xd7 or 1...♗xd7. 1.♘xg6 fxg6 → 2.♕h3 he takes my bishop. The knight on f6 guards h7, so I have to remove that knight with 3.♗xf6 ♗xf6. Doesn't work. 1.♕h3 with the idea of 2.♕h6. 1.♗xf6 ♗xf6 no good. 1.♗xf6 ♗xf6 2.♗xd5 exd5 3.♘xd5. Push clock.

Unlike many beginners, Subject F-1 did take his time, which is good. However, the density of his analysis per unit time is extremely low, indicating he was spending a lot of time just trying to figure out what might be possible. In the end, without verifying his analysis, he indicated a "principal variation" (his guess for best moves for both sides; PV) which involved trying to remove the guard. In his PV, he forgot about the bishop on c6:

de Groot A
Black to play after PV 1.♗xf6 ♗xf6 2.♗xd5 exd5 3.♘xd5?

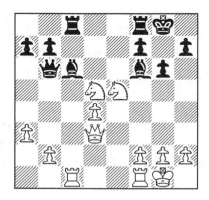

White's last move, the capture 3.♘xd5, is a visualization error since 3... ♗xd5 would win the knight.

Anyone can make this mistake in analysis. However, if you feel that you are winning material or giving checkmate, then this is a "red flag" indicating you should be extra careful. Whenever there is a "red flag" in your analysis, *you should verify that analysis before committing yourself to the first move of a critical sequence. If the sequence doesn't work, it can either cost you the game or just the opportunity to have played a much better move instead.*

In addition, if the subject were trying to get in ♘d7, then he is making the common mistake of sacrificing a piece to win the exchange, and that is not good, either. We will see this "give up a piece to win the exchange" mistake quite frequently among the de Groot A protocols of weaker players.

Protocol F-2 (de Groot A; adult; 800; 4.5 minutes)
1.♗h6 [no eval] 1...♘f4 attacks the queen, so better is 1.♕h3. Would like

> if you feel that you are winning material or giving checkmate, then this is a "red flag" indicating you should be extra careful. Whenever there is a "red flag" in your analysis, you should verify that analysis before committing yourself to the first move of a critical sequence. If the sequence doesn't work, it can either cost you the game or just the opportunity to have played a much better move instead.

the queen on h6. That leaves the pawn open on d4 for queen to capture so 1.♕h3 ♕xd4 not so great. How can I protect the d-pawn and make an offensive move at the same time? He could not do that [why?]. 1.♗h6 ♘f4 threatens queen then 2.♗xf4. So 1.♗h6 is decent. Still leaves pawn on d4 open — no it does not; ♕d3 stays. He has the bishop pair [sic]. So I could play 1.♘xc6 to win the bishop pair immediately and he could capture with the queen or rook. Let's see — game is tied [finally counts material]. OK. Pick off bishop pair with 1.♘xc6. Push clock.

This protocol contains some typical "beginner" thought process errors. The subject did not notice that Black was threatening 1...♕xb2 and did not consider all capturing sequences. At least the reason for the move — to win the bishop pair — is a lot better than those of many intermediate players! Notice that the subject's one big idea is to checkmate the black king on the dark squares. Therefore, he focuses on getting the queen and the bishop over there. Many weaker players go right for a checkmate pattern, no matter how hopeless or uncalled for by Steinitz's Rules, which require a player to have (or be able to generate) some advantage near the opponent's king before he can expect to successfully attack there. However, weaker players often get into bad habits of making otherwise counterproductive checkmate threats because their weak opponents sometimes allow such checkmates! At least in this case the subject properly saw that the checkmate attempt was hopeless. When the idea failed, his fallback — the bishop pair — was reasonable.

Protocol F-3 (de Groot A; age 11; 950; 2.5 minutes)
1.♗h6 [no eval] attacks the rook and then... or 1.♘xd5 exd5 2.♗xd5 ♗xd5 no good. 1.♗xf6 ♗xf6 something. 1.♖fe1 or something. 1.♘a4 to attack the queen. What other piece to move? 1.♘e4 ♘xe4 2.♕xe4 ♗xg5 not good. I think that's it [what's "it"?]. I think that's it. 1.♗h6. Push clock.

It's good that this subject considered the capture on d5. However, he rejected the capture simply because it did not win material. In other words, he treated the position as if it were a problem. This is a common error among players rated below ~1600.

The subject did not consider all of his opponent's recaptures after 1.♘xd5. But he is correct that, if you find one reply which does not suit you (as he did, although for the wrong reason), then you don't have to consider the others. That would be a waste of time.

As it turns out, the subject's chosen move — 1.♗h6 — forces the rook to a better position (d8). Therefore, unless there is a strong follow-up, this kind of threat should usually be eliminated quickly as a candidate move.

Protocol F-4 (de Groot A; adult; 900; 13 minutes)
Piece Safety — protected vs. adequately protected. Checks, captures. Knight takes pawn [?]. 1.♗xf6 ♗xf6. 1.♕xg6+ takes the pawn. 1.♘xd5. 1.♘e4 toward a knight fork. I had better make a move soon [7.5 minutes]. I can take the bishop on c6 [does not mention it wins the bishop pair]. I could play 1.♗h6. If I take the knight I am subject to a pawn fork [?]. Running out of things to think. I haven't come up with a good move. I am contemplating 1.♘e4. 1.♘e4 ♘xe4 2.♕xe4 ♘xc3 [sic] with discovered attack. I can't find the helpful move. I will play 1.♘e4.

The subject first looks at safety — good. Of course, counting the material would help, too! Then he considers checks and captures, again good. Unfortunately, he does not consider all captures and see how good each recapture is. This subject only had a few random thoughts in the first seven minutes and was, by far, the least verbal subject (per unit of time) in the book!

Protocol F-5 (de Groot A; adult; 850; several minutes)
1.♕xg6+ no good [no eval]. Captures: 1.♗xd5, 1.♗xf6 (lots of silence). 1.♖fe1 strengthens the center or 1.♖ce1 then 2.♘g6 ♖fe8. 1.♘e4 pressures f6 — protected. If 1...♘xe4 2.♕xe4 ♘xc3 [sic!].

de Groot A
Black to play after 1.♘e4 ♘xe4 2.♕xe4
Retained image; both F-4 and F-5 wish to play 2...♘xc3 but don't "see"
the real free piece 2...♗xg5

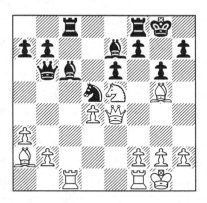

1.f4 to support the bishop and knight. 1...♘xf4 2.♖xf4 that's not bad. So 1.f4 ♘xf4 2.♖xf4 if he... If not 1...♘xf4 then I have the break move f4-f5. I think that is my best move so far [good!]. 1.♗h6 pressures the rook so 1.f4 hit clock.

When Subject F-5 considered 2...♘xc3 right before the diagram, he was making the same retained image error made by Subject F-4. Both "see" the discovered attack on the queen and want to capture the knight on c3 which is no longer there, and neither notices the bishop hanging on g5.

Despite some confusion, great credit to Subject F-5 for mentioning that a move was his best move so far! This use of the "King of the Hill" (see Chapter 10.2) is very rare among weaker players. Yet it was not beyond World Champion Max Euwe who, when considering 1.♘xc6, mentioned, "If I don't find anything better I can always do this." This is the equivalent of stating that the move is the King of the Hill (see Appendix A).

Protocol F-6 (de Groot A; adult; 700; 17 minutes)
White's knight, bishop on g5 both attack f6, the bishop is unprotected. The queen on d3 has OK diagonals. Black's knight on d5 is attacked and defended. ♖c1 has an open file; Black's rook also on c8; both sides castled. The pawn on g6 is advanced — there is a hole at h6, so 1.♗h6 is a candidate and 1.♗xf6.

1.♗h6 candidate; if 1...♘g4 then 2.♘xg4. 1.♗xf6 yield no advantage. There is an isolated queen's pawn; White has three pawn islands; Black has two. White's bishop on a2 attacks the knight on d5, defended by lesser pieces. 1.♗h6 is best so far. Let me do a sanity check on 1.♗h6. How would I follow that? 2.♘g4 ♘xg4; 2.♗xc6 — the bishop is protected — waste of time because the knight is good. The queen would be good on h6. I could play ♕h3-h6; have not looked any farther. Get pieces from White's queenside to the kingside. 1.♘a4 attacks the queen, but then he plays 1...♗xa4. Looking at various options — anything else? 1.♘xg6 hxg6 may be OK, but 1...fxg6 is good for Black. 1.♘d7 ♗xd7 but the bishop protects the knight at d5. 1.♘d7 ♗xd7 then d5 is less protected: 2.♘xd5 exd5 3.♗xd5 is nothing. 1.♕h3 and I can't coordinate the queen and the bishop. 1.♗h6, 1.♘a4 are candidates. The bishop at e7 is weak, so 1.♘e4. After 1.♗h6 what can happen? Can only be attacked. The rook is attacked — would move, so is viable. Am I missing some other great things? 1.♘xd5 (or 1.♗xd5) guarded three times — forget it — trying to take on c8. What is he threatening? d4 is attacked by the queen. [15 minutes] f2 is safe, back rank. 1...♗b5 attacks the queen and the rook; not good. 2.♗c4 ♖xc4 but 2.♘xb5 so 1.♗h6. Sanity check: seeing if ...♘d5 can do something dangerous. Can move queen. 1...♘f4 2.♗xf4. So 1.♗h6. Push clock.

This protocol shows that not all beginning-level players move extremely fast. Subject F-6 waited until 15 of his eventual 17 minutes had elapsed before considering the opponent's threats. Note the common error of assuming that just because d5 is guarded more times than it is attacked, capturing there is not good. Many weak players make the common mistake of treating each chess position like a "play and win" problem. They look for wins through forcing moves and, if the win is not there, reject the forcing move. But in a real game there may be no winning move and the best move can easily be a forcing move, such as a capture, which does not win material. So to reject a capture just because it does not win material can be a big mistake.

Protocol F-7 (de Groot A; adult; 950; 20 minutes)
♘g5[bishop] — Bishop[knight] on f6 backed by bishop at e7 protected by ♘d5. What is the lay of the land? 1.♘a4 threatens the queen. Is that good? If 1.♘a4 what would the queen do? [1...♗xa4]. 1...♕c7, 1...♕a6 — would not go to c5 — free queen. 1...♕b5 is possible. Oh, OK, 1.♘a4 ♕b5 is protected by the bishop. White's queen is protected by the knight at e5. Then 2.♕xb5 ♗xb5 and the rooks look at each other; pulling pieces might expose something. Other op-

tions? Don't like 1.♗xf6; don't like taking knights for bishops. 1.♗xf6 ♗xf6 now — do I have something going on here? ♘d7 is possible. Wait a minute. There is a bishop on a2; If I took...want ♘d5. If I take 1.♗xd5 and if 1...♗xd5 2.♗xf6 ♗xf6 3.♘d7 attacking the queen on b6 and the rook on f8.

de Groot A
Black to play after 1.♗xd5 ♗xd5? 2.♗xf6 ♗xf6 3.♘d7
The removal of the guard of d7 and then the fork:
a major attraction for tactics seekers

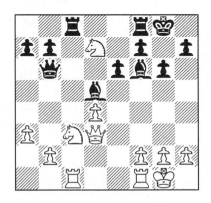

That's if he took — he would have to not see this. He can also take back with the pawn on e6 [good!]: 1.♗xd5 exd5 — he can see this. The knight on e5 can go to c4. 1.♘c4 hits the queen. Then 1...♕b5 pins the knight to the queen. Then the queen on d3 is not protected. So the knight is stuck on c4 but the queen is unprotected [sic ♘xb5]. Well, let's see... There is something. The rook on f1 is not developed. All pieces are not developed. The queen on d3 is halfway protected — it can't be moved out of the way. If Black were to drop... No; move the knight on f6 somewhere but that exposes the bishop on e7. The rook on f1 is undeveloped. The e-file is partially open. So 1.♖fe1. OK, now what else

Many weak players make the common mistake of treating each chess position like a "play and win" problem. They look for wins through forcing moves and, if the win is not there, reject the forcing move. But in a real game there may be no winning move and the best move can easily be a forcing move, such as a capture, which does not win material. So to reject a capture just because it does not win material can be a big mistake.

can I do? The bishop on a2 is in a hole, protected by the knight on c3. Things are not solidly protected. 1...♘xc3 then the bishop on a2 is loose. What to do. Like 1.♘c3-a4 then freebie! 1...♗xa4 [finally!]. Didn't see that at first. Feel like leading candidate is 1.♖fe1 – oh, yes – there is – Slick Willie – a pawn at b2 hanging out [finally!]. 1.♖fe1 ♕xb2 OK. So what do we do now? 1.♕c2 or 1.♕d2 or 1.♕e2 or 1.b4 – gotta protect the pawn. Lock knight onto ♕d3 – have to get into a defensive thing. Need to protect the pawn – queen move or 1.b4. Anybody else in trouble? Interesting. Just noticed 1.♘xc6 – lines me up 1.♘xc6 ♕xc6 or 1...♖xc6 – need to protect the pawn. Don't see alternatives to giving that pawn up. Gotta protect the pawn. Also 1.♖b1 or 1.♖c2. 1.♖c2 allows me to double rooks on the c-file. I need to be careful – then 1...♗a4 but 2.♘a4. 1.♖c2 protected by the queen. 1...♗a4 then I can exchange: 1.♖c2 ♗a4 2.♘xa4 ♖xc2 3.♕xc2 then ♖f8 is not guarded. He would not want to do that. 1.♖c2: pressure on the c-file – protects b2. No immediate threat. Looking at his knight on d5. 1.♖c2 not threatened by the bishop on c6 or the knight on d5. It helps develop the rook on f1. The knight on f6 is still pinned. OK. 1.♖c2. Push clock.

A very interesting protocol! For a player rated under 1000, he not only took his time, but saw the attraction of the fork at d7. What was interesting at that point was his comment, "That's if he took – he would have to not see this." I don't think he meant, "if he took" so much as, "if he took with the bishop on the first move." That's the part that is not forced. Black has two other ways to recapture. He then properly notes that 1.♗xd5 exd5 is possible and drops the analysis. When I was rated 1900, I made that same evaluation mistake, too! But World Champion Euwe (see Appendix A) evaluates much better and sees that 1...exd5 is bad for Black. We could hardly expect that of this subject. So he was doing very well to get that far, much better than some much more highly rated subjects in this book. After twenty minutes he finally plays Hope Chess (see the Glossary) and moves 1.♖c2 without looking to see if any check, capture, or threat can beat it. In fact 1.♖c2 is a bad move because after the only capturing reply, 1...♘xc3, White would have to spot 2.♘xc6! to avoid disaster. To not see this when playing 1.♖c2 is not only Hope Chess, but just lucky, since not anticipating such replies is often enough to lose on the spot.

Protocol F-8 (de Groot A; age 13; USCF 800/ICC 1260; 1.5 minutes)
There is a knight on e5. The bishop pins the knight on f6 [no eval]. Umm. 1.♕xg6+ No. Can't fork ♘e5-d7. 1.♘xd5 no. 1.♗xf6. Push clock.

This seems to be choosing a move by random process of elimination. The player finds a couple of moves he does not like and figures he will play the first one he sees which does not seem to lose. I would be curious to know why he thought 1.♘xd5 was a "no" – perhaps because it did not win material? If so, that would be the same error we have already seen several times: rejecting a capture just because it doesn't win material.

Protocol F-9 (de Groot A; age 9; USCF 600+; 4 minutes)
Interesting. Let's see. 1.♘xd5 ♗xd5. Both pieces can capture. 1.♘xd5 hmm. 1.♘xd5 ♕xb2 never mind. There I can take. 1.♘xd5 ♕xd4 [1...♕xb2?] 2.♘xe7+ is good for me. If 1.♗xd5 exd5.

de Groot A
White to play after 1.♗xd5 exd5
Good guess! Subject just assumes the move, correct in this case

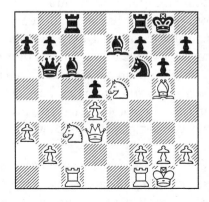

1.♖c2 and then ♖1c1 to pressure c8. 1.♗h6 attacks the rook on f8. Then there is, after I get rid of the bishop, ♘d7. I have to get rid of the knight on f6, so 1.♗xd5. Push clock.

Talk about making the right move for the wrong reasons! But this player *was* trying to be analytical and, although his analysis was all over the place, showed great promise for someone young and so low-rated. In fact, two years later, his USCF rating was up to 1019. Most youngsters show great rating gains as their deductive logic capabilities improve around the age of puberty. Notice how he came to his conclusion: he scanned the board for various ideas and then, without really analyzing the move actually played, just played it. That's better than playing the first move you see, but still a good recipe for disaster. It's always a good idea to check to see if the move you are going to play is at least safe. In this case (a capture of a piece) it's likely safe because Black is forced to recapture to maintain material equality.

Protocol F-10 (de Groot A; age 14; USCF 900+; 2 minutes)
Moving 1.♕f3 but the knight on f6 is well protected. His queen is attacking the pawn on d4 if I move the queen. Maybe 1.♘e4 to put pressure on the knight. Then ♕f3 would help. If he plays 1...♘xe4 2.♕xe4 – not better – if the knight on d5 moves he has a discovery with the bishop on c6. Let's see... I should be doing something with the knight on f6. 1.♘e4 ♘xe4 2.♕xe4 – would that get me anywhere? The rook is attacking the bishop on c6. Yeah I think I will go 1.♘e4. Push clock. [PV=1.♘e4 ♘xe4 ♕xe4].

Subject F-10 omits evaluating the position and does not look for opponent threats such as 1...♕xb2. Then, he did not start his examination of his candidate moves with checks, then captures, then threats. I guess he felt that 1.♘e4 was a threat but the forcing moves 1.♘xd5, 1.♗xd5, 1.♘xc6 were not even considered – quite the opposite of what Dr. Euwe selected to consider first (see Appendix A). Another curious aspect of this protocol was that Subject F-10 saw that after 2.♕xe4 the queen could be subjected to a discovered attack after the d5-knight moves – and still chose the move despite clear and present danger (see the diagram and discussion earlier with protocol F-5). Of course, besides a discovery, Black can just play 2...♗xg5, which was not mentioned.

Protocol F-11 (de Groot Zyme; age 14; unrated; 4 minutes)
The queen is on e4, the bishop on d6. Threats, checks, and attacks. The bishop is not under attack. The pawn on f2 is under attack. I can't play 1.♕e7: 1.♕e7+ ♕xe7. I can play 1.♕xa8 to win a piece. An alternative is 1.♖xa7, not good. I could play 1.h3 to attack the knight. What can my queen do? Black's queen can take on f2, guarded by the knight on g4 – I have to deal with that. 1.f3 prevents that. That's probably what I would do. 1.f3. Push clock.

Subject F-11 spots some of the threats like 1.♕xa8 and 1...♕xf2+, but not other critical ones like 1...♘xf2, 1...♕xc3+, and 1...♕xd6. Interestingly, he does not address the question of whether it is worth it to give up the check and the pawn to win the rook in the line 1.♕xa8 ♕xf2+, which would be very relevant and critical if that were Black's only threat. Unfortunately, he chooses 1.f3 to stop the only threat he found by Black, without attempting to find all of Black's checks in reply, one of which gives mate in two:

de Groot Zyme
1.f3 allows 1...♕xc3+ 2.♔d1 ♘f2#

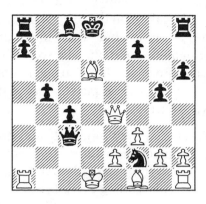

Summary of Class F and Below

Characteristics of the thought process at this level:

- Although in general weaker players play faster, this chapter contains examples of some very slow players. Nevertheless, as will be seen throughout the remaining chapters, higher-rated players usually play slower. Besides rating, there is also a correlation between time taken and overall personality. Players who are very patient in other endeavors usually play slowly and carefully. At the other end of the spectrum, players who are "in for the ride" often just play something quickly and see what happens. Although the net result occasionally comes out the same — or at least results in a similar rating — being careful is a very good trait in chess. Mercifully, some of the younger "fast" players end up slowing down as they become more mature in their understanding of, and approach to, playing chess.

- One thing that sticks out about the protocols in this chapter is their lack of focus and systematic consideration of alternatives for either player. The players, understandably, don't know how to find candidate moves or to analyze correctly. So their approach is very scattershot, even among the slower players. Rarely does a player stop and ask himself a basic question such as, "What are all my opponent's checks, captures, and threats?" or, "If I make this capture, what are *all* the ways my opponent can recapture and how good is each of them?" Instead, after a capture they just assume a recapture (or a reply) almost randomly and try to derive conclusions from that, even though that is illogical. In defense of weak players, they just don't have the tactical vision to see what is threatened and therefore what is forced, so their move choices are much more random and less critical to what actually is going on. The solutions are not only developing better thinking processes, but also solving basic tactics problems to better identify safety issues and playing lots of slow chess to improve board vision and visualization.

- Players at this level should think primarily about safety and much less about strategy but, in practice, it often is the other way around. They make moves without really trying to see the consequences and sometimes they don't even care. This leaning toward strategy over safety is true of players in many lower classes, not just the lowest class. If a move is not safe, then it does not matter if the move is positionally or strategically desirable. An unsafe move almost always has to be rejected as *not tactically justifiable*. The trait of choosing unsafe moves often comes from reading too many advanced chess books, where subtle differences are stressed but not the foundations of basic safety.

Improvements to the thought process that would help in getting to the next level:

- Start the thinking process by examining the opponent's threats arising from the last move, asking "What are *all* the things my opponent is trying to do?" In a de Groot exercise, one does not know the previous move. But outstanding threats by the opponent still have to be identified. If only one threat is missed, that could easily be enough to lose the game.

- Consider as candidate moves all checks, captures, and threats.

- Play more slowly in slower time-control games, especially for critical moves.

- Do repetitive study of basic tactical patterns to recognize safe and critical moves. Treat these patterns like the "multiplication tables" of chess – the basis for your sense of chess safety.

- Don't just consider one possible reply by the opponent, but stop to ask, "What are all the dangerous things my opponent could do if I did this, and can I meet them?"

- Try to evaluate resulting positions and learn to pick out the best move (assuming best replies by the opponent), rather than just finding a sequence which looks promising and playing it to see what happens.

- Practice visualizing pieces while looking ahead during slow moves. *While this is a skill at which some players are naturally better than others, with practice everyone can improve in this area.*

There will be a fair amount of overlap between the needs of one level and the needs of the next, but over several classes those needs will change, sometimes dramatically.

Chapter 3

Class E

This chapter includes players rated 1000-1200 USCF, or roughly 1150-1350 ICC standard.

For weaker players, I primarily gave them de Groot A. Giving a more complex line such as de Groot C or de Groot Ernie would be less indicative of their overall abilities. Giving them a more strategic position like de Groot Shafritz would not reveal their ability to analyze "simple" capturing sequences, which is an early skill to try to master.

For each protocol, I list the de Groot position (for example, de Groot A, de Groot B, de Groot C, etc.; see Chapter 1 for those positions); the age of the subject; the subject's rating; and the time the subject spent to choose his move.

Comments in parentheses indicate outside actions or comments that reflect the action of the player, such as (silent) if he paused for a long time. Comments in brackets are my thoughts. My frequent use of [*sic*] means that the subject is making a clear mistake in analysis or visualization. In contrast, [!] indicates that the player has made a comment that is either very insightful for their level of ability or a surprising error. A frequent note is [no eval], meaning that the subject did not try to evaluate which side stood better, by how much, and why.

Protocol E-1 (de Groot A; adult; 1000; short time)
The material is even. There is pressure on the black king. There is an idea of playing for ♘d7. If I play 1.♘xc6 I win the bishop pair.

de Groot A
Black to play after 1.♘xc6
Bravo! Simple move 1.♘xc6 wins the bishop pair

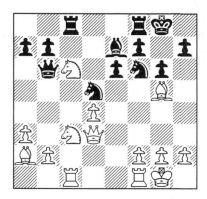

Suppose I play 1.♘xd5 with the idea of getting in ♘d7. Then after 1.♘xd5 exd5 I am not getting anywhere. Suppose I develop the king's rook. Then I can wait and see what Black wants to do. My move is 1.♖fe1.

There is some good promise in this protocol, but one can see why this player is currently weak. He does take the time to count the material (most weak players do not) but he quickly spots the removal-of-the-guard idea with ♘d7. Moreover, he is one of the few players at this level to clearly point out the opportunity to just procure the bishop pair with 1.♘xc6. It isn't the best move, but it's better than what he played. A major mistake was to skip looking for Black's threats, so that 1...♛xb2 was not spotted. This also had the effect of turning his move into Hope Chess since he did not bother to see what Black could do in reply to his proposed candidate 1.♖fe1. As noted many times, you should spend a fair amount of time seeing if the opponent can defeat your candidate move. If you don't, he surely will spend some time trying to defeat it and might succeed! Subject E-1 did not systematically consider all his captures — failing even to consider the best move 1.♗xd5, and rejecting 1.♘xd5 apparently just because 1...exd5 does not lose material. He made his move fairly quickly and pretty much "blind" — no analysis of 1.♖fe1 at all, much less a principal variation.

The following is another example of weak players not always being too fast:

Protocol E-2 (de Groot A; adult; 1170; 20 minutes)
Any threats? The bishop on g5 threatens the knight on f6 — it is guarded by

41

Chapter 3

the bishop on e7 and the knight on d5. The knight on e5 threatens the pawn on f7 and the bishop on c6. The bishop on c6 is guarded by the queen on b6, the pawn on b7, and the rook on c8. The knight at c3 threatens d5 with the rook on c1 behind it. There is then a double attack on c6 with the knight on e5 and the rook on c1. The bishop on a2 attacks d5, which is protected by the pawn on e6, the knight on f6. If the f-pawn moves, the king on g1 is indirectly attacked by the queen on b6 — I have to be careful.

The pawn on b2 is en prise to the queen on b6. Looking at the d4-pawn. The queen attacks it but it is protected by the queen on d3.

Do I have any good moves? 1.♗xf6. Ah! 1.♗h6 threatens the rook. Any combinations or sacrifices? 1.♘xg6 but it is protected by the pawns on h7 and f7. Can't get the queen in after the capture on g6. Any way to loosen the position up? 1.h4-h5 and then hxg6 hxg6 ♘xg6 fxg6 ♕xg6+ ♔h8 [waste of time to give White three moves in a row]. Then ♗h6 threatens mate. Look to see if Black can defend this combination. For example after h5, ...h6 threatens the knight for the final attack. But makes it easier for the queen. Looking at the bishop on a2 attacking g8. Too much blockage. One way is f2-f4-f5. Can be taken by ♘d5. ♖xf4 might be vulnerable.

The knight on f6 is guarded by two pieces and is OK. I am lulled into thinking without verbalizing. Candidates 1.f4 or 1.h4 with the idea of advancing to the fifth rank. 1.♗xf6 does not merit much; after 1...♗xf6 and there is no clear continuation. 1.♘xd5 — there is only one way to recapture as 1...♘xd5 leaves ♗e7 en prise [sic! A common error in analysis of de Groot A] so he has to retake with 1...♗xd5 [sic]. 1.♘xd5 threatens the queen and bishop.

What type of attack can I get? Tactical shot. Looking at 1.♘xd5, also attacked by bishop on a2, guarded by a pawn and two pieces (quiet). Attack d5; can all recapture back? Win a bishop on e7? 1.♘xd5 exd5 doesn't look too prosperous — just exchange bishop for a pawn. Can force him to take with the knight or bishop.

OK, just noticed I have a possible fork at the end: get knight from e5 to d7 to fork queen and rook. That might generate something. 1.♗xf6 removes a defender; 1...♘xf6 another defender. One knight can replace the other knight. So take d5 first — can capture with knight or bishop. If he recaptures with the knight then 2.♗xe7 wins [sic]. So 1...♗xd5 2.♗xd5 and then 3.♘d7. Is that accurate? On 1.♘xd5 he can just play 1...exd5. 1.♘xd5 exd5. I don't want to play 2.♗xd5;

42

he can take with knight or bishop. Back at 1.♘xd5 exd5 then before 2.♗xd5 play 2.♗xf6 ♗xf6 3.♗xd5 ♗xd5 4.♘d7. That's the sequence. I make 1.♘xd5. Push clock.

There is a lot to be learned from studying this protocol! Let's begin by examining his conclusions. The subject made the common mistake among weak players of believing that he is winning a rook when actually he is only winning the exchange (a rook for a bishop or a knight):

de Groot A
White to play after 1.♘xd5 exd5 2.♗xf6 ♗xf6

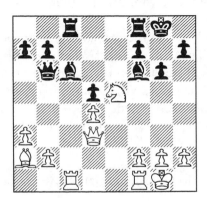

The subject's PV at this point is **3.♗xd5? ♗xd5** (not forced by the way; Black could consider 3...♗xe5 first) **4.♘d7** forking queen, bishop, and rook:

de Groot A
Black to play after 3.♗xd5? ♗xd5 4.♘d7

43

But if Black just guards the bishop, say with **4...♕d6,** then after the desired **5.♘xf8** Black can just recapture with **5...♕xf8** or **5...♖xf8** and have two bishops for a rook and a pawn, a fairly sizable advantage.

Beginners are taught that knights and bishops are, on the average, worth three pawns, but that is only a rough integer value. Actually knights and bishops are each worth — again on the average — more than three pawns, with a bonus for possessing the bishop pair of approximately an additional half-pawn (reference GM Larry Kaufman's scientific method for valuing pieces in "The Evaluation of Material Imbalances," *Chess Life,* March 1999), so winning two bishops for a rook and a pawn is an advantage of about a pawn, which is usually enough for a winning advantage.

The capture on f8 has won the exchange (worth only about 1¾ pawns), not a rook (worth 5). That's a big error! What the subject has done is to sacrifice a bishop on move three to win the exchange on move five. Because he uses the word "rook," he thinks White is coming out ahead. Over the years, probably a dozen subjects have made this same exact mistake when analyzing de Groot A. This "rook instead of exchange" mistake provides several insights:

- Weak players often do not differentiate between the following two situations:
  1. When they capture a piece worth more than the capturing piece and it can be captured back; and
  2. When they make the same capture but there is no recapture.

For example, there is a big difference between capturing a rook with a knight when the opponent captures back the knight ("winning the exchange") vs. capturing a rook with a knight and the opponent cannot capture the knight ("winning a rook").

> Beginners are taught that knights and bishops are, on the average, worth three pawns, but that is only a rough integer value. Actually knights and bishops are each worth — again on the average — more than three pawns, with a bonus for possessing the bishop pair of approximately an additional half-pawn, so winning two bishops for a rook and a pawn is an advantage of about a pawn, which is usually enough for a winning advantage.

I have seen this mistake made dozens of times, often with disastrous consequences. In the previous diagram, 5.♘xf8 wins the exchange, not a rook. If the subject saw the recapture but still misevaluated, then this is still incorrect.

One teaching trick I used was to perform the same exchange with money instead of piece value. This often worked wonders:

"Would you give up $3.25 for the opportunity to exchange a further $3.25 for $5? Would you do it if I gave you an extra $1 (pawn)?"

I think most everyone understood when I phrased it this way!

- The wording of your thoughts matters! The players say to themselves the appealing, "I am giving up a bishop but I am winning a *rook.*" More accurate would be, "I am giving up a bishop and then I am capturing a rook but he gets my knight," or "I am giving up a bishop but afterwards I am only winning the *exchange.*" With accurate wording, the trades don't look so appealing any more. See pages 266 and 270 for other word choices that mislead.

- Weak players are often OK until they have to calculate a critical sequence, when often they get very sloppy and sometimes make enormous errors. Yet they are often unaware that they might be making an error and don't double-check their analysis, especially analysis that contains several recaptures and precise counting. *Take more time for critical sequences, such as those involving multiple captures.*

This subject also thought he saw a winning line, but that did not send up a "warning flag." The applicable principle in Alburt and Lawrence's book *Chess Rules of Thumb* goes: *Whenever you see a winning line you need to stop, take time, and make sure it is right.* Don't just plow ahead. There are two reasons for this:

1. If the line is truly winning, then you probably don't need as much time or effort to finish the game. So making sure that it is winning now is more important than playing out an easily winning position; and
2. If the line is not winning (as was the case above), then you would like to know why. The reason your candidate does not win may be enough to convert your previously best move into a move which isn't very good, and you should not play that formerly "winning" move.

In this case, the subject had thought for a very reasonable twenty minutes. Yet once he spotted the "winning" line he did not double-check it or ask himself if it was truly winning. Instead he terminated the analysis instantly — a potentially gigantic mistake.

A common mistake Subject E-2 made was to assume, after 1.♘xd5 —

de Groot A
Black to play after 1.♘xd5

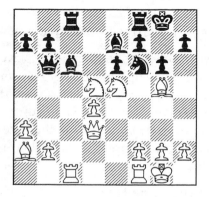

— that the recapture 1...♘xd5 is impossible because of 2.♗xe7 "winning a piece." This common error is due to one of two possibilities:

1. The player assumes that, by moving the pinned piece on f6, the piece behind it can be safely captured, since its original guard, the knight on d5, has been captured; or

2. The player does not attempt to visualize the position, and fails to see that the knight on d5 was replaced by another knight on d5, which is equally able to guard the bishop on e7.

As a result of this and other analytical problems, few players rated under 1800 USCF ever analyze the critical line 1.♘xd5 ♘xd5 2.♗xd5 (attempting to remove the guard on e7) 2...♗xg5 with complications. Players who don't get that far are not getting to the heart of whether de Groot A contains a winning tactic.

Notice that subjects E-1 and E-2 neither counted the material nor looked for threats. Subject E-2 eventually did notice his b2-pawn was attacked and not defended, but doing so near the beginning of the thought process often saves a lot of analysis time!

Let's contrast E-1 and E-2. They are both rated in the same class; although E-2 was rated higher at the time of the protocol, E-1 eventually surpassed him. At the time of the protocol, E-2 had been playing a long time and had a sophisticated but rather flawed thought process. On the other hand, E-1 had less tournament experience and did not know how to deeply attack the problem. Once E-1 learned how to handle this type of analysis, he slowed down and easily surpassed E-2, who was "mired" in his methods.

The next subject is very young and, at the time, probably somewhat over-rated. Consider his protocol as possibly belonging in the previous chapter:

Protocol E-3 (de Groot A; age 6; 1150; less than a minute)
1.♖fe1 — I want it in the game. 1.♕h3. I will move 1.♕h3. Push clock.

There is no check for safety or even a reason why the subject likes the move chosen. Perhaps he wanted the queen to head toward the weak square h6?! Of course, at this speed he did not consider any replies, much less such potentially dangerous ones as 1...♘xc3, 1...♕xd4, or 1...♕xb2. At least he considered more than one move and did give a reason for his first candidate.

Lest you start to believe that haste is primarily an attribute of youth, not all short protocols are youngsters:

Protocol E-4 (de Groot A; adult; 1050; 2 minutes)
I am looking at the piece positions. 1.♖fe1 — just on general principles. Hit clock. [no eval; no analysis; no PV]

Moving on general principles in positions with lots of checks, captures, or threats may be a fun way to spend an evening — but, without learning to recognize these positions and perform solid analysis on them, you won't become a good player!

This leads to the idea of *criticality assessment*. "Criticality assessment" is the ability to discern whether the current move is likely to have a major impact on the outcome of the game. A cousin of criticality assessment is a *sense of danger.* This subject seemed to have neither, and thus moved very quickly. However, de Groot A is a fairly tense and analytical position, so moving on general principles only works if you are very lucky.

Protocol E-5 (de Groot A; adult; 1200; short time)
The b-pawn is hanging. The center is important. 1.♗xd5 ♘xd5 2.♘xd5. 1.♘xd5. Push clock. ["What is your PV?"] My PV is 1.♘xd5 ♘xd5 2.♗xd5 and after Black recaptures on d5, 3.♗xe7.

Yet another case of assuming the opponent will make a move (like 1... ♘xd5 after 1.♗xd5) without considering whether it is the best move, or even the alternatives. Notice that Subject E-5, like many weak players, considers a second candidate 1.♘xd5 and chooses to play that second move, which he did not analyze, instead of the one he did analyze. At least he failed to analyze his second candidate *verbally,* which is all I can judge. That's why, after he pushed the clock, I asked him what his PV was. His analysis in the PV is also a mistake, as after 1.♘xd5 ♘xd5 2.♗xd5 – to remove the guard on e7 – he assumes Black must recapture on d5 and lose the bishop on e7. Instead Black can make the forced recapture 2...♗xg5.

de Groot A
Black to play after 1.♘xd5 ♘xd5 2.♗xd5
Black has 2...♗xg5

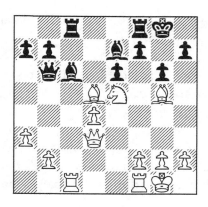

This is a key line that most players under 1800 never consider, even though it is critical for determining whether 1.♘xd5 is better than 1.♗xd5. See Euwe's analysis in Appendix A.

Protocol E-6 (de Groot A; ICC 1300; adult; 3-4 minutes)

Isolated queen's pawn. The material is equal. Black's king is slightly open. 1...♛xb2 is a threat. Can't push 1.b4 — doesn't look quite right. What else can I do? The rook is undeveloped, but I have to protect the pawn [?!]. OK, I think I can... hmm. Want to develop the rook at f1 but pawn under attack. After 1.b4 does he have any sacrificial attack with 1...♞xb4? Does not look like it. I get more space. Is there anything else under attack? OK. 1.b4. Push clock.

Again the familiar Hope Chess idea of not looking, after 1.b4, if captures like 1...♞xc3 can be safely met. Also, the subject takes a completely passive approach. His single-minded approach to b2 being threatened: move the pawn from b2.

de Groot A
Black to play after 1.b4
Settling for moving the attacked piece

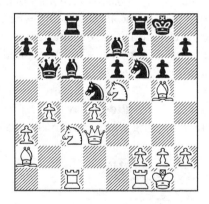

Instead, the subject could have taken Dr. Euwe's superior approach: "OK, b2 is threatened, but let's see if I can do something myself first." Hopefully players of all levels would play a *checkmate* instead of guarding a pawn, but that same logic applies to lesser initiatives as well.

Protocol E-7 (de Groot A; adult; 1050; 3 minutes)

1.♗h6. 1.♞d7 to remove guard. 1.♗xf6 followed by 2.♞xd5... ♞d7. In-between moves? 1.♕h3 so try to win material. 1.♞xd5 ♗xd5 I win a piece [?!]. Push clock. PV = 1.♗xf6 ♗xf6 2.♞xd5 ♗xd5 3.♗xd5 exd5 4.♞d7.

Once again we have a case where the subject assumes that the opponent will make moves that help the subject (rather than moves that will help the subject's opponent), even if they are not forced. For example, in his PV Black could easily vary by replying to 1.♗xf6 with 1...♘xf6 or, in the given sequence, 2...exd5 allowing the bishop on c6 to remain guarding d7. Note that the subject was only winning the exchange (a knight for a rook) in the PV, yet said he was winning a piece, which usually means obtaining a knight or a bishop for a pawn or less.

This subject could have done several things better. As happened with E-2, he thought he saw a winning move but then failed to re-analyze to see if this good fortune was correct. He should think, "Gee! I seem to be winning a piece by force — is that really true?", and re-check his analysis. *Any time you see a line which seems to win, you should always be very careful because there are only two possibilities: 1) You are correct, in which case the game is virtually over and the extra time you take will not cause future time-trouble difficulties; or 2) You are incorrect, in which case the move you are planning might not only not win, it might not even be the best move or, in the worst case, could be a monumental blunder.* An example of the latter occurs when you see a move that seems to checkmate with a queen, missing that a piece on the other side of the board could just capture it for free. This happened in an Internet game with a position similar to the following:

White to play
Not re-checking what appears to be a win

Despite having about an hour on his clock, White played **1.♕g7+??** almost immediately, thinking it was mate, and then resigned after **1...♗xg7.** Had White not been in such a rush, he might have seen the bishop on a1 and would have avoided such a rash mistake.

> Any time you see a line which seems to win, you should always be very careful because there are only two possibilities: 1) You are correct, in which case the game is virtually over and the extra time you take will not cause future time-trouble difficulties; or 2) You are incorrect, in which case the move you are planning might not only not win, it might not even be the best move or, in the worst case, could be a monumental blunder.

The next protocol is by a seven-year old-who, in a couple of years, ended up being one of the top players for his age group in the U.S. But at this point he was very much an 1100 player, which is great for age seven.

Protocol E-8 (de Groot A; age 7; 1100; 80 seconds)
1.♗h6 ♖fe8 not enough to exploit dark-square weaknesses. If 1.♘xd5 to exchange pieces but not so good so less pieces to attack king. 1.♖fe1 to go to e3 to h3 attacks h7 to attack or exchange. 1.♗xf6 to remove the defender or 1.♕f3 to hit both knights and that's what I'll do. Hit clock.

Unlike Subject E-7, Subject E-8 is all offense and no defense! He does not look to see if Black is threatening the b2-pawn and, just as bad, does not see that his planned 1.♕f3 abandons the d-pawn as well. And those threatened knights? The one on d5 is not less safe due to the additional attack by the queen on f3; the knight on f6 is already guarded twice as well. So any damage White can do after 1.♕f3 would take a lot more analysis than was provided. In a few years he will do a quite a bit better.

Subject E-8 jumps around until he hits on the idea 1.♕f3 and then plays it immediately. This "jumping around and then instantly playing upon seeing one attractive move" is indicative of a lot of low-rated players. Not only don't they look for a better move, but — more importantly — they don't take much time to analyze whether the move they are going to "bet the entire game" upon is as good as they think. Should Black have a good forcing move in reply (say, 1...♕xd4), the chosen move then turns out not to do all that the subject's initial analysis promised.

In his classic work *Think Like a Grandmaster,* Alexander Kotov suggested trusting your analysis and not re-checking your lines. But, scoffing at Kotov's suggestion, several strong players have advised that if you are going to play a critical analytical line, it *is* worth checking to make sure your analysis is correct. I might add that *the weaker you are, the less you should trust your initial lines. You should especially not trust the lines for the move you are actually going to play! So reviewing critical lines when you have plenty of time is an excellent habit.*

Protocol E-9 (de Groot A; adult; 1100; 6 minutes)
Counting material — even. His king is a little less safe — not too much. No imminent danger — no Black captures. ...♘xc3 not too scary. ...♕xd4 covered. Where else can he take?. Oh! ...♕xb2 is en prise. *Any tactics here? 1.♗h6 hits the rook — not bad. But the knight on f6 is pinned — hard to evaluate. [Looks for threats] What about ...♘f6 move? ♗c6 moves — opens c-file. Given that, I can't see anything too fancy — capture d5. Take with bishop, pawn, or knight, ...♗xd5 opens c-file. (silent)...♕xb2 so that's possible. Don't want to take the knight — gives up the two bishops [apparently 1.♗xd5]. Isolated queen's pawn — suppose to stay active and support the knight on d5. Protect b2-pawn. 1.♘b5 shaky. 1.♖c2; 1.♘b5 interesting. 1.♘b5 shaky. I'd be afraid to do that. Is 1.b4 safe? 1.b4 a5 2.bxa5 ...OK. 1.b4 a5 2.b5 is interesting. 1.b4 is... 1...♕xb2 is my main concern. 1.♕c2 ♕xd4 bad so I'm thinking 1.b4. Push clock.*

Subject E-9 did a much better job than some Class E players, but still was mostly passive. He did consider the capture on d5, but rejected it just because it did not win material. Weaker players often treat normal positions as if they were problems with possible solutions. When a capture fails to win, they reject it even if it turns out to yield a better position than the moves they actually choose! And a capture is more likely to be safe, as passive moves like 1.b4 require the player to analyze replies such as 1...♘xc3. A piece capture is much less likely to lose material. We have seen this mistake in almost half the protocols in Chapters 2 and 3.

To his credit, Subject E-10 did not completely play Hope Chess. Although he did not consider the critical capture 1...♘xc3 after his planned 1.b4, he did consider some replies such as 1...a5.

Protocol E-10 (de Groot A; adult; 1000; 8 minutes)
Look to activity on the kingside. What are Black's captures? c3 — can take back with a rook. White can take on d5 — would not do anything. Don't see any glaring weaknesses for Black so far. No piece undefended. First move to come to mind is 1.♕h3. The knight defends h7. 1.♘xd5 ♗xd5 — not going to take with the pawn — that makes it isolated. 1.♘xd5 ♗xd5 2.♗xf6 and then 3.♕h3 — the bishop on g5 hangs. 1.♘xd5 ♗xd5 2.♗xf6 ♗xf6 and I can't do anything on

♕h3. I need to work out some way to do damage on the kingside. A pawn storm with h4 to break open the g-file. 1.h4 h6 2.♗d2 ♘xc3 to prevent ♗c1 3.♖xc3 ♗b5 4.♕h3 ♖xc3 [4...♗xf1?!]. I'll sacrifice the pawn 5.bxc3. Push clock (PV = 1.h4 h6 2.♗d2).

Wow! This is an aggressive, attacking protocol. Too bad Subject E-10's analysis is not rooted in reality. He does not mention the hanging pawn on b2, nor does he consider Black's checks, captures, and threats after 1.h4. Of course, after 1.h4 h6 retreating the bishop to d2 is completely hazy. Why would Subject E-10 assume that Black should play 1...h6 when White can just play 2.♗xh6? Again, we are seeing a player assume an opponent's reply that is at best not forced and at worst just good for the thinking player, instead of trying to find the best move for the opponent. Maybe E-10 did not "see" 1.h4 h6 2.♗xh6, but that would be a good reason for going slowly and asking himself if each move were forced, or at least reasonable, before continuing the analysis. Many weaker players make the mistake of analyzing moves at some depth in their analysis tree that likely never would be reached for a variety of reasons (as in the above, where the subject assumes a somewhat random, non-best reply). Since Subject E-10 bases his final move on this sequence, it would be good to re-check to see if it was plausible.

Protocol E-11 (de Groot A; adult; ICC 1220; 2 minutes)
Looking at piece positions. I would play 1.♖fe1 on general principles. [No eval, no analysis, no PV] Push clock.

de Groot A
Black to play after 1.♖fe1
Just developing with no analysis

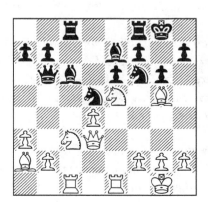

One shouldn't use general principles to make a move in an analytical position. Many weaker players make this mistake, but if they wish to improve, they will have to roll up their sleeves and attempt the analysis. It is true that most weaker players are not that proficient at analysis and may not have as much natural talent as Kasparov, but they will get better with practice.

I call making moves on general principles in an analytical position "Hand-waving" because one is waving his hands for effect instead of doing the work. In positions like de Groot A, it's great to develop your pieces, especially with one clearly less developed piece like the rook at f1. However, you should analyze the forcing sequences first, as any possible tactic or safety issue takes precedence over activity issues.

Protocol E-12 (de Groot A; adult; ICC 1150; 12 minutes)
(counts material) Even, both sides castled, White has a fianchettoed bishop on a2 [!]. Checks, captures, and threats: 1...♕xb2, 1...♘xc3, and capture 1... ♕xd4. Threats? If the knight on f6 moves, there is a discovery on the bishop on g5. I don't see any squares where that knight will move. Don't see any threats; not 1...♘g4 (silent). I don't see anything else. Look at black queen moves: 1... ♕xd4, 1...♕xb2 actually is loose. 1...♕xb2 I may need to meet – hits the bishop on a2. If 2.♖b1 then 2...♘xc3 grabs the bishop on a2 but also 2...♕xc3. If I pass then 1...♕xb2 is loose.

Candidate moves to stop that: 1.♖b1 don't like. 1.♖c2 would stop it and is more active. 1.♘a4 hangs to 1...♗xa4 [good!]. 1.♕d2 or 1.♕c2 protects. 1.♕c2 allows 1....♘b4, forking the queen and bishop – winning the bishop pair [? 2.axb4]. 1.b4 is a candidate – it gets space – any captures and threats after that? 1.b4 ♕xd4 no good, so 1.♕c2 is also no good – it loses the d-pawn.

My captures: 1.♘xc6 wins the bishop pair [good]. 1.♘xc6 ♕xc6 or 1...♖xc6. 1.♘xc6 ♕xb2 2.♘xe7+ wins a piece. 1.♘xc6 ♕xc6 looks good. Any forcing moves after that? 1.♘xc6 ♖xc6; b2 is still threatened – then 2.b4. 1.♘xc6 intermediate move? Checks? No tricky knight moves? 1...♘d5 → f4 hits the queen. 1.♘xc6 is safe – put it in my pocket.

1.♗xf6 ♗xf6 loses the bishop pair. 1.♘xf7 or 1.♘xg6 no continuation. 1.♘xg6 fxg6 2.♕xg6+ no good. Any forcing moves after that? 1.♘d7 forks but ...♗xd7 doesn't work. Other captures? 1.♘xd5 ♗xd5 file's open 2.♖xc8 ♖xc8 trades a lot of stuff. Then 3.b4 he grabs the open file. 1.♞xd5 ♞xd5 is also possible 2.♗xe7 then the rook moves [!] 3.♗b4 protects the b-pawn. 3...♞xb4 don't like so don't like 1.♞xd5 as much. 1.♞xc6 ♛xc6 or 1...♜xc6; 1...♜xc6 can play 2.b4, bishop pair — safe. Sanity check: no intermediate checks or captures. 1...♞f6 doesn't work. OK, so 1.♞xc6 ♛xc6 or 1...♜xc6 OK, so 1.♞xc6. Push clock.

In general, this is a very competent protocol from a player rated in this class. Of course, the thought process, while a large component of playing strength, is only one component. For example, this student admitted that one of his problems is letting down after a mistake — that's not the kind of issue we can easily spot via a de Groot exercise. In this protocol, Subject E-12 considered all his major captures (1.♞xc6, 1.♗xf6, 1.♞xd5) except the strongest one, 1.♗xd5. While it's true that even if he had considered it, he might not have figured out why it's so strong, the failure to consider it does lend credence to the idea of, "What are all my checks, captures, and threats?" as a helpful guide. Subject E-12 gets full credit for recognizing that 1.♞xc6 wins the bishop pair; he also gets credit for not playing it immediately once he values the move — he says, "...put it in my pocket," a euphemism for making it the King of the Hill (best move found so far). Then he properly looks for a better one. One big hitch is that he lost track of the material count in the sequence 1.♞xd5 ♞xd5 2.♗xe7, not only not seeing that Black now has the forced recapture 2...♞xe7, but also failing to notice that after 2..."rook moves"?? 3.♗b4, White has just won a piece. Many stronger players have chosen de Groot A moves much worse than 1.♞xc6; all in all, a better protocol than many players a class or two above.

Protocol E-13 (de Groot Zyme; adult; USCF 1010; 5 minutes)

Rook on half-open file. 1.♛xa8 possible, not defended [no eval] (silent). Black queen attacks the pawn on c3. The queen moves along the e-file — is anything there? 1.♜d1 hmm. Look at black knight moves: any forks or anything? 1.♛xa8 — can he trap the queen? 1.♛xa8 he can play 1...♛xd6. 1...♛xc3+ forks the rook — that could be a problem. Defending 1...♛xc3+: 1.♜c1 is the first thing that pops into my head. 1.♛c2. 1.♗b4 — back to 1.♜c1 umm. 1.♗b4 is best since it's not defended by anything and attacked by the queen. I'm thinking 1.♗b4 — Push clock.

de Groot Zyme
Black to play after 1.♗b4!

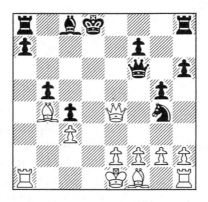

I could not resist including this protocol since Subject E-13 was the only subject ever to play 1.♗b4 in de Groot Zyme – this is actually a fantastically deep computer move that's almost as good as the normal "strong human" move of 1.♗e7+; see the analysis of 1.♗b4 by *Houdini* in the section of Appendix B that deals with de Groot Zyme. Of course, in this case Subject E-13 played that move for different reasons – he did not take the time to see that f2 was attacked more times than it was defended. For stronger humans, this is almost always enough to prefer a move like 1.♗e7+, but the computer finds that ignoring the threats to f2 with 1.♗b4 can be just as good – a fairly amazing result.

Protocol E-14 (de Groot A; adult; ICC 1200; 17 minutes)
White has six pawns, Black has six; the minors are equal so material is equal. The position is fairly critical – a lot of captures. Both sides have lots to do. The dark squares around the black king are weak so 1.♗h6 is possible. Look at captures first [no eval or threats]. 1.♘xd5 and then he has either 1... exd5 or 1...♗xd5 then 2.♖xc8 ♖xc8 ends up even. What does it do to the position? It's fairly open. Don't want to trade a knight for a bishop. He can move the dark-squared bishop to cover the weak squares. If 1.♗xf6 then 1...♗xf6 – not very good for White – gives up the bishop pair [good]. 1.♘xf6 loses the knight, ditto for 1...♘xg6 loses the knight and does not weaken the king that much. 1.♘xg6 hxg6 opens the h-file but I can't get the rook over there – I can get the queen to the h-file but no real attacking chances. 1.♕xg6+ loses the queen – ridiculous. 1.♗xd5 and if 1...exd5 I lose the bishop pair but it

obstructs the a8-h1 diagonal for Black. On 1.♗xd5 Black can recapture with the bishop and if 1...♗xd5 2.♘xd5 exd5 and then I can exchange the rooks but I don't see what that does for me — it gives him the file after 3.♖xc8 ♖xc8. Pawn moves?

I get space via 1.b4 the a-pawn is not protected, but I don't see any danger. In a game — oh 1.♘xc6 — Black can retake with the queen, pawn, or rook. If 1...♖xc6 then he just... it wins the bishop pair. It's a strong bishop, so it's candidate move "A" [King of the Hill]. 1.♘xc6 bxc6 is not dangerous for me. If 1...♕xc6 with a possible discovered attack but then the queen moves and ♖xc8 ♖xc8. I could fork the rook and queen with 1.♘d7 but he just takes — that loses the knight. So 1.♘xc6 but the knight on e5 is powerful, too. Trade a powerful knight for a powerful bishop, is it worth it? It might be, due to the bishop pair. He can drive the knight off with ...f7-f6, so it's not really an outpost. ...f6 can also fork the knight and the bishop if the knight on f6 moves, say ...♘g4. If so, I need to get one of my pieces out of there — I need ♗xf6 lose a piece [?].

What if I get rid of the bishop to set up the ♘d7 fork? 1.♗xd5 then checking the line 1...exd5. If 1...♘xd5 2.♗xe7 loses a piece [sic]. 1...♗xd5 then ♘d7 is not protected by the knight on f6 so 2.♘d7 ♘xd7 3.♗xe7 wins a piece [sic]. 1...exd5 solves problems other than inhibit the diagonal for the bishop on c6. 1.♗xd5 exd5 — don't see anything there that good. So I kind of decide 1.♘xc6 or 1.♗xd5 to obstruct the diagonal for the bishop. The king is safe so the bishop on c6 is not much of a problem but ...exd5 obstructs the bishop on c6 — the pawns are locked — I would need a later ♖d1 to keep them locked and free the queen. Umm. I would like to get rid of that bishop, though. I would rather get rid of the dark-squared bishop due to the weak dark squares — the only safe square for the king is h8 if I could target g7. Umm. 1.♘xc6 then 1...bxc6, 1...♖xc6, or 1...♕xc6. 1...♖xc6 looks OK — no — still no fork on d7 because the knight on e5 is gone. Hmm. Could... not thinking anything right now. 1...♕xc6 gives a discovered attack but 2.♘xd5 ♕xd5 no 3.♗xd5 so 2...♕xd5 no good. If 1...bxc6 Black makes the c-file semi-open for me. If he takes with the rook I don't see what that does for me. I think the move I would play is 1.♘xc6. Push clock.

Protocols E-12 and E-14 show promise for these E-class players. Subject E-14 was very thoughtful and weighed the options of winning the bishop pair vs. blocking the diagonal with 1.♗xd5. Unlike World Champion Euwe (see Appendix A), who made the same decision but clearly concluded that

1.♗xd5 was better, Subject E-14 eventually decided in favor of winning the bishop pair. But just the fact that he was able to arrive at and weigh the issues with 1.♗xd5 and 1.♘xc6 puts him ahead of players several classes above him. Despite some of his analytical mistakes (such as concluding he was winning a piece when he wasn't), it was a very reasonable effort. If more E-class players could think like this, their future would be bright as they got more experience analyzing positions carefully and improved their visualization so that large "Counting" errors were minimized.

Out of curiosity, I checked on the progress of Subject E-14, who performed this protocol in December 2010. Unfortunately, he never played another U.S. Chess Federation event after March 2011, when he attained a provisional 1070 rating. So we may never know what might have happened over a long period to see how he would have progressed.

Summary of Class E

Characteristics of the thought process at this level:

- The analysis is more concrete than Class F, but the subjects still do a lot of Hand-waving (using principles when only analysis will do).

- The subjects make many assumptions about their opponents' replies, but are either lacking a basis for these assumptions or are just making plain old bad guesses. At least they are considering these replies.

- The subjects are trying to see what moves are reasonable in the position. However, not only are many of their attempts incorrect, but they are sometimes also unnecessary as forcing moves should take precedence.

- The thought processes are all Hope Chess in that moves are made without seeing if all replies of checks, captures, and threats can be met. For example, in de Groot A, often a move was chosen that allowed an advantageous 1...♘xc3. The consequences of 1...♘xc3 were not even considered, much less seen as safe.

Improvements to the thought process that would help in getting to the next level:

- More systematic selection of candidate moves (this is true of most lower classes!).

- More checking to see if candidates are safe.

- Consideration of forcing moves first (for both sides).

- Taking more time to identify and evaluate the main candidates and, even if satisfied, looking for a better move.

Chapter 4

Class D

This chapter includes players rated 1200-1400 USCF, or roughly 1350-1550 ICC standard.

For each protocol, I list the de Groot position (for example, de Groot A, de Groot B, de Groot C, etc.; see Chapter 1 for those positions); the age of the subject; the subject's rating; and the time the subject spent to choose his move.

Comments in parentheses indicate outside actions or comments that reflect the action of the player, such as (silent) if he paused for a long time. Comments in brackets are my thoughts. My frequent use of [*sic*] means that the subject is making a clear mistake in analysis or visualization. In contrast, [!] indicates that the player has made a comment that is very insightful for their level of ability or a surprising error. A frequent note is [no eval], meaning that the subject did not try to evaluate which side stood better, by how much, and why.

Protocol D-1 (de Groot A; ICC 1350; adult; 5 minutes)
There is a fork ♘e5-d7. I am hitting the knight on f6 with the bishop on g5 but the bishop on c6 covers d5. I don't see the knight fork working [no eval]. Look at... no tactics. Look at moving a rook, like 1.♖fe1 [no checking for opponent threats].

Hmm. Can't see any immediate checks or direct threats on his part. He can take b2-pawn — maybe what to do with that. One solution is 1.b4. He wouldn't play 1...♘xb4 to lose a knight for two pawns. That might be good if I don't find a tactic. He can play 1...♗b5 to skewer queen and rook but then 2.♘xb5 so that's not really a threat.

Probably in this position I would play 1.b4 to save b2. I can't see any better so 1.b4 — longest I would have thought. Still looking at 1.b4 ♗xb4 2.axb4... so 1.b4. Push clock.

This subject, like many others rated below 1600, does no initial evaluation and thus has no goals or expectations to meet during the analysis. One big reason to evaluate a position is to figure out what your goals are. For example, if you think you are slightly better, then you are looking for a "best" continuation that leaves you at least slightly better.

Subject D-1 cleverly sees the fork possibility on d7. Yet he does not logically follow this observation with systematic analysis to discover whether any forcing sequence can take advantage of that possibility. Once he realizes that his pawn on b2 is in danger, he switches his focus exclusively to trying to make the pawn safe, ignoring possibilities to make a forcing move (check, capture, or threat) first. Many weaker players don't realize that if they can make a capture first, then defending the pawn may not be necessary as a series of forcing moves might keep the initiative and never allow the opponent time to capture the pawn. Instead, they tend to focus just on the defense of the pawn and ignore their own possibilities. Subject D-1 gets credit for spending some time seeing if the opponent can refute his final candidate move 1.b4. Most weak players never spend any time seeing if their opponent can defeat the move they are about to play, and thus play Hope Chess.

de Groot A
Black to play after 1.b4

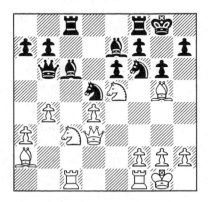

Unfortunately, the subject concentrates only on the pawn moved, and not on the square it had been guarding, c3. So he completely overlooks whether Black can defeat 1.b4 with a sequence starting with 1...♘xc3 and continuing with 2...♗b5 or 2...♘e4 or 2...♗e4. If White fails to examine Black's responses before playing 1.b4, then he is just lucky if Black does not defeat him with a series of captures!

The same subject a few months later:

Protocol D-2 (de Groot Zyme; ICC 1400; adult; 10 minutes)
"Equal in pieces [sic! Bishop pair] — one more pawn; black king exposed — may be about equal. Checks are 1.♗c7+ or 1.♗e7+. None looks that good — loses a piece. Captures: 1.♕xg4; 1.♗xg4; 1.♕xa8 interesting — can't recapture.

Threats for White: Maybe get knight away on g4. Black's checks: dangerous 1...♕xc3+ wins rook. 1...♕xf2+ dangerous. 1...♕xd6; 1...♘xf2. Lots of dangerous threats.

1.♕xa8 then 1...♕xc3+ 2.♔d1 only move 2...♕xa1+ or fork 2...♘xf2+ [mate]. Dangerous to take 1.♕xa8. 2...♕xa1+ and then ...♘xf2 loses two pawns by taking the rook. So 1.♕xa8 probably not possible. 1.♗e5 pins the queen to the rook but 1...♘xe5. A safe move to cover the square is 1.♕d4 to protect bishop on d6, c3, and f2. If I don't find anything better I can do that [King of the Hill].

Can also play 1.f3 but that does not cover 1...♕xd6 then 2.♖d1 but 1...♕xc3+ is not good. Hmm. Can't find anything much better than 1.♕d4. That threatens 2.♗e5+ winning the queen, so... I don't think I can find anything better so 1.♕d4. Push clock."

The de Groot Zyme exercise is even more tactical than de Groot A, and thus one would expect that weaker players should take more time on this protocol. The subject gets credit for starting by considering his checks, but his fatal flaw is not adding up two key pieces of information which he properly gathered: 1.♗e7+ is guarded by 1...♕xe7 and 1.♕xa8 fails to 1...♕xc3+. The key to this problem is realizing that if White can't take the rook because of the counterattack on c3, then the cost of deflecting this attack (a bishop) is less than the gain (the rook on a8). Thus the subject fails to realize that although each piece of information in itself seems enough to prevent 1.♗e7+ or 1.♕xa8, together they indicate that playing 1.♗e7+ first enables 2.♕xa8.

This type of deductive logic is partly learned, partly genetic. Even very brilliant people who have only been playing chess a short time often miss easy chess logic because they are not familiar with the paradigms of the game. Innate capabilities have to be cultivated with years of good experience to become a strong player.

The move played, 1.♕d4, is not acceptable, as after 1...♕xd4 2.cxd4 the endgame is promising for Black due to his queenside pawns:

de Groot Zyme
Black to play after 1.♕d4 ♕xd4 2.cxd4

Although this was Subject D-2's chosen move, he did not analyze the consequences of playing it. This is unfortunate because, although D-2 just spent 10 minutes finding this move, none of that time was devoted to investigating whether he could save the game after it was made. If your intended move leads to a lost position, then you should search for a better one. Of course, *if your candidate were the only legal move or the only move to save the game ("forced"), then you would just play it.* Since here White's move is not forced, the consequences should be weighed against those of other possible moves.

Protocol D-3 (de Groot A; 1250; age 17; 16 minutes)
Black's dark squares and king weak — I could have a fork on d7. 1.♗xf6 ♗xf6 2.♗xd5 exd5 fork at d7. 1.♗xf6 ♗xf6 2.♗xd5 exd5 3.♘xd5 ♗xd5 4.♘d7 fork wins the exchange but I gave up a piece for a pawn so I am worse giving up two pieces for a rook and pawn.

1.♗h6. Better to take knight on d5 first. 1.♘xd5 ♗xd5 2.♗xf6. 1.♘xd5 exd5 2.♗xf6. 1.♗xd5 exd5 ♗xf6 ♗xf6 don't want to give up dark-squared bishop.

Don't like giving up knight on e5. 1.♕f3 but he has threats. 1.♗xf6 and 2.♕f3. 1.♗xf6 ♗xf6 2.♕f3 not that good. 1.♕f3 and 2.♗xf6 ♘xf6 hits the queen.

1.♘xd5 ♘xd5 2.♗xd5 exd5. 1.♘xg6 does not look good. 1.♗b1 never mind. 1.♘xd5 then Black can't play 1...♘xd5 due to 2.♗xe7 [sic!]. 1.♘xd5 exd5 does not accomplish anything on 2.♗f6. 1.♕h3 not much. 1.♘xd5 exd5 1.♗h6 is King of the Hill [but no PV].

1.♖c2 don't know if it makes sense. 1.♖fe1 with the idea of ♖e3-h3 after 2.♘xd5 to remove knight. 1...♕xb2 is a threat. Then 2.♖b1 could be dangerous for him: 2...♕xa3 [2...♕xc3] 3.♖b3 escapes — no good for me. So 1.♖c2 protects pawn — allows doubling on the file.

1.b4 with the idea of a4-b5. 1.♖c2 is King of the Hill. 1.♖fe1 makes sense but 1...♕xb2. There must be something better than 1.♖c2.

1.♗h6 ♖fd8 no follow-up. 1.b4 defends — that threatens b4-b5 to hit bishop and then I can possibly get in ♘d7. 1.b4 weakens c3 and c4. 1.♖b1 helps advance — relinquishes file [not considering replies except on captures].

1.♘xd5 exd5 2.♖fe1 hits bishop on e7 on discovery. That's King of the Hill. 1.♘xd5 exd5 2.♖fe1 ♕xb2 no good. My PV is 1.♘xd5 exd5 2.♖fe1. Push clock.

Subject D-3 used less description and more "algebraic notation" than most. Like almost all others at this level, he does not begin by counting the material or making an evaluation — he begins by immediately identifying candidate moves without attempting to identify threats generated by the opponent's previous move. Subject D-3 gets very high marks for trying to make forcing moves work. But his approach is unsystematic and he does not list all possible recaptures with the goal of finding which recapture is best. This scattershot approach is not likely to find anything except by accident. Credit also goes to this subject for using the King of the Hill method, in which he identifies the best move found thus far. However, it is not clear how he compares candidate moves and their resulting positions to replace his King of the Hill. The process seems to happen almost by magic.

Protocol D-4 (de Groot Zyme; 1200; adult; 11 minutes)
Black is ahead a pawn. White has the bishop pair. The open center is helpful; need to finish my development. Black's rook on a8 is hanging. What hap-

pens if 1.♕xa8? He can check on f2 — I move away. 1.♕xa8... My checks, captures, and threats? Don't believe, so 1.♗c7+ ♔xc7 ruins his chances of castling [sic] but I lose the bishop. Any other checks? No [!]. 1.♕xa8 he has 1...♕xf2+. How would I respond? 2.♔d1 ♘e3+ then king moves: 3.♔c1 ♕e1+ chases me up the board. 4.♔b2 no more checks... 4...♘c1+ ♔a2 and the knight is pinned to the queen. 1...♕xc3+ is a fork, so 2.♔d1 ♕xa1+ 3.♔d2 what can he do? [Note: does not matter much — things are already bad]. 3...♕a2+ 4.♔c1 ♕a1+ is a challenge. Can he bring anyone else over to help? Not quickly. What else? 1...♘xf2 then 2.♖g1 can't castle kingside (silent). Going back looking at a check 1.♗e7+ forks king and queen but then 1...♕xe7 2.♕xe7+ [??] 2...♔xe7 is no good [!]. Threats are 1...♕xd6 and 1...♕xc3+. If 1.0-0-0 ♘xf2. 1.♕d5 protects the bishop. Two ways to protect the bishop. I can play 1.f3 to threaten the knight. 1...♕xd6 2.fxg4 threatening 3.♖d1 [!]. He can never take the bishop because of ♖d1. Is that true? 1.♕xa8 ♕xd6 2.♖d1 is no good for him. 1.♕xa8 ♕xf2+ been through that. What moves are better? 1.0-0-0 is possible — he can't check [?]. But there he has a fork — no good. So 1.♕xa8. Push clock.

Subject D-4 played 1.♕xa8 even though he saw the best reply 1...♕xc3+. Just the line 1.♕xa8 ♕xc3+ 2.♔d1 ♕xa1+ should have been enough to scare him away even though he (and many others drawn to the hanging rook on a1) missed the crushing move —

de Groot Zyme
Black to play after 1.♕xa8 ♕xc3+ 2.♔d1

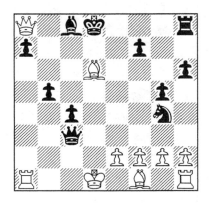

— 2...♘xf2#

Notice also how quickly Subject D-4 glossed over the best move, 1.♗e7+, which after the forced 1...♛xe7 now safely allows his actual move, 2.♛xa8. He listed the checks, incorrectly noting that 1.♗c7+ ♚xc7 stops castling, failing to notice that the black king is already on d8 and therefore could not castle anyway. The better check 1.♗e7+ is "seen" as so bad (or not seen at all) that the answer to "Any other checks?" is "No." This is probably an excellent example of a quiescence error: the player "saw" 1.♗e7+ without mentioning it, saw that the move appeared unsafe, but did not realize that the deflection of the queen plus the loose rook on a8 added up to quite a reasonable move.

Protocol D-5 (de Groot A; USCF 1380; adult; 3.5 minutes)
1.♘xd5 [no eval] ♘xd5 2.♗xd5 ♗xd5 3.♘d7. 1.♘xd5 ♘xd5 2.♗xd5 ♗xd5 3.♘d7 ♛a6 4.♛xa6 bxa6 5.♘xf8 wins the exchange. Push clock.

Subject D-5's brevity makes his protocol seem more like some of those in Class E. The subject correctly decides to consider a capture — after neither evaluating the position nor looking for the opponent's threats — but then just assumes one of the three recaptures. Worse, he analyzes his only line incorrectly, as he needed to spot 2...♗xg5:

de Groot A
White to play after 1.♘xd5 ♘xd5 2.♗xd5 ♗xg5

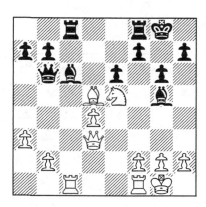

The subject does not consider any other recaptures on move 1, nor did he consider 2...exd5, leaving the bishop on c6 to guard d7. I guess, like many other weaker players, either he expects his opponent to play the moves which are good for him (White) or his unforced removal of the guard of d7 is wishful thinking. Later, if Black plays a better move, White's explanation will likely be, "I did not see it," rather than, "I did not even consider it."

Protocol D-6 (de Groot A; ICC 1500; adult; 7 minutes)
Count material. Seven pawns to six [?!]. Down material [!]. Isolated queen's pawn. Look at his checks, captures, and threats, then mine. 1...♛xb2 undefended. Queen attacks d4 — defended. Bishop attacks a3, defended. Threats? 1... ♛xb2, h6 not a threat. So. How would I defend the b-pawn or is that the right answer? My pawn structure is OK. Three pawn islands. Probably protect the b-pawn and perhaps attack on the dark squares double on the c-file. OK. I think I'll look at 1.b4 then 1...a5 trade there. 1.♖c2 with the idea of 2.♖1c1 protects b-pawn. I like that better. I can play 1.h4. Trade knight on c3 for knight d5. I can trade 1.♘xc6. I don't... 1.♘xd5 is defended three times, attacked twice. Does not work. Although ♗g5 pins knight to bishop on e7. So really only defended twice, and d5 attacked twice. Like better 1.♖c2 with the idea of 2.♖1c1 although... If I double he could play ...♗c6-a4 but then ♘xa4. Going to play 1.♖c2. Push clock.

Subject D-6 did a great job by beginning with a material count. Unfortunately, he miscounted and thought he was losing. Of course, if that were so, then a good player would know to look for aggressive moves first (not a bad idea at any time) and not settle on passive moves which just defend the b-pawn. As many low-rated players did, he dismissed the capture 1.♘xd5 primarily because it is defended adequately, as if this were a "play and win" problem. In most cases it is ironic that the players who reject captures often choose a move (in this case 1.♖c2) which also does not "win" material. Apparently they more highly value non-captures that don't win material over captures that don't win material. Captures and non-captures should be weighed at least equally to see which produces the better position.

Protocol D-7 (de Groot A; 1350; adult; ½ minute)
I need to do 1.b4 to protect b2. Push clock.

This was perhaps the shortest protocol, but not the worst. At least Subject D-7 took the time to determine the opponent's threats and meet them. Unfortunately he did not follow World Champion Emanuel Lasker's advice: "If you see a good move, look for a better one." Nor did he attempt to see if he had anything better than passive defense. If he'd had an easy combination to win, he would have missed it while concentrating on defending the b2-pawn!

Protocol D-8 (de Groot A; 1300; adult; 5 minutes)
*1.♘xc6. Messy. The bishop at e7 is vulnerable. 1.♘xd5 ♝xd5; if instead 1...
♘xd5 then 2.♝xe7.*

de Groot A
White to play after 1.♘xd5 ♘xd5

The recapturing knight on d5 now guards e7. Yet many weaker players
either visualize this incorrectly or assume that, with the piece on f6 gone
and the knight on d5 taken, the bishop on e7 must hang

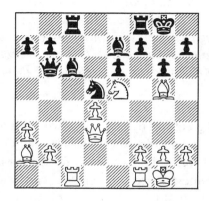

*After 1...♘xd5 2.♝xd5 exd5. Is that good? Isolating the d-pawn. Other
weaknesses? 1.b4 loosens c3. 1.♘xc6 wins the bishop pair; is the knight stronger
than the bishop? The bishop on c6 hits g2, so it is a good idea to win the bishop
pair. He can take back with the rook — no problem. 1.♘xc6. Looking for better.
1.♘xc6. Push clock.*

Before giving the de Groot exercise to my students, I almost always
make sure they understand the value of the bishop pair. As we have seen,
according to GM Larry Kaufman the bishop pair is worth, on the average,
about a ½-pawn bonus. In de Groot A, one can win the bishop pair with
1.♘xc6. Yet most weaker players don't even mention this candidate, much
less play it. So a lot of credit to Subject D-8, who, although he did not look
for a better move, at least chose one resulting in something positive. It
would have been much better to thoroughly analyze *all* the forcing moves

to see if one was better than 1.♘xc6. Like many other subjects, D-8 did not perform an evaluation at the start (who stands better, by how much, and why?) nor did he look for his opponent's threats. So 1.♘xc6 may have been "lucky" in that he did not notice that 1...♕xb2 — or anything else — was threatened.

The following subject was a youngster who was just starting lessons and USCF play. By age 16 he was a USCF expert and Pennsylvania State High School Co-Champion.

Protocol D-9 (de Groot A; 1200+; age 11; 6 minutes)
The square h6 is weak. 1.♘xg6 fxg6. No [no eval]. 1.♘xd5 ♗xd5. 1.♘xc6 ♖xc6 2.♘xd5 shows how little I think. 1.♖fe1 develops. 1.♘xg6 no, so 1.♖fe1 — no — 1...♕xb2 is a threat. 1.♖c2 to double. What does Black have? 1...♘xc3 and skewer (on b5)? 2.bxc3 skewer [sic?] and 2.♖xc3 ♕xb2. The d-pawn is weak; maybe 1.b4. If I let him play 1...♕xb2 then 2.♖b1 ♕xc3 so guard him with 1.b4. 1.♘c4 ♗b5? Guess not: 2.♘xb5 ♕xb5 the knight is pinned; does not look good. So 1.b4 hit clock.

Subject D-9 shows very early signs of becoming a good player. Although there was no evaluation and the identification of threats came a little late, he begins by looking at his aggressive captures, although he cuts 1.♘xd5 short, does not mention winning the bishop pair on 1.♘xc6, and never considers the best move 1.♗xd5. A big dose of Hope Chess as he does not consider whether Black has any check, capture, or threat that can beat 1.b4 — especially the dangerous 1...♘xc3. The analysis given, while sketchy and incomplete, is at least almost entirely accurate.

Protocol D-10 (de Groot A; 1200; age 9; 1 minute)
1.♗xf6 ♗xf6 2.♘xd5 ♗xd5 3.♗xd5 exd5 4.♘d7. Push clock

This protocol, wherein the youngster stops analyzing after seeing a fork, encapsulates in one line what is wrong with many fast, weak, and/or young players:

- They don't follow Lasker's Rule: "When you see a good move, look for a better one."

- When they see a winning line, they just play it instead of following the advice (from GM Alburt and others): "If you see a winning line, then that is a critical move and you should spend lots of time." The idea is simple: if it really is winning, then using extra time won't hurt. If it is not winning, then the move may not even be a good one, so it is important to look for a better one.

- They play a line that is completely unforced, expecting the opponent will gladly play bad moves for them. Of course, the opponent is trying to find his best moves, so assuming they will play the ones you want will not lead to accurate conclusions. For example, here Black can vary on the very first move, recapturing on f6 with 1...♘xf6 instead of 1...♗xf6. Or, on move 2, Black can retain his bishop as a defender of d7 by recapturing on d5 with the pawn with 2...exd5 instead of with the anticipated 2...♗xd5. When you have a winning line, it has to be winning in *all* variations, not just the ones that you would like.

- They play very quickly as if to see what happens, rather than trying to figure out what could happen if the opponent played well. When you ask players who have this problem why they played so quickly, you often get an answer like, "I thought the line won," which, of course it did not. But even if it did, they should have all the more reason to check it and make sure.

If you want to play quickly and superficially for fun, by all means go ahead. But if you purchased this book with the idea that it could make you a better player, then avoiding the thought process displayed in protocols like this one is definitely a step in the right direction!

The next two protocols, done back-to-back, were by a normally very slow player. The first one was uncharacteristically very fast. His haste shows that not only do some players "show off" by moving uncharacteristically slowly for the exercise (understandable, but not helpful in diagnosing their "normal" problems), but the opposite is also occasionally true: slow players sometimes play too quickly.

Protocol D-11 (de Groot Zyme; 1200; adult; 2 minutes)
Looking at a mate in one — my bishop is attacked, so... Do I have any checks, captures, or threats here? No. I am going to save my bishop and prevent mate with 1.♗g3. Push clock (after moving: "Oh! I lose a pawn...").

de Groot Zyme
Black to play after 1.♗g3

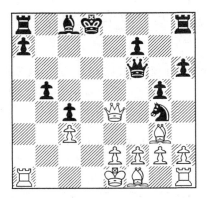

The subject not only did not count the pieces or do an evaluation, but he did not look for all the threats, such as 1...♛xc3+ 2.♔d1 ♘xf2#, and he did not even see he could possibly play 1.♛xa8. Purely defensive, and not much of a defense at that. Subject D-11 did exclaim, "Oh! I lose a pawn," immediately after moving when he belatedly spotted 1...♛xc3+. Many players play like this. To get to the next level, they have to consistently play more slowly and become more systematic in searching for both sides' forcing moves. A wise move is to realize, "I am a fairly weak player, so I should take my time, because when I move fast I often make big tactical mistakes."

Protocol D-12 (de Groot Ernie; 1200; adult; 2 minutes)
White is a pawn ahead, 6-5. I am looking at the board and trying not to miss any pieces. The two rooks are on open files. I have a centralized queen and a well-placed bishop. His rook attacks my bishop and his knight attacks my queen. There are light-square holes around his king for my queen and bishop. I need to get in there. How do I save my bishop and queen at the same time? Umm. Let's consider the queen first: where can she move? Anywhere on the fifth rank? Looks like the a-, b-, and e-files. Umm. Or she could retreat to d4, d2, or d1 (silent). Can't put... If I keep the queen on the a- or b-files I can protect the bishop, but the problem is that the pawns on a7 and b7 can chase me — so that won't do any good. I can move 1.♛e4 to protect the bishop that way — the attacked knight is covered by the black queen. Do I have any threats right now? Black's king is protected by the pawns at h6 and g7, which are both dark squares — I have a light-squared bishop — I can't move the rooks or check, else I lose my queen.

So... (silent) Umm. Need to move the queen to e4 to protect the bishop and get the queen out of the attack with the knight. I think that's the best I can do right now. No checks — can't capture anything. 1.♗xd7 is not good — he just takes. My knight is too far away to do any good right now. So I will play 1.♕e4 (hesitates; silent). 1.♕e4.

This is an excellent example of Hope Chess, as Subject D-12 never considered what Black could do to defeat his intended move. Indeed, after 1.♕e4 the reply 1...d5!:

de Groot Ernie
White to play after 1.♕e4? d5!

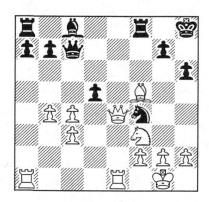

hits the queen and attacks the bishop a second time, winning a piece. An important tip: *in analytical positions, your opponent will spend almost 100% of his time trying to defeat your move, so to make a move and not spend* any *of your time trying to see if he would be successful (and, if so, discarding your candidate move) is often quite disastrous.*

The next two protocols are a little different. I gave the same position to the same subject twice in a row (!). After his first protocol, I gave him some generic suggestions on what he did incorrectly (see below), but did not supply any correcting analysis. I then gave him a second chance...

Protocol D-13 (de Groot Zyme; 1200; adult; 5 minutes)
White has a centralized queen and bishop, is underdeveloped on the kingside. I could... Any checks? 1.♗e7+ ♕xe7 loses the bishop; 1.♗e7+ ♕xe7.

1.♖d1 sets up a discovered attack. [no eval] He can't castle. After 1.♖d1 he could play 1...♗d7. Yes, his knight is guarded by his bishop on c8, so 1.♕xg4 is bad due to 1...♗xg4. I could ... check him 1.♗c7+ then 1...♔xc7 but I can take his rook 2.♕xa8.

de Groot Zyme
Black to play after 1.♗c7+ ♔xc7 2.♕xa8

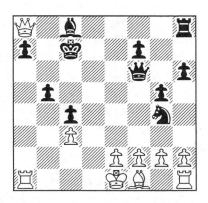

1.♗c7+ ♔xc7 2.♕xa8 with the idea of 3.♖xa7+ when he has to run to b6 or c6 — he can't interpose 3...♗b7 because then I take. 1.♗c7+ hit clock.

After this protocol, I first asked Subject D-13 to play out his main line against me. So he played 1.♗c7+ ♔xc7 2.♕xa8, but I surprised him with 2...♕xc3+ and, after the forced 3.♔d1, asked him what he thought Black would do. He then saw 3...♕xa1+ but I pointed out that 3...♘xf2# is even better.

After that sobering experience, I asked him why he sacrificed the bishop on c7 first? — if he did not see the threat of ...♕xc3+, why not just take the rook with 1.♕xa8 instead? He said that he wanted to play 1.♗c7+ to expose the black king and was worried about 1...♕xd6, but he did not realize that would cost him a tempo — after 1.♕xa8 ♕xd6?, it is White's move and he can play something like 2.♖d1. But after 1.♗c7+ ♔xc7 2.♕xa8 it is Black's move and White cannot play 3.♖xa7 as analyzed — it is not his move, falling instead into the mating sequence with 2...♕xc3+ 3.♔d1 ♘xf2#.

So I suggested to Subject D-13 that he should first count the material — Black is ahead a pawn for the bishop pair — and then look and see what kind of forcing moves both sides are threatening like White's 1.♕xa8 and Black's 1...♕xd6, 1...♕xc3+, 1...♕xf2+, and 1...♘xf2. Once he was aware of these ideas, then he could start looking for candidate moves, keeping these in mind. I also suggested that such a complicated position was a "red flag" that indicates that he should take more time. I then stated that I had not given away too much of what he should have done, so I would give him a second chance:

Protocol D-14 (de Groot Zyme; 1200; adult; 5 minutes)
Material: Black is ahead a pawn for the bishop pair. Black threatens 1...♕xc3+ and 1...♕xf2+ and 1...♕xd6. I can play 1.♕d4 — it guards the bishop on d6, and also guards c3 and f2. So if 1.♕d4 ♕xd4 2.cxd4 then he...(silent) — equal in... I have guarded his threats. Can he win material? The f-pawn is guarded on 1.♕d4. If not 1...♕xd4 what can he do? 1...♕xf2+ 2.♕xf2 ♘xf2 3.♔xf2 is no good for him. Are there other checks or threats for him? He could activate his rooks, but what is the point? I have to guard c3, f2, and the bishop on d6. The only move doing that is 1.♕d4:

de Groot Zyme
Black to play after 1.♕d4 ♕xd4 2.cxd4

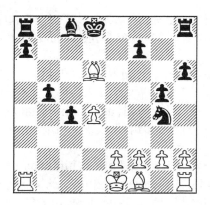

— so, 1.♕d4. Push clock.

Given the D-13 "post-mortem" information as a start, Subject D-13/14 does better in his second try, but still plays too quickly. He settles for a purely defensive move and completely ignores the fact that, after 1.♕d4 ♕xd4 2.cxd4, Black enjoys an endgame ahead a pawn with three connected passed pawns on the a- to c-files. He also ignores the motto, *When you see a good move, look for a better one.* The computer rates 1.♕d4 as only the fifth-best move. Even though I had pointed out that 1...♕xd6 was not much of a threat due to 2.♖d1, the subject forgot that and thus overlooked that the superior 1.♕f3 would also be an adequate defensive move. The possibility of winning the exchange with the deflection 1.♗e7+ never made it onto his radar. I suggested to Subject D-13/14 that he play much slower when he sees all those pieces hanging...

Protocol D-15 (de Groot A; ICC 1450; adult; 9.5 minutes)

The material is even. The white king is safely castled. The black king has weak dark squares around it. The white bishop on g5 and the white bishop on a2 are good. Calculate a move. What was his move? Any threats? 1...♕xb2 is a threat − not sure it's real. 1...♕xb2 2.♖b1 can the queen save herself? 2...♕xc3 − safety on d6. So 1...♕xb2 is a real threat [good]. Other threats? d4 is weak − only the queen defends. The knight at e5 is a good piece. The knight on f6 − if I get rid of the knight on d5, the knight on f6 is pinned, so 1.♘xd5 ♗xd5 is forced. 1.♘xd5 ♗xd5 2.♗xd5 exd5 − trying best to get rid of d5 pieces. 1.♘xd5 ♗b5 − the queen is pinned to the rook on f1. 1.♘xd5 exd5 and have to move the queen, I guess. Still have to protect the b-pawn. Other threats? 1.♖b1 protects the b-pawn 1.♕c2, 1.♕d2, 1.♕e2, 1.♘a4 ♗xa4. 1.♘xd5 ♗xd5 2.♖xc8 ♖xc8 3.♗xd5 exd5 is a problem. If I can rid of 1.♘xd5 exd5 2.♕f3 is good [good!] − can set a double attack on the knight: 1.♘xd5 ♗xd5 2.♗xd5 exd5 3.♕xd5. 1.♘xd5 is it safe? 1.♘xd5 ♘xd5 2.♗xe7 ♘xe7 ah! So 1.♘xd5 ♘xd5 2.♗xd5 ♗xd5 3.♗xe7 is complicated. 1.♘xd5 ♘xd5 2.♗xd5 ♗xg5 [good!]

de Groot A
White to play after 1.♘xd5 ♘xd5 2.♗xd5 ♗xg5

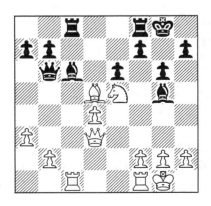

3.♗xc6 bxc6 – of course. 1.♘xd5 ♗xd5 2.♗xf6 ♗xa2 3.♘xa2. 1.♘xd5 exd5 2.♗xf6 ♗xf6 3.♕f3. I think 1.♘xd5 is probably the move. No checks. A series of captures looks favorable for White. I'll do that. 1.♘xd5. Push clock.

Despite anything else Subject D-15 did, he was one of the very few players rated below 1800 that I have tested ever (!) to reach the critical position 1.♘xd5 ♘xd5 2.♗xd5 ♗xg5. Not only that, Subject D-15's rating isn't even close to 1800: bravo! Of course, it takes a lot more than just reaching one critical position to have a good analytical protocol. Here Subject D-15 convinced himself that the series of captures is good for White, when in fact the very sequence he discovered at the diagram is the one that proves that 1.♘xd5 is not so good. Of course, the astute reader already knows that 1.♗xd5 is better – when you see a good move, look for a better one...

Summary of Class D

Characteristics of the thought process at this level:

- Good: A lot more analysis and less Hand-waving than at the Class E level. In accordance with those better actions, more time is taken to make a move.

- Bad: The analysis is often slipshod, illogical, and/or unsystematic.

- Hope Chess still reigns; hardly anyone spends any time seeing if the opponent can defeat his selected candidate move. This leads to the #1 lesson I learned as a beginning tournament player: *It's not enough to be smart and to be able to solve "problems" better than your opponent. Some problems are insoluble and some threats are unstoppable. So, to allow such problems/threats just loses instantly – they have to be foreseen and prevented because to wait for, "I didn't see that!" is too late.*

Improvements to the thought process that would help in getting to the next level:

- Less assumption of what the likely reply is by the opponent and more consideration (or listing) of all the reasonable replies. For example, in de Groot A after 1.♘xd5, it would be good to list the three recaptures and figure out which one is best for Black. 1.♘xd5 is only as good as the best recapture allows it to be.

- Don't eliminate captures just because they don't win material. They often keep the initiative. Chess is not always a "play and win" puzzle.

- Take time to evaluate (who's winning, by how much, and why) at the start of exercises. That provides a strong basis for deciding what needs to be done.

- Take some time to see if the chosen move can be defeated by a tactic. If so, discard the move.

- Search for all of your opponent's threats before beginning the selection of candidates. Don't take an inordinate amount of time, but don't stop after you see the first threat either.

Chapter 5

Class C

This chapter includes players rated 1400-1600 USCF, or roughly 1550-1750 ICC standard.

For each protocol, I list the de Groot position (for example, de Groot A, de Groot B, de Groot C, etc.; see Chapter 1 for those positions); the age of the subject; the subject's rating; and the time the subject spent to choose his move.

Comments in parentheses indicate outside actions or comments that reflect the action of the player, such as (silent) if he paused for a long time. Comments in brackets are my thoughts. My frequent use of [*sic*] means that the subject is making a clear mistake in analysis or visualization. In contrast, [!] indicates that the player has made a comment that is either very insightful for their level of ability or a surprising error. A frequent note is [no eval], meaning that the subject did not try to evaluate which side stood better, by how much, and why.

The first two protocols are by the same student a couple months apart, as he was pushing past the upper end of the class:

Protocol C-1 (de Groot Zyme; 1570+; adult; ~10 minutes)
If 1.♕xa8 then 1...♕xd6 OK. 1...♕xf2+ 2.♔d1 ♘e3+ does not add anything. 1...♕xf2+ seems only reasonable. 2.♔d1 ♘e3+ don't see anything good for Black after 2.♔d2. So what? Any others? 1.♕xa8 ♕xf2+ 2.♔d1 everything else is guarded. No queen checks, Black can't castle. 1...♘e3+ doesn't do anything. What am I missing? 1.♕xa8 ♕xc3+ 2.♔d1:

de Groot Zyme
Black to play after 1.♕xa8 ♕xc3+ 2.♔d1
The "big appeal" of 2...♕xa1+ causes players to miss 2...♘xf2#

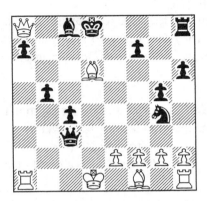

2...♕xa1+ 3.♔c2 or ♔d2. Then 3...♘xf2 rook moves not so good for White. 1.♕xa8 ♕xc3+ 2.♔d1 ♕xa1+ ♔d2 Black is up three pawns. No continuation for White. 1.♕xa8 ♕xc3+ 2.♔d1 ♕xa1+ 3.♔d2 ♘xf2 White is not threatening ♗e7+. Bad for White. 1.♗e7+ ♕xe7 2.♕xe7+ ♔xe7 can't be good for White [sic]. 1.♗c7+ not decent. 1.h3 hits knight — bishop still hangs. 1.♕d5 then still 1...♕xc3+. 1.♕d4 stops the threats. Black's king is in trouble.

1.♕d4 ♕xd4 2.cxd4 not bad for Black. White is down a pawn. Not particularly desirable. Three connected passed pawns and the knight is not trapped. Can go to f6. Hmm. Don't like any of this. 1.♕xa8 ♕xc3+ 2.♔d1 ♕xa1+ 3.♔d2 doesn't seem good. So I don't like 1.♕xa8. 1.♕d5 then c3 is vulnerable. 1.♕d4 holds but a bad endgame. Chasing knight is no good — no other tactical threats. So choose between 1.♕xa8+, loses pawn, and bad position, interesting. But 1.♕d4 is just sedately losing. 1.♕xa8 is wild and woolly but bad. 1.♕xa8 ♕xc3+ 2.♔d1 ♕xa1+ 3.♔d2 ♘xf2. Push clock.

As we have seen with weaker players, they are so enamored with the opponent's 1.♕xa8 ♕xc3+ 2.♔d1 ♕xa1+ (which *should* be enough to dissuade them from 1.♕xa8) that they don't look for the better 2...♘xf2#. What's interesting is that since 2...♕xa1+ is strong enough to eliminate the entire line, the need to find 2...♘xf2# is moot. The only time it would *not* be moot would be the case illustrated by C-1, where for some reason 2...♕xa1+ is not enough to dissuade the subject, and he chooses that line anyway. In that case, finding 2...♘xf2# *is* important to eliminate 1.♕xa8.

Note that even at the Class C level the players don't always start by evaluating the position. Subject C-1 had no idea that Black was ahead a pawn at the start, and so just trading down was not necessarily good for White. Even in a game, where players should have a better handle on what is going on, this same problem persists: weaker players trade down even though it is bad for them because they don't stop to evaluate the position. *If your "best" move makes the resulting position easier for your opponent to win, that is a great reason to question it.*

Finally, kudos to C-1 for correctly evaluating that 1.♕d4, while stopping all of Black's threats, is insufficient due to 1...♕xd4 2.cxd4 with a good endgame for Black. It is not enough to stop all the threats — if the result is a likely loss, then searching for something better is a good idea.

Protocol C-2 (de Groot C; 1590+; adult; 11 minutes)
Material: no pieces trapped, no tactics. White's king is open. Is White threatening? He threatens the e-pawn. 1...e5 2.♗xc8 with the idea of 3.dxe5 loses a pawn. Does not seem to work. Like to activate the light-squared bishop. How about 1...b6? Still leaves the e-pawn hanging. If 2.♗xe6+ ♗xe6 3.♕xe6 but knight on f3 hangs [does not see check].

de Groot C
Black to play after 1...b6 2.♗xe6+ ♗xe6 3.♕xe6+

So don't have to worry about it yet, so ...♖e8 is possible. Then 1...♖e8 2.d5 ♕d7 doesn't work — no it does — it doesn't. How to defend? 1...♖e8 2.d5 exd5 is OK. So 1...♖e8 2.d5 exd5 is good for Black. So 1...♖e8 with the idea of 2...

e5. 1...♖e8 2.♘g5 what is the move after 1...♖e8? 1...♖e8 2...e5 3.♗xc8 exd4 4.♘xd4. Tough to think through. 1...♖e8 2.any e5 Oh, 1...♖e8 2.any e5 3.♗xc8 ♖axc8 4.dxe5 dxe5 5.♘xe5 ♕xh1 6.♖xh1 ♖xe5 7.♕xe5 ♘d3. But what if he does not capture on e5? Not good. Oh, bugger! Complex so analysis is meaningless. So 1...♖e8 hit clock.

I must have mentioned something about evaluating the position between protocols C-1 and C-2 because this time the subject counted the material first. The difficult de Groot C position causes everyone problems and he handled it passively. After a couple of initial attempts to look at ideas like 1...e5 (reasonable) and 1...b6 (strange), he honed in on the passive 1...♖e8 and never really tried to find a better move. He was trying to prove that his move was reasonable rather than making any attempt to show it was best.

In many situations (especially in quiet positions or faster games), it is OK to just to find a "good" — or at least a reasonable — move. But to do so in sharp positions is often a crucial mistake. In sharp positions, the expected result of the game after the best move may differ greatly from that of the second-best move. For example, the best move might be the only winner, while the second-best move draws. Or the best move might ensure an easy win whereas the second-best move requires great technique. In these protocols, most of the positions are more critical than the average position, so at least some attempt to find a very good move is justified.

Note that Subject C-2 terminates his thought process not because he feels he has found the best move or has taken enough time, but rather because, "Complex so analysis is meaningless." However, the right idea is to play relatively quickly in non-complex (non-critical) positions so as to save your time for analyzing complex, critical positions. If you find yourself giving up because the analysis is too complex, but have lots of time remaining which can be applied to this move, perhaps a short break to get water might be better than picking a random move! Remember, *you may never be as good as Kasparov at analysis, but that does not mean you can't get better with practice. Practice may not make perfect, but it sure helps, so practice as much as you can.*

Protocol C-3 (de Groot A; 1500; adult; 11 minutes)
Hanging? Immediate attention knight c3 attacked by knight d5. Pawn hangs at b2. His knight at f6 is under attack; the bishop at c6 is attacked. Probably not going to worry too much about b2 — not an immediate concern. I like 1.♘xc6

to get the bishop pair [!]. There are immediate tactics which come to mind. Fair amount points to king. g6 weakens king. 1.♘xg6 or something to make it better. 1...fxg6 not exciting to follow up. So 1.h4 is a candidate. I like it as a possibility. 1.♘xc6 and 1.h4 candidates — both forcing enough that 1...♕xb2 is OK. Think more. Prefer 1.♘xc6 less so 1.♘xc6. I am thinking he might lose a pawn if... If 1.♖xc6 can I win a pawn on d5? [!?]. No, f6-knight is on it. So 1...♖xc6 is possible. So think about 1.♘xc6 bxc6 what would be the follow-up? Don't see anything exciting. Bishop pair. The knight on e5 is in a good spot, but bishop c6 was pointing at my king. On the whole, probably not my best move. Back to 1.h4. Is h5 a good follow? No, because of the knight at f6. So what is the follow? Want to play h5. So I need to get knight on f6 to get off defense of h5. So 1.♘xd5 ♘xd5 but 1.h4 with the idea of 2.♘xd5 so I like h4 more. 1.h4 response? 1...h5 any follow-up? [not captures] 1.h4 h5 2.♘xg6 fxg6 ♕xg6+ may be OK. So 1...h5 likely not good. What is good after 1.h4? Think ahead: 1.h4 ♕xb2 2.♗b1 is on g6, too. Not sure what the bishop on a2 does. If I am going after the king, then the bishop is better on b1. So 1.h4 ♕xb2 2.♗b1. I don't know. He plays...? 2...♘xc3 3.♖xc3. It's all getting wild and I don't see the consequences. My play is still on the kingside — 1.h4 still looks good. I could set it up with 1.♗b1 first but 1.h4 looks more interesting. So 1.h4. Push clock. (PV = 1.h4 ♕xb2 2.♗b1...?)

Subject C-3 did not count the material, but did survey the position and found that b2 was attacked. He gets good marks for deciding not to worry too much about b2 (yet) and noticing he can win the bishop pair. However, he quickly fixates on trying to make a pawn break with h4-h5, which in many fianchetto positions is reasonable. In positions like these with so many forcing moves, such slower considerations are usually secondary to the immediate forcing moves: checks, captures, and threats. Not considering any capturing sequence other than 1.♘xc6 is inefficient and lowers the probability of finding the best move.

Here are three in a row from another student. On the first he is almost Class C, but by the third he is almost above it!

Protocol C-4 (de Groot A; 1350; age 10; 2 minutes)
The knight on f6 is pinned by the bishop if you get rid of the knight on d5 [No eval]. 1.♗h6 weak dark squares. Can move open to half-open file. May need to protect b2. Can move 1.♘e4 — set knight up to a good square. Don't see anything else. 1.♘xd5. Push clock.

A spotty protocol that was not completely finished, but that happens when you are ten years old, talented, and not so verbal. Sometimes talking out loud is distracting, especially for a process that one usually does silently. Subject C-4 did not count material but did do a rough assessment before mentioning a candidate move. Also to his credit is that he spotted the hanging b2-pawn and did not state that he had to defend it — he properly noted that he *may* need to do so. Far more experienced players have made the mistake of being too black-or-white on such issues — keeping an open mind with "may" is a great idea.

Protocol C-5 (de Groot Zyme; USCF 1500; age 12; <5 minutes)

The rook on a8 hangs. Black threatens f2 with the queen and the knight. 1.f3. Wait, he also threatens 1...♛xc3+ winning the rook. 1.♝e7+ to win the queen? No, need to stop 1...♛xc3+ by ♖c1, ♖a3, or ♔d2. If there was not a knight on g4, then ♝e5 skewers queen and rook. 1.♛d4 stops 1...♛xc3+. Could play 1.♝c7+ ♔xc7 don't know if that's good. Then — no 2.♖a6, no ...♝xa6. 1.♝e7+ ♛xe7 2.♖d1+ ♝d7 3.♛xa8+ and 2...♔e8 3.♛xa8 and no attack on c3 or f2. That's about it. 1.♝e7+ hit clock.

de Groot Zyme
Black to play after 1.♝e7+!

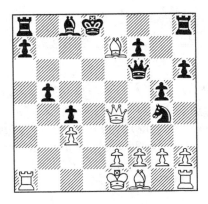

The two years meant a lot! The subject still does not count material, but he quickly spots all the key tactical issues. Although at one point he finds the passive 1.♛d4 to meet all the threats, unlike Subject D-2 he properly looks for a better and more aggressive answer and surveys his checks. In doing so he does not commit the quiescence error that weaker players make and instead deduces the right idea 1.♗e7+. Bravo! I suspect this player will be well above 1600 in a few years...

Protocol C-6 (de Groot Ernie; 1550; age 12; 7 minutes)

White's queen is threatened by knight on f4. If 1.♕e5 ♕xc4 2.♖e4 wins the knight — no, then 2...♘e2+ or 2...♕xc3 — doesn't work. 1.♕c5 ♕xc5 2.bxc5 ♖xf5 tripled isolated pawns and down a bishop — hopeless. 1.♕d4 pressures g7 and allows ♖e7. Wait! 1.♕d4 ♖xf5 2.♖e8+ ♔h7 3.♕e4 pins the rook. Then ... f6 [sic: ...g6] holds piece. 3...g6 4.♕e7+ wins. 1.♕d4 ♖xf5 2.♖e8+ ♔h7:

de Groot Ernie
White to play after 1.♕d4! ♖xf5 2.♖e8+ ♔h7
Subject wants to play 3.♕e4, but 3.♖e7! is stronger

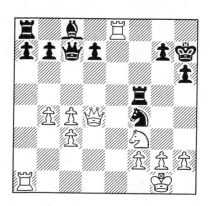

3.♕e4 g6 4.♕e7+ rook moves 5. Takes — checkmate so he can't take the bishop. 1.♕d4 ♖f7 2.♖e8+ ♖f8 3.♖xf8#. 1.♕d4 then 1...d6 or 1...d5. 1...d6 2.♕xf4 ♖xf5. White is up a pawn. I am not even in material, I just noticed. Play 1.♖e8 ♖xe8 or 1...♘xd5. 1.♕g8+ ♖xg8 no tactics. Back to 1.♕e5 ♕xc4 never mind (silent). 1.♕d4. Push clock. PV = 1.♕d4 d6; if 1.♕d4 ♖xf5 2.♖e8+ ♔h7 3.♕e4 g6 wins.

Again the youngster hits a quick bull's-eye with the computer's top move! This time, though, he was quite a bit lucky because he played it without correctly analyzing several of the main lines. If you see a move like that, you need to work out some of the lines. If there is one big defensive idea, that may be enough to cause that line to be discarded, much less considered best. While the idea is to find the best move you can, in volatile positions one analytical mistake can make all the difference between a great move and a terrible one. Still, an A+ for finding a pretty difficult idea fairly quickly.

Protocol C-7 (de Groot A; 1550; adult; 5 minutes)

Black is threatening 1...♕xb2. Nothing is en prise. He threatens to capture 1...♘xc3. I can capture 1.♗xf6, or 1.♘xc6 gets the bishop pair, but that trades a good knight for a bishop that is not active. Do I have any tactics? No tactics. Count material; isolated pawn. He's weak on the kingside dark squares. Candidate moves: 1.b4 – against the threat 1.♘xd5 ♘xd5 2.♗xd5 wins the bishop on e7 [wrong].

de Groot A
Black to play after 1.♘xd5 ♘xd5 2.♗xd5

Missing that 2...♗xd5?? 3.♗xe7 is not forced; instead 2...♗xg5

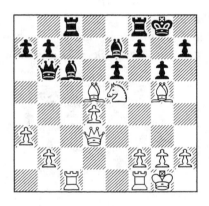

1.♘xd5 ♗xd5 nothing that benefits [wrong]. 1.♖fe1; 1.♘a4 ♗xa4; 1.♕d2 guards b2. I can double rooks with 1.♖c2. That's a candidate – to double rooks. 1.♖c2. Push clock.

Subject C-7 begins with a decent assessment but no evaluation – for example, there is no indication of which side stands better. Notice the strange logic: First, Subject C-7 says that if 1.♘xd5 then if 1...♘xd5 2.♗xd5 wins the bishop. This is incorrect, but he does not check it. Then he correctly tries to find a better reply for Black and sees 1...♗xd5, but then again incorrectly concludes that White has nothing, missing the removal-of-the-guard and then fork idea 2.♗xd5 ♘xd5 3.♗xe7 ♘xe7 4.♘d7.

At the end of his protocol, Subject C-7's process is pure Hope Chess. He sees a move that does two things — it prepares to double rooks and also guards the b-pawn — and plays it without checking to see if it is safe. Players who play Hope Chess and then have to reply to 1...♞xc3 usually think, "Hmm! I wonder how I should take back — maybe I am in danger..."

Protocol C-8 (de Groot A; 1500+; adult; 7 minutes)
1.♗xf6 or 1.♗xd5. [no eval] 1.♞xc6 but not sure if it's best. What's going on? Material — White down a piece. No exchanges. No, pieces even. White has an extra pawn — no, even. If 1.♗xf6 ♞xf6 is best; after 1...♗xf6 2.♞xd5 ♗xd5 then 3.♞d7 is a fork. But 1.♗xf6 ♞xf6 is OK. Trying to affect ♞d7. 1.♗xd5 ♞xd5 2.♞xd5. Back up. 1.♞xd5 If 1...♗xd5 2.♗xd5; 1...exd5 2.♗xf6 ♗xf6 3.♞d7 [missing 3...♗xd7]:

de Groot A
Black to play after 1.♞xd5 exd5 2.♗xf6 ♗xf6 3.♞d7
C-8 commits a visualization error; because the bishop on c6 moved
in another variation, he thinks that it is no longer there

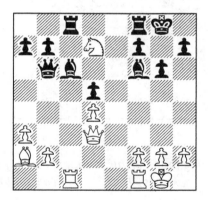

1...♞xd5 2.♗xe7 ♞xe7 3.♞d7 [again 3...♗xd7]. 1.♞xd5 ♗xd5 2.♗xd5. If 1.♞xd5 ♞xd5 2.♗xd5 ♞xd5 and 3.♞d7. So 1.♞xd5 hit clock.

For clarification, at this point I asked the subject, "What is your PV?" and he replied, "1.♞xd5 ♗xd5 2.♗xd5 ♞xd5 3.♗xe7 ♞xe7 4.♞d7."

Subject C-8 makes a mistake similar to the one shown in the diagram for C-7. C-8 incorrectly assumes that, after 1.♞xd5, 1...♞xd5 is not possible due to the "win" of the bishop on e7. As for the PV, he made another com-mon mistake by assuming he was winning and entering a critical line without double-checking his analysis. In this case the mistake was a retained image error, forgetting that the bishop on c6 is still guarding d7. *When you see a move which wins, jam on the brakes and make sure — don't just play it and then say, "Whoops!"*

Protocol C-9 (de Groot A; USCF 1550; adult; 16 minutes)
Count material — White has more space. Isolated queen's pawn. Rook has open file, queen is centralized, White's dark bishop is a "bad" bishop, actively placed. Black has moved a pawn in front of his king, has a rook on the open file, the queen threatens ...♛xb2, the knights are roughly centrally located. Black's dark-squared bishop is not protected [sic], so the knight on f6 is pinned. So White, with more active pieces, should attack. Can White win anything? To calculate: 1.♞xd5 to remove guard of bishop on d7: knight on f6 is protected twice. 1.♞xd5 ♝xd5 2.♞d7 ♞xd7 3.♝xe7 just trade a bunch of pieces [?!]. Is there a combination here? 1.♝xd5 ♝xd5 2.♞xd5 exd5 — I don't see a way to win material [?!]. 1.♝xf6 ♝xf6 2.♞xd5 or 2.♝xd5 ♝xd5 3.♞xd5 exd5 4.♞d7 forks bishop [rook?] and queen or ♞d7 fork. 1.♝xf6 ♝xf6 2.♝xd5 ♝xe5 is forced [sic] 3.dxe5. I don't think that is going to work. Now I am just looking to improve the position. Black's plan? I don't know Black's plan; ...♝b5 with skewer, but the knight on c3 can just capture on b5. 1...♞xc3 and I take with the queen to avoid the skewer, so if I take the knight on d5, ...♝b5 is troublesome, but perhaps not a real threat. Need a plan. More space — pieces more active. I could challenge for the c-file or attack his king. 1.♖c2 followed by 2.♖1c1 lines the rooks on the c-file. He could... double his rooks also and end up trading. If 1...♞xc3 2.bxc3 ♝b5 is kind of nasty [sic]. It's a threat I need to deal with. Also, I have a pawn in take at b2; that's an issue that needs to be dealt with. So maybe I just take the knight... The more I look at this, the more I think it is a problem that needs to be dealt with. So I suppose I just move 1.♛c2 or 1.♛b1 but that leaves d4 unprotected. So I see more and more problems as I go. Do I move 1.♛d2 to avoid all problems? 1.♛d2 ♞xc3 2.bxc3 ♝b5, so avoid attack of b5 and f1, so 1.♛d2 hit clock.

Subject C-9 is more verbal than most — he was able to put his concerns out loud more readily. That should not preclude one from doing concrete analysis, and there he had several problems. He often had trouble figuring out what was forced during the capturing sequences. Subject C-9 had typical basic tactical-vision problems seeing the discovered attacks and figuring out the removal of the guards. Like almost all players under 1800, he did not see the key line after 1.♘xd5, e.g. 1...♘xd5 2.♗xd5 (to remove the guard on e7) 2...♗xg5 with complications not unfavorable to Black. He never considered the best move, 1.♗xd5, even though it is a major capture. So, like many C-class players, his analysis was neither systematic nor correct. His final move, 1.♕d2, is defeated decisively by 1...♘xc3 (which, to his credit, he did consider, so it was not completely Hope Chess!) but then, after his intended 2.bxc3, Black can play 2...♘e4:

de Groot A
White to play after 1.♕d2? ♘xc3 2.bxc3? ♘e4

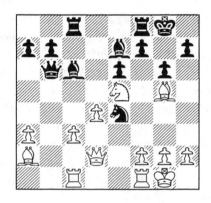

which double-attacks the queen and bishop and also makes a discovered attack on the bishop on g5. White cannot meet all these threats, and thus loses a piece.

So long as we are covering C players who like 1.♕d2:

Protocol C-10 (de Groot A; 1500; adult; 9 minutes)
Pawn structure; king safe; light-square bishop long diagonal − not that active. Knight on e5, bishop on g5 both attacking. Black's g7 is weak − no bishop on g7 − ♖c8 balances ♖c1. Checks and captures for Black: 1...♕xb2; 1... ♘d5xc3 − might not exchange. If 1...♘xc3 opens ♗a2 diagonal. Black's ♘fg5 [sic] attacks the bishop on g5. Protect the b2-pawn? 1.♖b1 or 1.♖c2 or 1.b4 gets space. Attacker 1.♗h6 is beginning but weakens king − maybe combine by ♕f6 later. 1.♘f3 protects the king. Left with 1.h3 [White is not considering his checks, captures, and threats]. 1.♗e3 guards d4. Long range: Trade off Black's

dark-squared bishop. Don't like his knight on d5, so 1.♘xd5 is possible. Look at 1.b4 or 1.♘xd5. Maybe exchange ♗a2 on d5 as well: isolate his pawns. Hanging pawn has to be dealt with. 1.♘xd5 attacks queen but after the exchange the pawn is still attacked so that is not a good idea [?!]. 1.♖c2: swing to e2 to attack the bishop on e7 eventually. I remember that b2 is attacked. 1.h3 removes ... ♘g4. Drop queen to d2: guards b2 and d4 and g5. If 1.♕d2 not a bad idea. Check 1.♕d2 a little further. Any tactical shots? So 1.♕d2 or 1.b4. Don't want to take the rook off the c-file — converging a little on 1.♕d2. Gives up the light squares. 1...♗b5 skewers the rook but 2.♘xb5. I like 1.♕d2 is what I'd like to do. Push clock.

Again a great example of Hope Chess, as Subject C-10 does not consider the winning sequence in response for Black given in C-9. It is also interesting that Subject C-10 spent so little time on his forcing moves, briefly considering 1.♘xd5 but not systematically examining Black's three possible recaptures to see if something good could be forced. Notice that after first considering 1.♕d2 he properly asks, "Any tactical shots?" but misses the glaring 1...♘xc3, removing the guard on e4. *You can have a good process but that does not mean your analysis will be good. On the other hand, if you have a bad process then it is highly unlikely your analysis will be consistently good.*

The following protocol was by an accomplished Internet Chess Club (ICC) player who was about to start playing over-the-board chess. His first USCF ratings, around the time he did this protocol, were in the Class C range. He later quickly rose to B level, at one point even getting his rating just above 1800.

Protocol C-11 (de Groot A; 1500+; adult; 10 minutes)
What's going on? Equal? Count material: equal. Isolated queen's pawn. More of a position to protect. I need to defend d4. I see 1.♘xd5 or ...♘xc3. Which is better for me? ...♕xd4 1.♘xd5 ♘xd5 2.♗xe7 is good? Then 2...♘xe7. Is that good for me? Would simplify the game. He has nothing better than 2...♘xe7. Is that good for me? 1.♘xd5 ♘xd5 2.♗xe7 ♘xe7 — worried about his rook going to d8 to pressure d4. Lost opportunity to play ♗e3. I don't think it is good to exchange because d4 becomes more exposed. What else can I do? ...♘xc3 2.♖xc3 or 2.bxc3. If 2.♖xc3 is an open file — not terrible. Am I blatantly missing something? Do I lose a piece? Position looks equal. I want to better my position. Consider 1.♖fd1 to strengthen d4. If 1.♖fe1 ♗a4 2.♘xa4. Well, all right I am waiting for a move to jump at me. 1.♖fe1. Push clock [then 1...♕xb2?].

89

This protocol contains some very interesting pros and cons. Subject C-11 never considered all of Black's threats. My note about 1...♛xb2 at the end expressed my surprise at his omission, although 1.♖fe1 ♛xb2 can be met by 2.♘c4.

de Groot A
Black to play after 1.♖fe1 ♛xb2 2.♘c4
Even grandmasters never mentioned 1...♛xb2 2.♘c4

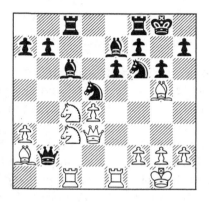

No grandmaster who performed this exercise with Dr. de Groot mentioned the possibility of 2.♘c4, but that is not an omission since it was irrelevant in the PV for the best move 1.♗xd5. However, it turns out that 2.♘c4 is more complicated than good after 2...♗b5!. See the analysis in Appendix B.

Subject C-11 was very conscious of evaluation ("Is that good for me?"), which other players at this level sometimes lack. As players improve, this conscious concern about evaluation grows.

Note his extensive use of the "null move" technique (where one assumes a player "passes" — makes no move — for the purpose of determining the threat of the previous move) to find what would happen after ...♘xc3, which makes his missing ...♛xb2 all the more puzzling. Although this subject seemed unaware of the principle, "When you have the isolated queen's pawn, avoid trading all (or most of) the minor pieces," he still came to the correct conclusion that trading for trading's sake would be bad for him.

Another good trait of Subject C-11 was his excellent use of comparisons, asking "Which is better for me?" This kind of question, which often directs the analysis, is usually lacking at lower levels. Unfortunately, his focus was primarily defensive, and he did not systematically consider his captures — a big mistake. His actual move (1.♖fe1) was made with very little analysis.

Protocol C-12 (de Groot A; 1570+; adult; 15 minutes)

The material is even. White has an isolated queen's pawn. All minor pieces are in play, fully developed. Nothing is unprotected on either side — on my side I think everything is protected, yes [sic: b2]. Attacks on d5, f6, knights. 1.♘xc6 gives the bishop pair:

de Groot A
Black to play after 1.♘xc6
Just win the bishop pair

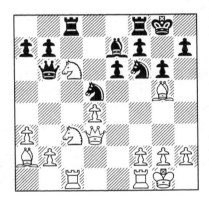

1.♘xc6 and try to get the bishop pair; the rook or queen recaptures — can give him an isolated pawn. For one 1.♘xc6 — not to worry about 1.♘xc6 ♛xc6 and I get a discovered attack on his queen. 1.♘xc6 ♛xc6 2.♘e4 he can save on c1 but the bishop on g5 guards c1.

Looking for ways to trade off pieces. ♘xc6 with the idea of ♘xd5 then the bishop at e7 has no defenders. 1.♘xc6 ♖xc6. If 1...bxc6 the isolated pawn is not so good. 2.♘xd5 exd5 giving him an isolated pawn, not 2...♘xd5 hanging the bishop on e7 [sic]. 1.♘xc6 ♛xc6 2.♘xd5 ♛xd5 then no tricks. Umm. (silent)

There's a fork potential. I was missing that the bishop on a2 was hitting d5. Looking for tactics where I can get my knight to d7. 1.♗xd5 ♘xd5 2.♘xd5 exd5 hmm [missing 3.♗xe7]. Let's see — don't like the bishop on g5 though if it goes the queen sac on c1 is possible. On tough moves give me 9-10 minutes ["taken 6, the equivalent of 3"]. I don't think my calculation's good enough to figure all this out. There are enough defenders on d5 — defended three times due to the pawn on e6 — can I can get rid of the two defenders of d7? 1.♗xf6 ♗xf6 2.♘xd5 ♗xd5. 1.♘xd5 hits the queen. So 1.♗xf6 then probably 1...♗xf6 2.♘xd5 probably 2...♗xd5 3.♗xd5 exd5 4.♘d7 forks the queen and rook. I like that idea. Black (illegible text) f6. 1.♘xd5 exd5 then I don't have a lot — the bishop is in worse shape. No fork opportunity.

But oh! b2 is hanging [!]. So 1.♘a4 is good — I could easily lose a pawn here. Is it safe for him? a3 hangs. 1.♗xf6 ♗xf6 2.♘xd5 ♗xd5 3.♖xc8 ♖xc8 4.♘d7 ♕xb2 — it's ugly. Trade pieces for simplification so I can better figure out the position. 1.♘xc6 ♕xc6 2.♘a4 no. 1.♘e4, I don't like that. 1.♘e4 ♘xe4 bad — all sorts of possibilities for discovered attacks. No 1.♘e4. 1.♘xc6 is significant — I get the bishop pair. The queen can't take on b2 — there are possibilities of... no mate threat on the c-file.

1.♘xd5 ♗xd5 — looking for simplification. 1.♘xc6 queen or rook take on c6 with the idea of 2.♘xd5 or 1.♘xd5 possible but the bishop hangs on g5 if he moves the knight on f6. Hmm. I guess 1.f4 to protect the bishop on g5 exposes the king to the queen on b6 — on the same diagonal as the king on g1. I guess I — boom — 1.♗xf6 — doesn't make sense to give up the bishop if I can get the bishop pair. So 1.♘xc6 — he has to take back with the queen or rook. Probably then 2.♘xd5 ♘xd5 and the bishop on e7 hangs [sic]. At this point I play 1.♘xc6 hit clock.

Subject C-12 has some very good moments. He correctly understands than winning the bishop pair with 1.♘xc6 has some value. Like most players under 2000, he does not calculate that, after 1.♗xd5, 1...exd5 is forced and, like almost all players under 2000, does not notice that this is key because the resulting position is so brittle for Black. But he does make an interesting point. Some players have learned in rote manner that trading minor pieces when you have an isolated pawn is bad; thus they avoid capturing sequences for this reason (a bad reason, since a capturing sequence might be excellent — as at least one is in this case — for reasons which supersede the isolated-pawn issue; for one, they might also isolate opponent's pawns). However, Subject C-12 states, *"Trade pieces for simplification so I can better figure out the position."* This is worthy of discussion:

First, we can applaud Subject C-12 for being honest with himself. He does not pretend to be able to correctly figure out all the capturing possibilities, but he does recognize the complexity.

More interesting is the question of whether simplification does allow one to better figure out the position. In some positions this supposition is clearly true, but is it true that positions with less pieces are generally easier to calculate? I have long held that, with many pieces on the board, humans often shortcut calculations with Hand-waving (making a move on principle in an analytical position); weaker players do it detrimentally, but even some strong players might make a move largely based on an idea such as, "It's a complicated position but it can't be bad to activate my rook onto the open file" — many of our chess principles were invented to help guide ourselves in positions where it's impossible for a human to calculate all the ramifications.

Moreover, the endgame (where the most simplification has taken place) is where the most precise calculation is often required. Hand-waving in the endgame is often disastrous. So, ironically, the very simplification that was sought creates positions that are calculable within human capabilities and which often need to be carefully analyzed. For example, an endgame of a rook and four pawns vs. a rook and four pawns might be easily drawn with a little care by both players — but, if they trade rooks, the resulting king-and-pawn endgame might be very tricky indeed, and more easily won or lost for one side. For these reasons, I conclude that simplifying the position very often results in positions that require *more* careful calculation.

The next subject, C-13, has almost the identical rating of Subject C-12 (pushing toward B class) but he produces one of the most amazing protocols I have ever taken (and I've taken well over 1,000 by now). I took it just as I was finishing the manuscript for the second edition but there was no doubt I had to include it:

Protocol C-13 (de Groot A; 1580+; adult; 11 minutes)
Counting material — equal. The black king is behind some dark-squared weaknesses. I can't see how to exploit that now — it may be an issue later. There are lots of exchanges on the board: 1...♛xb2 and the queen is attacking the d4-pawn so I have to be careful where I move my queen. There is an isolated queen's pawn. The black pieces are defending each other and important squares like the fork on d7. I'm thinking — some sequences of exchanges might be able to remove

the guard on d7 or e7. The bishop on g5 is vulnerable on some exchanges. I have to be careful about ...♗b5, e.g. 1...♘xc3 removes the guard and then ...♗b5. If 1...♘xc3 2.♕xc3 then 2...♘e4 is a double attack. OK.

For White exchanges to remove the guard. The possibilities are 1.♘xd5, 1.♗xd5, or 1.♗xf6 or 1.♘xc6, but 1.♘xc6 takes away the knight from d7. Looking at each: if 1.♘xd5, 1...♘xd5 is the most natural of the three recaptures. If 1.♘xd5 ♘xd5 2.♗xd5 ♗xg5 [good] — it gets complicated but I have not achieved my goal.

Better to recapture on the second move on d5 with the knight to hit the queen. 1.♗xd5 ♘xd5 2.♘xd5 hits the queen — that seems to win a piece [good]. Other recaptures: 1.♗xd5 ♗xd5 2.♘xd5 hits the queen and then if 2...♘xd5 leads to 3.♘d7 winning the exchange. After 1.♗xd5 the final option is 1...exd5; that makes his d-pawn isolated. I stand OK — I can play for example 2.♕f3:

de Groot A
Black to play after 1.♗xd5 exd5 2.♕f3
Dr. Euwe mentions this possibility in Appendix A

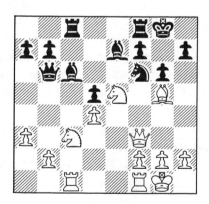

1.♗xd5 exd5 2.♕f3 and the dark-squared weaknesses are an issue. He has to defend the knight. If he moves the bishop on c6 he might lose a pawn. 2...♔g7. 1.♗xd5 exd5 Black's dark-squared bishop is worse — this is more clearly to my advantage than the original position [!].

Other options 1.♗xf6 if 1...♘xf6 keep solid. 1.♘xc6 and after the exchange of the pieces there is the bishop pair at least. 1.♗xd5 exd5 gives him the bishop pair but his bishop on c6 is not that good so I'm still happy with that. Did I miss any threats? What is my time? ["10 minutes which is the equivalent of 5"] 1.♗h6 with the idea of h4, h5 or ♘xg6 takes time. 1.♗h6 ♖fd8 seems OK there's no fork on d7. In the short term 1.♗h6 does not do anything. OK. 1.♗xd5 looks good but the reply 1...exd5 then maybe 2.♕f3. Black has to protect the knight on f6 — that gives time to shore up the pawns on the queenside. OK, 1.♗xd5 hit clock.

Wow! In my 40-plus years of giving de Groot A, I have never had a player rated so far under 2000 do so well! If you compare his protocol with that of Dr. Euwe's in Appendix A, it isn't that bad! Sure, Dr. Euwe was more comprehensive and detailed, but just the fact that you can compare them at all is amazing, given the 1000+ point difference. If Subject C-13 was performing this well in a tournament we might suspect him of cheating but, before we did this, as is usual I checked his familiarity and he had barely heard of a de Groot exercise and did not have the first edition of this book.

Protocol C-14 (de Groot Zyme; 1450; adult; 22 minutes)
Counting material — Black is up a pawn; White has the bishop pair. Both kings are relatively exposed. Black is more developed/has more activity and a potential passed a-pawn. White has an isolated pawn on c3, Black is backward on b5. Black threatens, among other things, 1...♕xf2+.

Plan: Attack the backward b-pawn, development, 1.e3 to develop, with eventual castling or 1.g3 to get the bishop into the game via g2 or h3 — get the kingside into play. Candidates 1.e3 and 1.g3. Problem with both is the bishop on d6 and the f2-pawn are both hanging, as is the c3-pawn [now we are getting there] (silent). Another move 1.♖d1 to line up a discovered attack on the black king to take advantage of its lack of safety. Another candidate is to fork the king and queen with 1.♗e7+; can this be made to work? Make the black knight move to skewer the queen and rook with ♗e5.

Those I guess for completeness — checks, captures, and threats. Only available check is on e7; the knight on g4 is protected from 1.♕xg4. Checks and captures: 1.♕e7+ ♕xe7 2.♗xe7+ ♔xe7 does not look good. 1.♕xg4 ♗xg4 no good. 1.♖d1 next most forcing; protects the d6-bishop — he can play 1...♗d7 or 1...♕xf2+ and 2.♔d2 then 2...♕xd6+ [sic!]. 1.♖d1 ♕xf2+ 2.♔d2 (sees his error on 2...♕xd6+ and then silent). Not clear about what Black's follow-up is. Not likely attractive. Looks less good. Can try to get knight to move.

1.f3 unattractive because of 1...♛xd6 [?] 2.hxg4 White has lost an active piece. 1.e3 ♛xd6 2.♖d1 skewers the queen and king so perhaps the bishop is protected [missing 2...♛xd1+ 3.♔xd1 ♞xf2+ in a quiescence error]. Back to making the knight move: 1.h3 forces 1...♞xf2 — it's the only safe square for the knight. But what about 1.f3? Then the knight has no obvious safe square so 1.f3 is attractive. 1.f3 ♛xd6 2.♖d1 skewer. If 1...♛xd6 is not good then 1...♞e5 2.♗xd5 — can he counterattack the queen? 1.f3 ♗b7 2.♛xb7 attacks the rook on a8 — Black can't move the knight to f2 or h2 without being taken. Best candidate.

Safety check: the rook on a8 is hanging. 1.♛xa8 obvious — couple of responses is 1...♛xc3+ 2.♔d1 forced then 2...♞xf2 is mate. 1.♛xa8 ♛xc3+ 2.♔d1 ♞xf2# killer move:

de Groot Zyme
Position after 1.♛xa8 ♛xc3+ 2.♔d1 ♞xf2#
A sequence that also defeats other first moves like 1.f3

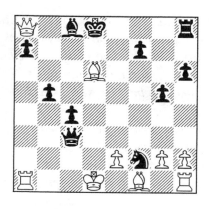

1.f3 doesn't do, so that goes out the window [good!].

So 1.♖c1 or 1.♗b4 — does nothing for 1...♛xf2+ still open (silent). Look at b1 — not attractive. 1.♗e5 not attractive 1...♞xe5 2.♖d1+ ♗d7 then 3.♛xa8+ does not block potential mate [!?] (silent) Again the candidates 1.♗b4, 1.♖c1, 1.♗e5: 1.♗e5 ♞xe5 2.♖d1+ king moves no help. 2...♗d7 3.♛xa8+ ♔e7 4.♛xh8. The knight on e5 blocks the queen from playing ...♛xc3+. 1.♗e5 ♞xe5 2.♖d1+ ♞d7 still allows 3.♛xa8 but not with check so 3...♛xc3+ could be blocked by 4.♖d2 but pins the rook to the king, then 4...♛c1+ followed by 5...♛c3+ is a perpetual — that's a possibility — complicated. 1.♗b4 leaves 1...

♕xf2+ 2.♔d1 or 2.♔d2. 2.♔d1 ♘e3+ *not attractive. 1.♖c1 guards c3 but allows 1...♕xf2+ forces the king out — not good.*

Need to block mate threat and protect the f2-pawn. Difficult. Another move is 1.♕f3 to protect f2 and c3. If 1...♕xd6 2.♖d1. It does allow a trade of queens, allowed that Black's queen is more active. 1.♕f3 rules out 1...♕xc3+; 1...♕xd6 2.♖d1 no obvious defense. Look at the knight moves for Black: 1.♕f3 ♘e5 2.♗xe5. 1...♕xf3 is fine. Again, 1.♕f3 ♕xd6 2.♖d1 ♕xd1+ 3.♔xd1 then a knight fork on f2; but no, the queen is on f3 [good]. 1.♕f3 ♕xd6 2.♖d1 ♕xd1+ 3.♖xd1 and no knight fork. What about 1...♗b7 2.♕xf6 ♘xf6 ultimately fine — not the problem. 1...♖e8 OK — one last look at all the potential safety issues. 1.♕f3. Push clock.

Subject C-14 was certainly taking his time but he was all over the place, sometimes forgetting his earlier analysis. He certainly would have been much better off if he had started by noting White's one big threat of 1.♕xa8 and Black's four main tactical ideas of 1...♕xd6, 1...♕xc3+, 1...♕xf2+, and 1...♘xf2 and then starting to analyze with those in mind. He would have saved himself a lot of time and realized that many of his lines would not have worked if he had kept all of Black's threats as possible answers. He gets very high marks for finally deducing that, if 1.♕xa8 doesn't work due to 1...♕xc3+ 2.♔d1 ♘xf2# (a line many other lower-rated players miss), then other moves which allow this sequence also lose, e.g. 1.f3 ♕xc3+ 2.♔d1 ♘f2#. This idea is called the "killer move" idea because it kills all the lines which allow it. It would also have been nice if he had seen that 1.♕d4 is similar to 1.♕f3 and compared the moves (his 1.♕f3 is better but he did not even see the other possibility). Of course, he briefly saw 1.♗e7+ but, like many near and below his rating, was not able to put "1+1" together and realize that this pseudo-sacrificial move would indeed deflect Black's queen with 1...♕xe7 and thus allow the otherwise disastrous 2.♕xa8 (or 2.♖d1+ first and then 3.♕xa8).

Summary of Class C

Characteristics of the thought process at this level:

- On the average, C players are much more detailed and analytical than Class D, and consequently, on the average, they take more time. C players do a much better job of looking at specific sequences and trying to figure out how far to look before making an evaluation.

- With some exceptions, C players seem to have trouble listing all the opponent's recaptures, and also have trouble figuring out which ones are forced (these two issues are related).

- By looking deeper, C players make more visualization mistakes since they are trying to hold those positions in their heads. They actually visualize better than Class D players, but the additional lines being visualized result in more total errors.

- Players at this level often miss hanging pieces at the end of analytical lines, or come to "big error" conclusions because of a missed capture or visualization error.

- As with most players under 1700, C players play Hope Chess (don't consistently check to see if a candidate move can be defeated by an opponent's check, capture, or threat in reply), but at least they start to check their moves for safety more frequently than players in classes below them.

Improvements to the thought process that would help in getting to the next level:

- Ask more frequently about analysis moves, "Is that forced?" or "Is that all of the opponent's possibilities?" Frequently, players at this level either jump to conclusions or don't stop to make sure they have considered all the key lines;

- Double-check key lines to make sure that the analysis is correct, or that the line is really quiescent. Often the players make a key mistake and don't check it, or stop too soon;

- Do lots of basic tactics problems to work on visualization and quiescence. As players get near 1600 they think they are too good for basic tactics. But this chapter shows that's clearly not so!

- Be more consistent in the process. Start by evaluating the situation, then find the threats, then assess candidate moves, etc. Sometimes C players know what to do, but skip steps in the excitement of the position, or too quickly gravitate to one idea without searching for all the good ones;

- Make sure to understand the situation. The candidate moves have to fit the needs of the position. When the player doesn't correctly identify those needs, candidate-move selection is more random. If you are losing, you want to play more aggressively and avoid trades. If you are winning, you usually want to avoid complications and play simply.

Chapter 6

Class B

This chapter includes players rated 1600-1800 USCF, or roughly 1750-1950 ICC standard.

For each protocol, I list the de Groot position (for example, de Groot A, de Groot B, de Groot C, etc.; see Chapter 1 for those positions); the age of the subject; the subject's rating; and the time the subject spent to choose his move.

Comments in parentheses indicate outside actions or comments that reflect the action of the player, such as (silent) if he paused for a long time. Comments in brackets are my thoughts. My frequent use of [*sic*] means that the subject is making a clear mistake in analysis or visualization. In contrast, [!] indicates that the player has made a comment that is very insightful for their level of ability or a surprising error. A frequent note is [no eval], meaning that the subject did not try to evaluate which side stood better, by how much, and why.

The first two protocols are by the same student roughly six months apart:

Protocol B-1 (de Groot A; 1600; adult; ~2 minutes)
Isolated queen's pawn. Not down. Opponent OK. All major pieces are on the board. A fake pin at f6 and e7. I can take on d5 with knight on c3; b2 hangs. 1...♛xb2 (hmm). Rooks developed. d4 attacked. So... I can take bishop pair but now. Looking for something to catch my eye. All pieces except b2 safe. I can play 1.♘xc6 to get the bishop pair. Then I can protect b2. So 1.♘xc6. Push clock.

I can never fully condemn the "Let's grab the bishop pair" idea in de Groot A. Subject B-1's thought process is not very thorough for such a complicated position and does not follow the maxim, "When you see a good move, look for a better one," so I can't fully endorse it, either. At this level we see more frequently that the players notice that the pawn on b2 is hanging, but understand that it does not necessarily need immediate attention.

Subject B-1 makes an interesting use of the term "fake pin" — I have used a similar term, "phantom pin," so perhaps that's the same thing.

Protocol B-2 (de Groot Ernie; 1630; adult; 6 minutes)

(counts material) Six pawns to five pawns. Bishops and knights even; my rooks have open files. Black's a-rook and his bishop are trapped. His knight on f4 is near my king. He threatens the queen. The queen protects the c-pawn. The bishop is protected by the queen and in take. Queen also guards c4. Where can I put the queen to guard the c-pawn and the bishop? 1.♕b5 allows 1...a6 so might not be too good. Let's see. Make sure to guard bishop because I am up a pawn anyway. 1.♕e4 protects both after all. 1.♕e4 let's see. 1.♕e4 opponent's options? Hmm. The knight doesn't have...1...♘e6 or 1...♘h5. If I take the knight... opponent can't push g5 and pin the bishop to the queen but that is no good. So... the knight can stay on f4 guarded by the queen. It is good to make the queen guard the knight. No threats besides those two. Want to keep bishop on b1-h7 diagonal. I have used six minutes; that is good enough. 1.♕e4. Push clock.

Players who want to use the following logic: "1) My queen is attacked, 2) My bishop is attacked, and 3) My queen needs to move and guard the bishop, so 1.♕e4 is a great idea" are playing Hope Chess. That is, they don't attempt to see if their main candidate (1.♕e4) is safe before playing it. Of course, give half those players the black pieces and say "Black to play and win":

de Groot "Ernie"
Black to play after 1.♕e4?

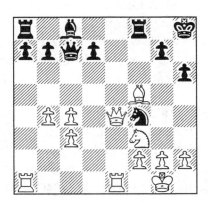

and they will find 1...d5! in a minute or less. That means their analysis, in a nutshell, is Hope Chess. Their moves can be defeated easily by forcing moves (check, capture, or threat) which they don't even attempt to find. Instead they are surprised (unhappily) when their opponents do. To see this in a Class B protocol tells you that even B players sometimes play this way. This partially explains why they may know so much about chess but aren't experts. Subject B-2 makes the same mistake as Subject D-12.

Protocol B-3 (de Groot A; 1650; adult; 9.5 minutes)

Even material. White has a little more space — good. The knight has an outpost on e5; I don't want to trade that. The rook has an open file — I'd like to get my rook on f1 to e1. Umm — the bishop on a2 is pretty good. Possibly some tactics later at f7. Black has dark-square weaknesses on the kingside. He's got a bad bishop — no, dark-square weaknesses so getting rid of his dark-squared bishop is good. Moves: exchanges. I can capture the knight on d5: 1.♘xd5. He's got that square guarded three times so there is no way to win anything on d5. If I don't take him and he takes me 1...♘xc3 then that strengthens my pawns by bringing a pawn to the center. My d-pawn is isolated on an open file, so I would want to win in the middlegame, possibly with a kingside attack. It is not apparent that there is any way to take advantage of tactics, so 1.♖fe1. Hmm. OK. Another is 1.♘xc6 because it gives me... no. Bishops are better than knights. But in this position the knight is probably better. 1.♗h6 with the idea of f4. Hmm. Need a moment (silent). Not seeing any tactics — how to improve the position? 1.♘xc6 gives the two bishops but costs my best minor piece. Moves like 1.f4 don't do anything. Don't see a way to weaken his dark-squared bishop. 1.♖fe1 and 1.♗h6 are best — the only moves to improve the position. The idea of 1.b4-b5 to hit the bishop on c6. So 1.b4 is a candidate. Hmm. Yeah I might play 1.♖fe1 followed by ♕h3 so ♘xf7 with the idea of ♕xe6. No, that's not even playable. All right, 1.♘xd5 exd5 and my pawn is no longer isolated [sic]. 1...♗xd5 2.♗xd5 exd5 then I no longer have an isolated pawn — the e-file is open. So 3.♖fe1. 1.♘xd5 ♘xd5 2.♗xd5 ♗xd5. 1.♘xd5. No, all those exchanges on d5 would be bad for me. So 1.♖fe1. Push clock.

Subject B-3 started with a good evaluation. Nevertheless, except for the length, this seems more like a C-player protocol as Subject B-3 never searched for his opponent's threats and did not spot the b2-pawn hanging. Once you see it's hanging, you either consciously have to ignore it while looking for something offensive (as World Champion Euwe aptly noted in

Appendix A) or look for moves to guard it. Otherwise, if it turns out that the b-pawn cannot be taken, then you are just lucky!

Subject B-3 first dismissed capturing on d5 because it did not win anything and then later just because "all those exchanges would be bad for me." When you have a typical isolated queen's pawn position, equal trades of minor pieces generally favor the player attacking the isolated pawn. Although White has the isolated pawn, the trades are not "equal." Such principles ironically take a back seat to concrete forcing lines, and it turns out the "bad" trade of minor pieces is actually the right idea! Playing more by general principles than by solid analysis and evaluation can be very dangerous in analytical positions.

Protocol B-4 (de Groot A; USCF 1600; adult; 12 minutes)
Plusses/advantages: isolated queen's pawn. My queen is better; the d-pawn is pressured, blockaded. I have more room on the kingside; his black bishop is out of place. He threatens ...♛xb2. I'd like to double on the c-file, so 1.♖c2 is a candidate. The bishop at g5 is undefended. If 1.♖c2 ♖fd8 I can defend easily. 1.♗h6 or 1.♛h3. 1.♘e4 drops a bishop. 1.♘xc6 wins the bishop pair but gives up the centralized knight. 1.♘xd5 but I don't like exchanges — that helps the player playing against the isolated pawn — I would probably avoid without a tactical reason. 1.♘xd5 ♘xd5 2.♗xd5:

de Groot A
Black to play after 1.♘xd5 ♘xd5 2.♗xd5
A most common problem: missing the forced capture on g5

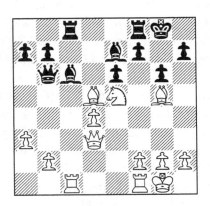

2...♗xd5 3.♗xe7. 1.♘xd5. With the rook on e1 I would have an attack on... get rid of the isolated pawn because his piece is hanging. 1.♘xd5 ♘xd5 2.♗xd5 ♘xd7 3.♗xe7 ♘xe7 4.♘xc6 ♘xc6 5.d5 ♘e5 6.♕e4 and the pawn is hanging: ...♕xb2. 1.♖c2 is best for if exchanges then the pawn hangs. 2.♖fc1. 1.♗h6 with the idea of ♘f3-♘g5. 1.♗xf6 with the idea of 2.♘e4 ♗e7. 1.♘e4 hangs the bishop. 1.♗xf6 ♗xf6 2.♘e4 with the idea of going to c5 or g5. 1.♗xf6 ♘xf6 is not as good — it opens the diagonal for the c6-bishop. 1.♖c2. Push clock.

Subject B-4 was all over the place. (I don't know what he intended for Black's second move in the line 1.♘xd5 ♘xd5 2.♗xd5 ♘xd7 — occasionally I transcribe moves incorrectly and occasionally my subjects misspeak.) After jumping around, suddenly he returned to his original idea and played it without even checking to see if it was safe (Hope Chess!). Jumping and guessing would seem indicative of a player closer to 1600 than 1800. On the positive side, his 1600+ traits included knowing that trades usually help the side attacking the isolated pawn (see the comments to B-3). Also, to his credit, Subject B-4 tried to have an evaluation at the end of most analytical lines, which players at his level rarely do, although sometimes his conclusions were not very clear.

The following subject was one of the country's top eight-year-old players, and soon reached Class A. He is now an expert and rising. Here are his two protocols:

Protocol B-5 (de Groot A; USCF 1600; age 8; 2.5 minutes)
Force something on c-file. Pressure his knight on d5 is supported by the bishop at c6 and the knight at f6. His dark squares on the kingside are weak. The knight on f6 cannot be protected by pawns — ...♕xb2 is a threat. 1.♖fd1; 1.♖fe1 to try. Not 1.♖b1 to protect pawn. So 1.b4 is good. 1.b4 hit clock.

Subject B-5 provides another purely defensive protocol, with the main intention being to safeguard the b2-pawn. It could be worse, but at age eight there are always some big deficits to one's overall approach. On the other hand, to be 1600 at age 8 means many of those deficits will soon be overcome! For example, at age 10 this same player would probably take Dr. Euwe's approach and think "OK, I can guard the pawn, but first let's see if I can do something offensive instead." He would also play more slowly.

Protocol B-6 (de Groot C; 1600+; age 8; a few minutes)

White's queenside pawns are up the board. 1...d5 because c4 is pinned. The queen and rook can attack f3. 1...♘fd5 with pressure on the f3-knight. 1...♗d7 — the e6-pawn is attacked. 1...d5 with the idea of ...♘e4. 1...d5 2.♘e5 is bad for Black. 1...♘e4 with the idea of a queenside fork. 1...♘e4 2.♘g5 no good: 2...d5 exd5. 2.♖he1 d5 3.♘e5 ♕b6. No good for Black; 3...♕a6 4.♘xc7. 3... ♕b6 4.c5 ♕a6 pins queen, so ♘xc7 ♕xe2 with the idea of ...c6. 1...♘e4:

de Groot C
White to play after 1...♘e4

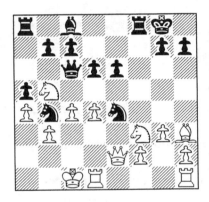

2.♖he1 d5 3.♘e5 ♕b6 4.c5 ♕a6. Push clock.

Subject B-6 is quite a bit hasty and judgmental in such a complicated position! But again youth will be served. Overall, he exhibits a decent tactical feel, and the final selection of 1...♘e4 is commendable. Several moves are reasonable and worthy of consideration in this difficult exercise. However, the logic that led to 1...♘e4 is at best questionable, and some of the moves in the lines are not as forced as Subject B-6 seemed to think.

Protocol B-7 (de Groot A; 1600; adult; 7 minutes)

Middlegame. The knight on f6 is pinned [no eval]. If I can remove the guard I can apply more pressure to that knight. So if I capture on d5 there are two pieces covering d5 and possibly I can fork on d7. Looking at 1.♗h6 — no purpose in that. The rook on the c-file would be nice to win. 1.♘xd5 if 1...♘xd5 then bishop attacks g5. 2.♗xd5 ♗xg5 3.♗xc6 and 3...♖xc6. No, I think — I think I need to think quiet [?!]. 1.♘xd5 ♘xd5 2.♗xd5 ♗xg5:

de Groot A
White to play after 1.♘xd5 ♘xd5 2.♗xd5 ♗xg5
Avoiding a common omission: Subject B-7 finds 2...♗xg5

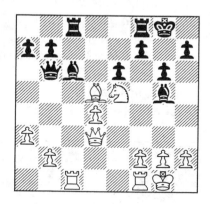

OK, so I think [no conclusion!] I will play 1.♗xd5. That way the knight... 1.♗xd5 then if 1...♘xd5 2.♘xd5 to attack the queen. Then if 2...♗xd5 3.♗xe7, so 1.♗xd5 [PV = 1.♗xd5 exd5 gives him a bad pawn and then maybe 2.♕f3].

This is an unbelievably good, if lucky, protocol from a 1600 player. Without fully analyzing or evaluating the position he hits on exceptionally good and key points. For example, he does a good job of discussing why 1.♘xd5 might not work, but then skips to 1.♗xd5 without showing how it does. He completely overlooks the key evaluation after 1.♗xd5 exd5 until I ask him about his PV, and even then it's at best shaky. It's not really a case of a blind squirrel finding an acorn, but this does happen. There really was a lot missing, so this is not a great analysis. However, it was *like* great analysis in one sense: it came to some of the same conclusions and moves!

Protocol B-8 (de Groot Zyme; 1640; age 10; 4.5 minutes)

I can take 1.♕xa8 but then 1...♕xc3+ wins the rook on a1. So don't allow 1...♕xc3+. Move such as 1.♖c1 looks good — then the rook on a8 is trapped — can't move. So far 1.♖c1 looks best. Oh! He has 1...♕xf2+. So he has two threats! So 1.♕f3 stopping both threats is a candidate. But if 1...♕xf3 I don't have a pleasant choice. 2.exf3 and I have a wide open queenside. Anything besides 1.♕f3? Whew! I can distract with 1.♗e7+ ♕xe7 2.♕xa8 — that looks best now. Is there anything better? He is attacking the bishop now. All right. Let's see. All right, well. My bishop is not really threat-

ened. *If 1...♕xd6 then 2.♖d1 but then 2...♕xd1+ wins a queen for a bishop and a rook — but then:*

de Groot Zyme
Checking a threat: White to play after 1...♕xd6 2.♖d1 ♕xd1+
Finding out the bishop on d6 might be hanging after all

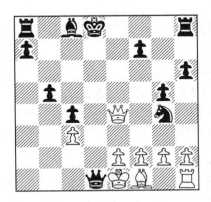

3.♔xd1 ♘xf2+ and 4...♘xe4. Is there anything better than 1.♗e7+? Don't see. Let's evaluate. White has five pawns, Black has six — otherwise the same: Black is ahead a pawn. So winning the exchange would help, but not that much. I like 1.♗e7+. The check is forcing — he can't decline. All right 1.♗e7+ (hits clock).

Subject B-8 is obviously a talented player, but some additional thinking discipline would make him much more efficient. First, if he had first counted material then, knowing he was down a pawn, he could have made further evaluations more efficiently. Second, after an early identification of his opponent's threats, if he had then systematically considered his checks, captures, and threats, he would have found 1.♗e7+ more quickly. The capabilities are all there; he just has to organize them better to be more efficient.

Protocol B-9 (de Groot A; USCF 1600; adult; 21 minutes)
Material is equal. Is there anything of White which is hanging? The bishop at a2 is loose but not attacked. The d4-pawn is OK. The dark-squared bishop is hanging but not attacked. The b2-pawn is the only one loose. I am double-attacked on c3, but no problem. Black's knight on f6 when moved can discover attack on g5. No checks or mating threats for Black. Who is better? Does Black

have anything hanging? No. Who's in better shape? White king is a little safer. Both queens are OK. White's light-squared bishop is better, dark-squared bishop is better. The knight on e5 is better than the one on f6; Black's knight on d5 is better than the one on c3. White has more space. So the position is roughly equal, maybe slightly better for White.

Either save the b2-pawn or sacrifice it for something better. 1.♗h6 attacks the rook on f8. 1...♕xb2 2.♗xf8 ♘xc3 3.♖xc3 ♕xc3 4.♗h6 No! 4.♗xe7 ♕xd4 5.♗xf6. What a mess. I have captured a rook, bishop, and knight and he has captured a rook, knight, and two pawns. Not correct. 1.♗h6 ♕xb2 2.♗xf8. None of this works because the queen is protected so Black loses the exchange for a pawn. 1.♗h6 ♕xb2 2.♘xc6 ♖xc6 3.♕xa2 [Ed. note: The subject apparently analyzed two moves in a row for Black, skipping White's third move, and then made an impossible capture for Black on the following move] *♗xe7 4.♘d5 [♘d5xe7?].* White has captured a rook and bishop; Black has captured a pawn and bishop, so 1.♗h6 is decent so what would happen? Black will not take the pawn so 1...♖fd8 to overprotect ♘d5, Black's minor piece 2.♘xd5 to remove the hit piece. 2...♘xd5. Is there some way to take advantage of the dark squares around Black's king? Is there any way to get rid of his dark-squared bishop? 1.♘xd5. Let's see what happens. Black is forced to recapture 1...♗xd5 because the knight is pinned [sic]:*

de Groot A
White to play after 1.♘xd5 ♘xd5
Another subject who visualizes this incorrectly or assumes that with the
piece on f6 gone and the knight on d5 taken,
then the bishop on e7 must hang

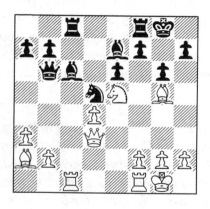

2.♗xd5 exd5 isolates both pawns. I've got to protect b2, say 3.b4 but the bishop is still hanging. The immediate 1.b4 gets to the same place — it's a complicated position. 1.♗h6 ♖fd8 2.♘xd5. The knight can't take on d5 because of the pin [same mistake as in the diagram]. 2...♗xd5 or 2...exd5. Is there any way to get another piece in? Yes, 3.♘d7 wins material — or does it? [sic ♖xd7] 1.♗h6 ♖fd8 2.♘xd5 ♗xd5: Black can trade rooks or take with the pawn. Trading rooks doesn't help. 2.♘xd5 ♗xd5 3.♗xd5 exd5 4.♘d7 attacks the rook [sic] and pinned knight. Oh! The rook has moved! That does not work. But 1.♗h6 ♖fd8 2.♘xd5 ♗xd5 3.♗xd5 exd5 4.♖xc8 ♖xc8 5.♘d7 Hmm. 5...♕d8 and I can't play 6.♘xb7 [sic?]. I should move the queen back to the first rank. I get a knight and bishop for a knight and bishop, pair of rooks. White has won a pawn on b7 — is this a drawish position? I felt the position was equal, so I am not terribly excited. Don't see a winning combination anywhere. The knight on c3 is unprotected. 1.♘xd5 ♗xd5 2.♗xd5 exd5 3.b4 and...(silent) Having a rough time figuring out a better move. This is all very messy. I think I like the idea of getting my bishop to h6 even if it leads to an equal position. So I would play 1.♗h6 ♖fd8 2.b4. I have improved my position slightly. So 1.♗h6. Push clock. (PV = 1.♗h6 ♖fd8 2.b4)

Subject B-9's protocol exhibits several interesting points:

- There are two primary ways to keep track of material during a series of exchanges: A) keep a running count (the method I use the majority of the time), and B) visualize the final position and count the material. This subject uses a third, slightly different method: he recounts the material captured during the sequence at the end. I rarely see this third method employed as it seems slightly less efficient and possibly more prone to error. If you go through a series of exchanges and are not sure of the material count, it is important to double-check, either with the same method or with a different one.

- The key to this subject's entire plan was to safely establish the bishop on h6. He never really asked himself if getting the bishop to h6 at the expense of forcing Black's rook to the center, where it attacks the key d5 and d4 squares, was worth it. Instead he took significant time justifying 1.♗h6 on the tactical idea that the 1...♕xb2 counterattack did not work! So he was assuming that if he could justify 1.♗h6 and force the rook on f8 to move, he would have accomplished something positive. Yet when his combinations with ♘d7 failed to work because either d7 was covered by a rook or the rook was not available on f8 to be forked, he never put one and one together and deduced, "Hey! If I don't force that rook to d8

I can do lots of extra stuff after ♘xd5. So instead of 1.♗h6 ♖fd8 2.♘xd5 I should be looking at just 1.♘xd5 first!"

• Subject B-9 did an extraordinarily good job of attempting to evaluate the position before analyzing. In this book, very few players rated below 1800 (and even below 2000) try to come to some "static" conclusion of who stands better, by how much, and why before trying to figure out what to do. This evaluation sets a "bar" for analysis. If you stand better, then you would not want to force perpetual check, or even settle for a line that is dead even. Although the subject was wrong to think the initial position was even (see Appendices A and B), his *logic* in comparing how good his best line is with *how good he thinks the position should be* is excellent. This initial evaluation and comparison with the outcome of lines is rarely found among players at this level (or even a level above)!

Protocol B-10 (de Groot A; FIDE 1700; adult; 10 minutes)

Assess position: White has the initiative on the queenside. The bishop would be better on g7. The knight on d5 protects the bishop on e7. Material: nothing off except two pawns. My move – can he do checks, attack the queen? ...♘f4 loses to the bishop capture, ...♘b4 loses – can attack with the bishop ...♗b5 ♘xb5 or ♕xb5. Can attack with the queen. My rooks can't be attacked. What's undefended? Every piece but the bishop on g5, which is undefended but is subject to discovered attacks with the movement of the knight on f6. All Black's pieces defended. Is my bishop on g5 in danger? If the knight on f6 retreats, then ♗xe7; ...♘g4 ♗xe7 – prefer not to swap bishops. Potential discovery on c3 with the bishop on c6. Keep dark-squared bishop so 1.♗h6 maybe with h4-h5 with the idea of using the queen on the kingside. His initiative is on the queenside: ...♕xb2 is undefended [!], threatens to swap off on c3. Attention to b2-pawn. Two things: 1) Defend with a piece – not good, or 2) b4 – I like this better. It leaves the bishop open on the a2-g8 diagonal but the c3-knight is not protected by a pawn so 1.b4 is possible. Quickly check: Can he do nasty knight forks? ...♘d5 retreats is not a bother; going to f4 and e3 loses; ...♘g4 loses, and 1...♘xc3 2.♖xc3 and don't think he... 1...♘xc3 2.♖xc3 ♗b5 pins queen to rook and can't take with knight – not so good. 2.♗c4 or 2.♘c4 attacks queen. 1.♘c4 attacks queen and guards b2. Not too attractive: 1.♘c4 clogs the c-file. How am I going to defend the b-pawn or sacrifice it for a kingside attack? If he takes with the queen, is the queen in trouble? a3 would be hanging – don't want to sacrifice that (a3) pawn. Honest, I would have a long think – I'm not sure what to do. I like 1.b4 – worried about 1...♘xc3:

de Groot A
White to play after 1.b4 ♘xc3
Analyzing the reply: that's *not* Hope Chess!

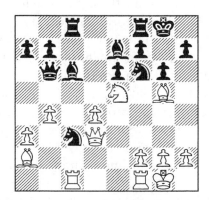

2.♖xc3 ♗b5. *I could play 1.♕d2 — it defends b2 and removes the skewers on the b5-f1 diagonal. I don't like 1.♕b1 or 1.♕c2, the latter putting the queen on the same line with the rook on c8. So 1.♕d2 or 1.♕e2. The queen on e2 can still get skewered so 1.♕d2 (silent). What am I thinking? I quite have begun to like 1.♕d2 ♘xc3 2.♖xc3 — have the option of f4 or h6 — can't attack d2 by ...♘e4 because of ♘c3xe4. Quickly. 1.♕d2. Ah, ♘xe4 both the knight and the queen defend g5. That reinforces the only hanging piece on g5, so 1.♕d2. Push clock.*

See the comments to Protocol C-9 for the refutation of 1.♕d2. Amazingly, Subject B-10 saw both the idea of 1...♘xc3 and ...♘e4 but did not put them together and realize that the combination of the two refutes his move outright.

Interestingly, the subject mentioned 1.♘c4 to *guard* b2, but did not find that 1...♕xb2 would not have been possible anyway due to 2.♘c4 trapping the queen. (As mentioned in Protocol C-11, though, even the grandmasters in de Groot's book missed this possibility.) The diagram position is noteworthy also: the subject did not just look at 1.b4, but tried to see if it was safe after 1...♘xc3. I believe Subject C-9 was the lowest-rated player in the book to find the refutation of 1.b4 systematically. This is consistent with my conjecture that Hope Chess is practiced by most players until their rating rises to 1600-1700.

Protocol B-11 (de Groot A; 1660; adult; a few minutes)
The material is even. White has a free hand. Black is weak on d7 and f6. My worst piece is the bishop on a2 and Black's best piece is his knight on d5, so

let's consider 1.♗xd5. 1.♗xd5 ♘xd5 (proceeding slowly) ...wins a piece. Push clock.

This is the classic case of playing the right move for mostly the wrong reasons. Here Subject B-11 is happy to win a piece on 1.♗xd5 ♘xd5 but does not even consider the other recaptures 1...♗xd5 or 1...exd5. *If* he had looked at 1...♗xd5 and found the eventual knight fork *and* considered 1...exd5 and decided it was good for White on positional grounds *and* had considered other moves and seen that indeed 1.♗xd5 led to the best position, then his analysis would have been perfect. Moreover, if you see a winning move, the next thing you should do is ask yourself whether or not this good fortune is really true and proceed slowly and carefully. Many weak players do exactly the opposite and play the "winning move" immediately, as in this protocol.

When I bought de Groot's book I was a Class A player and, to the best of my recollection, I too saw that 1.♗xd5 ♘xd5 won a piece but, unlike Subject B-11, I also saw that 1...♗xd5 loses the exchange. Unfortunately, I think my reaction to 1.♗xd5 exd5 was, "Darn! If 1...exd5 had lost material too, I would be winning, but 1...exd5 is OK for Black, so that doesn't seem to be my best move."

Dr. Euwe evaluated 1...exd5 much better than I did! (See Appendix A.)

Protocol B-12 (de Groot Ernie; 1800 ICC; adult; ~20 minutes)
Material — White has an extra pawn — it's doubled. Threats? No harmful checks. The queen is en prise *and can't take the knight. I need to move the queen. 1.♕f7 ♖xf7? 2.♖e8+ will mate. So that is possible — threatens — can play 1... ♘e6 but then 2.♖xe6 removes the guard, so I probably have to move the rook. What else can I do? Better is 1...♕d8 but then 2.♖e7 threatens mate — no, 2... ♖xf7 so 1.♕f7 ♕d8 threatens the queen. Is there anything better? 1.♕e5 d6 and Black threatens the bishop on f5. If the queen moves off the fifth rank then the bishop is loose. 1.♕d3 is not possible so 1.♕e4. Hmm (silent). What else? 1.♕e4 then what would he do? 1...d5 attacking the queen and double-attacking the bishop. Not so appealing. 1.♕e4 d5 anything else? Not really. So 1.♕e4 is not a good idea at all. 1.♕e5 probably fails to 1...d6. 1.♕c5 or 1.♕a5. 1.♕c5 ♕xc5 and the bishop goes. 1.♕a5 ♕xa5 2.♖xa5 covers the bishop but then a removal of the guard with ...b6. Umm. Can move the rook to b5, d5, or e5. d5 is no good. 1.♕a5 ♕xa5 2.♖xa5 b6 3.♗b5 or ♖e5 but 3.♖e5 d6 or 3.♗b5 a6 4.♖xb6 ♖xf5 5.♖e8+ ♔h7 and I am down a piece although Black's kingside is messy, but eventually he will free his game so I'm not too keen on that. Back to 1.♕f7. At first 1...♕d8 is the*

answer. The white queen is short of squares. Tactics? Well, 2.♘e5 ♖xf7 3.♘xf7+
wins the queen. 1.♕f7 ♕d8 2.♘e5 threatens 3.♘g6+ too — it looks more prom-
ising than the others. Anything else besides 1...♕d8? 1...♖g8 2.♘e5 is stronger so
1...♕d8 looks strongest. Then 2.♘e5, what has Black got? (silent) Hmm. I sup-
pose something like 2...d6 3.♘g6+ ♘xg6 4.♕xg6 ♗xf5 wins the bishop. 1.♕f7
♕d8 2.♘e5 d6 3.♗xc8 ♕xc8 then the queen's en prise and 4...♖xf7 5.♘xf7+
no longer hits the queen. Is there anything I can do? ♘g6 exchanges the knight.
What does that leave me? Just a pawn up. 1.♕f7 ♕d8 2.♘e5 d6 3.♗xc8 ♕xc8
4.♘g6+ ♘xg6 5.♕xg6 ♕xc4 but then 6.♖e7 ♕xc3 attacks a1 and guards the
mate on g7 — I may have to protect the pawn then. Anything better? (silent) Don't
think I've...(silent) Hmm. Anything else I can do to protect the... Alternatives to
the 1.♕f7 sequence? 1.♕d4 ♖xf5 2.♖e8+ ♔h7 then pin the rook to the king.
Wondering what options Black has if I do that? (silent) 1.♕e5 ♕xe5 2.♕xe5 d6
looked at that before (silent). The best line I can see is 1.♕f7 — looks fairly even
from White's point of view. Wait a minute. 1.♘e5 ♘xd5 2.♘f7+ ♔g8 works (si-
lent) ["Please do your analysis out loud if possible."] OK, umm. OK, so looking
at 1.♘e5 ♘xd5 2.♘f7+ ♔g8 is just winning the queen. So I do have to move the
queen. 1.♕f7 ♕d8... (silent) No, I can't see anything better than that. Maybe I
am missing something...(silent) 1.♕f7. Push clock.

Wow! This analysis shows that the difference between being a great ana-
lyzer and a decent one is not that big. Let's consider the three key lines of
Subject B-12's analysis and identify the mistake in each:

A) First, his PV of **1.♕f7 ♕d8 2.♘e5 d6 3.♗xc8**:

de Groot Ernie
Black to play after 1.♕f7 ♕d8 2.♘e5 d6 3.♗xc8

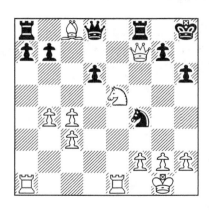

Here Subject B-12 only considered the move 3...♛xc8 and concluded that after 4.♘g6+ the position was more or less equal. But suppose Black makes the "other" capture **3...dxe5!**. Then White still has his queen and bishop attacked and loses a piece. *Probable cause of error:* Not considering all the forcing moves at a critical node of the analysis.

B) His rejection of the second-best move **1.♕e5** was based upon the key removal-of-the-guard idea **1...♛xe5 2.♖xe5 d6**:

de Groot Ernie
White to play after 1.♕e5 ♛xe5 2.♖xe5 d6

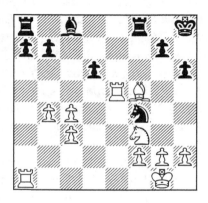

But here White has the forced **3.♗xc8 dxe5 4.♗xb7,** when White already has more than enough for the exchange (two pawns) plus both the a7- and e5-pawns are vulnerable and the c-pawns are strong passers. *Probable cause of error:* Quiescence error – assuming that, after 2...d6, the case was closed and Black was doing well, when in fact the exchange sacrifice was good for White.

C) Finally, in the best line he rejected White's play after **1.♕d4! ♖xf5 2.♖e8+ ♔h7:**

de Groot Ernie
White to play after 1. ♕d4 ♖xf5 2.♖e8+ ♔h7

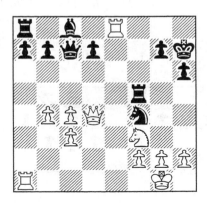

— noting correctly that White could pin the rook with 3.♕e4. But even better is to threaten mate with **3.♖e7.** For a full analysis of this see Appendix B. *Probable cause of error:* A combination of quiescence and not considering all the forcing moves, as there was no further investigation of how good 3.♕e4 was, nor any realization that 3.♖e7 had to be investigated to properly evaluate the strength of 1.♕d4!.

Subject B-12's analysis, in general, was very good. But that one little missed move here or there, or misevaluation, was just enough to cause another move to be played. Just these subtle errors caused Subject B-12 to misevaluate each line: the move chosen (Line A) loses, while the moves rejected (B and C) are both good for White. Contrast this near-miss analysis to that of much weaker players, who can't find the main forcing moves and don't get anywhere near as close to the truth as did Subject B-12.

Protocol B-13 (de Groot A; 1600 Canadian; adult; 5 minutes)
Material equal — c-file open. So many pieces on the board. d7 is a square for the knight but two pieces are protecting it — that doesn't work. Can I attack some of your pieces? 1.♘xd5: if 1...♘xd5 I get the bishop on e7 [sic] but you can take back with other pieces. Don't see any easy win of pieces here. 1.♕h3 doesn't go anywhere — not enough pieces to attack the black king. The bishop on a2 is not doing much but it's on the diagonal to the black king. Which piece is doing the least? I'm fascinated that this is a classic position to examine. 1.♘e2 — nowhere to go due to the pawn on g6. Is Black attacking anything? 1...♘xc3 what to take

with? Probably 2.♖xc3. Ah, Black is attacking the pawn on b2 — that would force me to move the bishop, so I probably need to save it. If 1...♛xb2 2.♖b1 ♛xa3 or 2...♛xc3 — I don't want you taking that pawn. I can play 1.♘c4:

de Groot A
Black to play after 1.♘c4

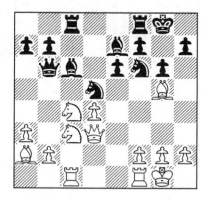

— that saves the pawn and attacks the queen. I am going to do 1.♘c4. Push clock.

Subject B-13 did examine the one capture 1.♘xd5 but quickly lost interest, apparently because it was well protected. Same thing with the idea of trying to get a knight to d7. Interestingly, as soon as he ran across the idea of saving the pawn and attacking the queen with 1.♘c4, that was sufficient for him. Unfortunately, he did not take this logic one step further and examine if he made another move first and then replied to 1...♛xb2 with 2.♘c4 — that would have been quite remarkable for this position (how many players have actually tried this? — not many!) — see the computer analysis in Appendix B.

Protocol B-14 (de Groot Zyme; 1720; adult; 18 minutes)
I have 1.♛xa8 — what is Black doing? Can I checkmate him? No. He's got 1...♛xf2+ 2.♔d1 ♘e3+ 3.♔d2 probably. Looks like Black is running out of steam. OK. 1.♛xa8 is a move. Then 1...♛xc3+ 2.♔d1 ♛xa1+ and so that doesn't look — Black gets a strong initiative. Black threatens 1...♛xc3+: did not see that at first. Material? Black is ahead a pawn but Black has more active pieces. Let's see. I think 1.♛xa8 ♛xc3+ Black has a dangerous game going but the bishop on c8 is pinned. Probably advance the c-pawn: 1.♛xa8 ♛xc3+ 2.♔d1

♛xa1+ ♚c2 or possibly 1.♛xa8 ♛xc3+ 2.♚d1 ♛b3+. 1.♛xa8 ♛xc3+ 2.♚d1 ♞xf2# is... mate! [too much time on 1.♛xa8]. Candidates: 1.♛d4 – I threaten a discovered check with the bishop and guards c3 and f2. Black has to stop the discovered check. 1.♛f3 is also possible, but 1.♛d4 is stronger because it threatens a discovered check. 1...♛xd4 2.cxd4 and Black's queenside is dangerous. Hmm, OK, what if the ugly 1.e3 ♛xf2+ 2.♚d2 [illegal] – don't see a killer there. 1.♜c1 ♛xf2+ or 1...♞xf2. 1.♜c1 ♛xf2+ 2.♚d2 and White has several threats like 3.♛xa8. 1.♛d4 ♛xd4 cxd4 and Black's queenside pawns are dangerous and has more pieces active as well – I don't like 1.♛d4. 1.♛f3 I like better. Then he has 1...♛xd6 or 1.e3 ♛xd6. 1.♛f3 ♛xf3 2.pawn takes queen – not sure which. If 2.exf3 then the bishop on f1 hits the pawns. I can go ♝e2-d1-c2 or something. So after 1.♛f3 that stops both 1...♛xf2 and 1...♛xc3+. The bishop on d6 is protected. If 1...♛xd6 then 2.♛xa8. I'm starting to like 1.♛f3 more than any other move. I don't think Black will exchange queens. I could defend c3 with 1.♜c1 but that does not look good at all – 1...♛xf2+ or 1...♞xc2. I like 1.♛f3 but here. Hmm. 1.♛f3. Push clock.

Subject B-14 had some good moments. He finally figured out that 1.♛xa8 is no good – that has to be the first task once candidate moves are tried. He did take a while to count material and he never quite figured out that in some lines ...♛xd6 can be met by ♜d1. The biggest error he made was not seriously looking at all the checks and then eventually figuring out that 1.♝e7+, ostensibly a move that loses a piece, would be the one that allows 1...♛xe7 2.♛xa8 by deflecting the black queen away from its threats. 1.♛f3 is better than 1.♛d4 but inferior to 1.♝e7+ and the surprising 1.♝b4 – see the computer analysis in Appendix B.

Summary of Class B

Characteristics of the thought process at this level:

- The first sign that Hope Chess is disappearing! For example, Subject B-10 considered 1.b4 and then tried to determine if that was playable after 1...♞xc3!.

- The players in this class start to show the characteristics of much stronger players, but they all seem to have a fatal flaw or two: one is too young to do all the deductive logic, a second assumes too much in opponent replies, another knows too much and uses general principles where only analysis will do. Finally, we have one subject who gets the right move for the right reason even if he didn't go through the entire proof process in a way that would make it repeatable.

- Players are not as defensive and are more aggressive, looking for wins and not settling for purely "safe" or "saving" moves.

Improvements to the thought process that would help in getting to the next level:

- As at all lower levels, consistency is a key. Class B players have the rudiments of better play but jump around too much and don't consider all the key possibilities in a reasonable order.

- B players have a tendency to play a winning idea as soon as they "think" they see it! Better to follow GM Lev Alburt and Al Lawrence's advice in *Chess Rules of Thumb,* "If you see a move which seems to win, that is a critical move; a critical move is one about which you should think long and hard!" Many players get excited when they think they find a winning line and translate that excitement into quick play. It would be better for them to take that excitement and use it to generate extreme caution against believing something that may be too good to be true! *Be more cautious when you have more to lose — it is worse to throw away a win and lose than to throw away a draw.*

- More than players above them, B players seem to analyze various candidates and then settle on their final move without double-checking to make sure it is good, or at least safe. If you are going to play a move, then your opponent is going to spend 100% of his effort trying to defeat it. So spend at least a decent percentage of your time making sure that the move you play is not easily defeated.

Chapter 7

Class A

This chapter includes players rated 1800-2000 USCF, or roughly 1950-2150 ICC standard. At this level the average reader should start to focus on what these players do correctly and how best to emulate them.

For each protocol, I list the de Groot position (for example, de Groot A, de Groot B, de Groot C, etc.; see Chapter 1 for those positions); the age of the subject; the subject's rating; and the time the subject spent to choose his move.

Comments in parentheses indicate outside actions or comments that reflect the action of the player, such as (silent) if he paused for a long time. Comments in brackets are my thoughts. My frequent use of [*sic*] means that the subject is making a clear mistake in analysis or visualization. In contrast, [!] indicates that the player has made a comment that is very insightful for their level of ability or a surprising error. A frequent note is [no eval], meaning that the subject did not try to evaluate which side stood better, by how much, and why.

In the following two Internet protocols, the subject was hard of hearing. So he typed his "thought process" in real time. There is something lost in doing this, but there is also something gained. It is very interesting to compare these written protocols to the others, which I transcribed, so I made sure to include them.

Protocols A-1 and A-2 are edited only for readability.

Protocol A-1 (de Groot A; adult; 1800 FIDE; 30+ minutes)
OK, look at the material situation... it's even... No checks... but b2-pawn is loose...

Potentially g5-bishop is loose, subject to discovered attack, but knight at f6 can't go somewhere else to attack bigger game like a queen or king. OK, let's carry on with identifying threats to White... b2-pawn is loose, anything else? Black could play knight takes c3... ah, if bxc3 then ...♗xa3.

Thinking about 1.♘xc6, as that would attack Black's bishop at e7. But after 1...♖xc6 Black still has his threat on b2 plus he can double on c-file. OK, what happens on 1.b4 or even 1.b3? If 1.b4, ♗xb4 axb4 ♘xb4 forking queen and bishop, but queen d2 or e2 defends the bishop on a2. [Perhaps the subject doesn't see the knight on c3 already lends some protection to the bishop on a2.]

So far 1.b4 seems reasonable. I'll hold that and see if there are any other moves... 1.b3 no good as 1...♗xa3. 1.♖b1 another possibility. Thinking of 1.♘xc6 now... 1...♖xc6 in reply doesn't get me anywhere and Black looks better... Perhaps 1.♘xd5? Sort of feeling some possibility of tactics based on knight attacking c6, bishop g5 on e7, knight c3 on d5. Thinking 1.♘xd5 ♗xd5 2.♗xd5 ♘xd5 3.♗xe7 ♘xe7. Hmm, then 4.♘d7 forking queen and rook at f8.

de Groot A
White to play after 1.♘xd5 ♗xd5? 2.♗xd5 ♘xd5 3.♗xe7 ♘xe7
Removing the guard for the 4.♘d7 fork is the Holy Grail for many subjects in de Groot A

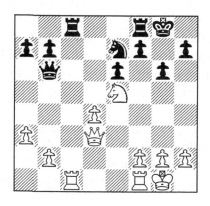

But [going back to move 1.♘xd5] bishop at c6 doesn't have to move, guarding d7 square. Let's try again, 1.♘xd5 maybe 1... exd5. No, doesn't seem to get anywhere for me... If I have to make a move now, I would do 1.♖b1. Check this first to see if safe and keep that as reserve... 1...♘xc3 2.bxc3 uncovers attack on ♕... Queen can go a6 or a5 but looks OK for Black. Don't want to move knight on e5 – outpost.

Let's try again, 1.♘xd5... Getting complex for me... don't like 1.b4 because of 1...a5 in reply...

de Groot A
White to play after 1.b4 a5

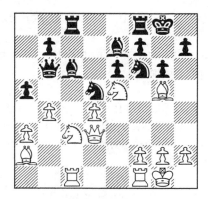

1.♖b1 still my best move... Do I want to grab the bishop on c6 with the knight? No, remember ♘e5 is in quite a nice position. 1.♗h6 ? 1...♖fd8 in reply, covers d7 square so knight can't go there... 1.♖c2? Can it be attacked? For example, by Black's knight on d5? Hmm, I like 1.♖c2 and maybe 2.♖fc1 to follow. Check for tactics... Looks OK, 1...♗xa3 2.bxa3 and knight can't fork queen and rook on b4 because of the pawn at a3.

And I don't mind knight at f6 moving as I have ♗xe7 in response. Prefer 1.♖c2 to 1.♖b1 as it's more active. Ah, what about 1...♘xc3 and then 2...♗a4? Well, I can do b2-b3 in reply or do ♖xc3 instead of bxc3 after ...♘xc3. 1.♖c2 is my No. 1 move so far. Thinking 1...♗xa3 and possible Black's queen zooming down b-file for a double attack... no it's OK for White. Anything better than ♖c2? No, I'll cut off here and play ♖c2. 1.♖c2 Push clock.

Summary after the protocol:

Dan: Let's take a look at your PV. After 1.♖c2 ♘xc3, what were you planning to play? [The subject moves 2.♖xc3.] Yes, but what about 2...♛xb2?

Subject: Argh!

Dan: (My student continued playing White and I, with help from *Rybka*, played Black: 3.♖c2 ♛b5 4.♛xb5 ♗xb5 5.♖fc1 ♖xc2 6.♖xc2 ♖d8 and my student admitted that Black was pretty much winning.)

Subject: I've lost one pawn already, so yes.

Dan: But I can't say you played Hope Chess because you did try to find this. You did try to make sure 1.♖c2 did not lose to any check, capture, or threat.

Subject: Well, I couldn't see anything better and my mind was getting fogged up with all the possibilities...

Dan: Note that you saw Black's idea of ...♕xb2 but planned to recapture with the rook on c3 anyway. This should raise a flag. Your earlier "King of the Hill" 1.♘xc6 just wins the bishop pair, so it is much better than 1.♖c2. Half a pawn is not bad.

Subject: True, but I lost the e5-outpost knight.

Dan: Well, although ♘xc6 was not the best move, all the grandmasters who analyzed this position said it was a good move. Outpost knights are great for things like winning the bishop pair! Anyway, back to the start. You did count material at the beginning — you counted the pieces but stopped there. Much clearer would be to evaluate the position statically before you analyze: Who stands better, by how much, and why?

Dan: For example, suppose 1.♘xg6 led to perpetual check by 1.♘xg6 hxg6 2.♕xg6+ ♔h8 3.♕h6+ ♔g8 4.♕g6+ ♔h8 5.♕h6+. If so, would you do it?

Subject: Depends on if I felt Black were better.

Dan: Exactly, but you never let me know! Most grandmasters at the start try to get a feel which side is better (statically). That gives them a "hoop" to jump through during analysis.

Subject: Yes, you're right I didn't do a static analysis [evaluation].

Dan: For example, if they feel White is a lot better, they are looking for a move which leaves them a lot better. If they feel the position is equal, then they are thrilled if they can force a line with a slight advantage, showing they were wrong. Theoretically, if your static evaluation is perfect, then your PV's evaluation, if also perfect, should match it. Does that make sense?

Subject: Yes. If you make no mistakes, your position can't get worse.

Dan: Let's move on. You did pretty well when it came to picking out a "King of the Hill." When you saw a good move, you looked for a better one. The main problems were: 1) your analysis did not examine all checks, captures, and threats before moves like 1.♖c2, and 2) when you did make a capture, you didn't systematically attempt to find your opponent's best recapture.

Subject: Yes, I found it hard work, so I probably held back from examining every possibility.

Dan: For example, you would have to make sure Black's best reply after 1.♘xc6, 1.♘xd5, 1.♗xd5, and 1.♗xf6 led to a good position for Black before settling for 1.♖c2. And after 1.♘xd5 instead of saying, "Now Black has three recaptures: 1...exd5, 1...♘xd5, and 1...♗xd5; which would he do?" you first assumed 1.♗xd5 and later 1...exd5, never mentioning ...♘xd5. Now that would make sense if 1.♘xd5 exd5 was so good for Black that you needn't consider 1...♘xd5 but you did not make that clear.

Subject: Yes, I need to be more systematic in looking along analysis trees.

Dan: I would guess from reading in between the lines that you liked Black's position better after 1.♘xd5 exd5 than you did after 1.♖c2 ♘xc3, right?

Subject: Er, I can't quite recall.

Dan: Otherwise you would never play 1.♖c2!

Subject: ♖c2 felt safer to me...

Dan: But that's exactly what you need to do to decide to play 1.♖c2 — make sure your position after Black's best reply is better for you than it would be after any other candidate and his best reply, right?

Subject: Yes, do the analysis tree.

Dan: So therefore 1.♖c2 ♘xc3 is better for White than 1.♘xd5 exd5, I would guess. The problem is that your process in showing this was not clear

— it did not look as though that was what you were deciding, when that is exactly what you are supposed to be weighing: Do I want the position after line A or line B? Does that make sense? Of course, that only applies to an analytical position like this. In a non-analytical position you play much faster and by general principles, usually. I am going to email you World Champion Max Euwe analyzing this position. As a math professor, Dr. Euwe is very systematic — compare what he did with what you did and it should be very helpful in pointing out clearer ways to approach the problem.

Subject: Okay, I will look forward to that!

Now, here is the same subject a couple of months later:

Protocol A-2 (de Groot Ernie; adult; 1800 FIDE; ~30 minutes)
OK, White has 6 pawns vs. Black's 5 pawns, else material is same. The knight at f4 is attacking white's queen. White doesn't have an immediate mate, also no safe checks. Can't ignore knight attack on queen, as have nothing to seriously threaten Black with. See that the rook at f8 is loose but can't see easy way to take advantage of it. OK, some possible initial candidate moves 1.♕d4, er... 1.♕d2, 1.♕c5 (don't like it), hmm, 1.♘e5 a possibility... OK, take each in turn...

1.♕d4, then... 1...♖xf5!. Forgot that the bishop at f5 was under attack by the rook, so have to hang onto it. New initial candidates 1.♕e4, 1.♕e5 (loses c4-pawn?), 1.♘e5(??)

Look at ♘e5 first. 1...♘xd5, 2.♘g6+ ♔g8 and that's it. Can't do ♘e7+ so forget ♘e5 possibility. Just remembered, ought to really get a feel for who is better here. Looks like White has an advantage one pawn up, queen centralized, both minor pieces out, both rooks on open files. Need to make the most of it. 1.♕e5 ♕xc4, 1...♖e4. 1.♕e5 ♕xe5 ♖xe5 — that looks good for White as can do ♖ae1...

Now look at 1.♕e4. What about 1...d5 in reply? Hits the queen and uncovers an attack on f5-bishop by the bishop at c8... Doesn't look good. I see that d5 or d6 is a possibility to consider for my ♕e5 initial move. So... 1.♕e5 ♕xe5 2.♖xe5 and d6... Not good for White... Hmm, not only I have to think about the knight at f4 attacking White's queen, but also ...d6 or ...d5. Might even have to think about 1.♕c5... No, that's no good as after 1...♕xc5 2.bxc5 ♖xf5. So the position is proving a little tricky...

Looking at possibility of knight forks or bishop skewers or rook at back rank but can't see at moment any way of luring Black's pieces to their doom... At the moment, my best shot seems to be 1.♕e5 ♕xe5 2.♖xe5 d6 3.♗xc8 dxe5 4.♗xb7... At the end of that I have two pawns for the exchange... but need to make sure position is quiescent... Hmm, after 4.♗xb7 ♖b8, 5.♖xa7 getting another pawn? Can't see a better initial try than 1.♕e5 as 1.♕e4 fails to 1...d5, 1.♕c5 to 1...♕xc5 and 2...♖xf5... think some more... Think about 1.♕e5 d6... but that's OK after 2.♕xf4 ♖xf5 queen moves away... So my king of the hill is 1.♕e5 (ugh) ♕xe5 2.♖xe5 d6 3.♗xc8 dxe5 4.♗xb7 ♖b8 5.♖xa7. At the moment no other likely sounding first move comes to mind... recheck my best line... Thinking 1.♖e8, with 1...♖xe8 in reply... no, not getting anywhere... OK, recheck first line... 1.♕e5 ♕xe5 ♖xe5 d6 ♗xc8 dxe5 ♗xb7... Yes, I'll go for 1.♕e5 and press clock.

Summary after the protocol:

Dan: If we can improve your analysis skills you become a better player, and positions like this can force you to stretch yourself. OK, let's look at some key points:

1) You did not explain why a simple move guarding the bishop like 1.♕a5 was bad (or good);

2) You did not look at the interesting threat 1.♕f7.

de Groot Ernie
Black to play after 1.♕f7

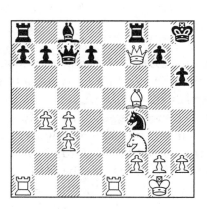

3) After 1.♕d4 ♖xf5 you didn't look much to see if you could get away with sacrificing the bishop — you seemed to assume that it was just pretty bad.

On the other hand, you get an A for your analysis of 1.♕e5 and, indeed, the computer says that your PV is the 2nd best line for White and does retain an advantage. Take a look at 1.♕f7 and tell me what you think.

Subject: Yes, I was looking at 1.♕f7 (and 1.♕a5)... That is, when you mentioned these and not before! 1.♕f7, clearly 1...♖xf7 loses to 2.♖e8+ as the bishop at f5 is covering escape square at h7. So 1.♕f7, look at 1...♕d8 but 2.♕g6 looks good. Looks like 2...♖xf5 forced. So 1.♕f7, 1...♕d6 covers f8 and g6... but 2.♖e8 puts the kibosh on it... Try 1...♘e6 in response to 1.♕f7... 2.♖xe6 looks strong... Yes, 1...♕d8 looks the best defense for Black for 1.♕f7... Thinking about 1.♕f7 ♕d6 2.♖e8 ♘e6...

All in all, a very good, workmanlike job by Subject A1/A2, and I thank him for his extra insight via his typed post-protocol comments.

Protocol A-3 (de Groot A; adult; 1850; moderate time)
Static features: isolated queen's pawn, material even [but no evaluation]. ... ♕xb2 is a threat. Black has dark-squared weaknesses. I would exchange dark-squared bishops. 1.♘xc6 ♖xc6 wrecks the queenside pawns. Minor pieces OK; the knight on e5 is the best. The bishop on a2 is posted but hits granite. At some point ♖fe1 to overprotect e5. 1.♗xf6 to remove d7 defender. 1.♗xd5 ♗xd5 2.♗xf6 and then ♘d7 wins the exchange. 1.♗xd5 ♘xd5 2.♗xe7 ♘xe7 allows 3.♘xc6 ♕xc6 does not work. ...♘xd5 is a good antidote. 1.♗xd5 ♘xd5 2.♘xd5 ♗xd5 3.♗xe7 wins the exchange with ♘d7 [sic]. 1.♗xd5 ♘xd5 2.♘xd5 exd5 3.♗xe7 and exchange the bad bishop with b4 or b3. Double check. 1.♗xd5. Push clock.

Another "right move for the wrong reason" protocol. It is true that 1.♗xd5 is the best move, but not only did Subject A-3 fail to consider Black's best reply 1...exd5, but after 1.♗xd5 ♘xd5 2.♘xd5 ♗xd5 3.♗xe7 he said he wins the exchange when it is "twice" as good: he is winning a piece. Full credit to A-3 for double-checking a line where he thinks he is winning — but then he didn't find any corrections! For if 1.♗xd5 is indeed winning you would want to make extra sure: if so, the game is basically over; but if not, then the idea that you are missing might mean that the candidate is not even a good move! If for some reason he thought 1.♗xd5 exd5 were bad for Black (and I did not when I was at his level), then he certainly did not say so, or why. And if it were bad for Black, the part of the "proof" where you show that your leading candidate is better than any other move, say 1.♘xd5, is missing as well. Compare this protocol to how Euwe found 1.♗xd5 best in Appendix A. Euwe was convincing; Subject A-3 less so.

Protocol A-4 (de Groot A; adult; 1840; 20 minutes)

Material: White is one pawn up [sic]. Weakness on dark squares for Black's king. If the knight on d5 is off, then the bishop is the only one guarding d7, and ♘d7 can fork rook and queen. The bishop on c6 and the knight on f6 which are guarding d7 can possibly be exchanged on d5. I have a hanging pawn on b2. Now consider moves. I have no checks or attacks on the king. Consider 1.♘xd5, 1.♗xd5, 1.♗xf6. Another is to get in ♘d7 in some combinations. Another is 1.♘xf7. Candidates: captures on d5, f6 with the idea of ♘d7. So 1.♗xd5 then 1...♘xd5 or 1...♗xd5. 1.♗xd5 and then if 1...♗xd5 2.♘xd5 ♘xd5 3.♗xe7 with the idea of playing ♘d7. 2...exd5 3.♗xf6 with the idea of 4.♘d7 so I am good. Two other options: 1...♘xd5 2.♗xe7 ♘xe7 and I cannot fork. I can consider the sacrifice on f7 then ...♖xf7. If 1.♗xd5 ♗xd5 then I am happy — can get in ♘d7. 1.♗xd5 ♘xd5 no refutation so far.

de Groot A
White to play after 1.♗xd5 ♘xd5
Missing 2.♘xd5 winning a piece

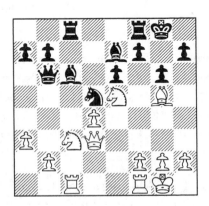

He's not going to capture with the bishop. He can capture with the pawn. On 1.♘xd5 he can capture with the bishop, knight, or pawn. 1.♘xd5 I don't see anything good over there. Don't see any captures on d5 with the idea of ♘d7

too appealing. So 1.♘e4 hangs a pawn on b2 — don't see anything. 1.♘e4 ♘xe4 is OK for Black. 1.♗xf6 If 1...♗xf6 2.♘e4 not really threatening anything. Maybe ♗xd5. Not good. Overall — I am a pawn up still — I can go for simplification [!]. Can I just play 1.b4? My position is better on the kingside. Maybe just simplify — Oh! I am not a pawn up, so there is no reason to simplify (silent). Kind of stuck but I have to play a move. So 1.b4 to gain space and potentially bring the knight to c5. Does Black have a threat? 1...♘xc3 helps me double rooks [?!]. He has a queen and rook aiming at that. OK, so I just now don't like 1.b4 because of 1...♘xc3. Need to protect the pawn. 1.♖c2 maybe? Can double rooks on the c-file. That's an option. Can't find tactics in exchanges over there. 1.♘xc6 so knight on e5 is good. No reason to exchange. Any tactics? 1.♘xc6 can play 1...♖xc6 or 1...bxc6. 1...♖xc6 2.♘xd5 can play 2...exd5. OK. Idea: 1.♘xc6 ♖xc6 2.♘a4. If capture with queen can't play 2.♘a4 — yeah. 1...♕xc6 2.♗xd5 exd5 3.♘e4 and the queen on the sixth rank protects the knight. Have to make a move. b2 is annoying. Want an improving move. Go back to 1.b4. 1.b4 ♘xc3 seems bad to me. Can move my queen to f3 on the diagonal but the d4-pawn hangs. Let's see 1.♗h6 then 1...♘xc3 or 1...rook on f-file moves. Already fifteen minutes. Back to 1.b4 — protects pawn and gains space — c5 an outpost 1.♗xf6 but 1...♘xf6. 1.♗xf6 ♗xf6 2.♘e4 don't want to let his bishop get to g7. What about 1.♕h3 with the idea of ♗h6? But d4 hangs. OK. Hmm (silent). The line I'm thinking of is 1.♗xd5. 1.♗xd5 ♗xd5 is no good. 1.♗xd5 ♘xd5 I'm OK: 2.♗xe7 ♘xe7 3.♘e4 — can have a strong knight. I don't have a dark-squared bishop — my knights are OK. 1.♗xd5 ♘xd5 2.♗xe7 ♘xe7 then b2 hangs. I can play 3.b4 and then play ♘e4 later. So 1.♗xd5. Push clock.

At the end this protocol is remarkably similar to that of Subject A-3: Subject A-4 did not consider 1.♗xd5 exd5 and he also played 1.♗xd5 ♘xd5? 2. ♗xe7 or 2.♘xe7, missing 2.♘xd5! which wins a piece. Yet, despite these lapses, 1.♗xd5 emerged as clearly best. In chess it is *not* better to be lucky than good, although on the way to being good one gets lucky more and more often!

Notice that, when Subject A-4 considered 1.♘xd5, he next stated: "...he [Black] can recapture with the bishop, knight, or pawn." This is the way to begin the kind of systematic analysis missing in almost all protocols in the previous chapters. Unfortunately, Subject A-4 then dismisses the entire line without further analysis!

Without mentioning the bishop pair, he carefully considers 1.♘xc6 and this time does consider the various captures. Careful analysis takes time, and it is noticeable now that the Class A players' average protocol length is longer than those in the preceding chapters.

Protocol A-5 (de Groot Ernie; adult; 1834; 34 minutes)

Pawn structure? Two islands to three. Black is worse. White's more developed. White's in a predicament. The bishop at f5 is attacked — is it really? Back-rank thing prevailing. Let's see (silent). Well, back rank comes into play 1.♕f7 ♖xf7? 2.♖e8+ and leads to mate. 1.♕f7 then the bishop on c8 can't develop so he must play 1...♕d8 or 1...♖g8. Usually not good to have to move 1...♖g8. That gives White has a free move, so to speak. 1.♕f7 ♕d8... Queen moves: 2.♕e7 ♕xe7 3.♖xe7 ♖xf5 and Black is doing well. 4.♖e8+ ♔h7. 1.♕f7 ♕d8 Black can't develop the queenside. Maybe...hmm. As White needs a way to stop him from developing his queenside. Let's see (silent) ["Do out loud"]. 1.♕f7 ♕d8 hard to continue for White. The bishop on f5 is a problem; the bishop is somewhat a problem. There are cases where ♘h4 comes to mind — a lot of possibilities, but not right away. So...(silent). If White just moves his queen, wants to move to attack the knight on f4 to prevent ...d6, for example. Let's see. Umm. Candidates 1.♕f7, 1.♕e4 — what else? (silent). Looking at forcing moves like 1.♖e8 — trying to force a conclusion. May be some type of forceful conclusion — Black is awkward. Candidates 1.♕f7, 1.♕e4. Two moves to look at first. If not good for me, then analyze other moves. 1.♕f7 ♕d8 and doesn't seem like 2.♕e7 ♕xe7 3.♖xe7 ♖xf5 4.♖e8+ ♔h7... question there — not a good variation — Black can play ...b6 and ...♗b7. If 1.♕e4 then 1...d5 even if it sacrifices a pawn which it doesn't. 1.♕e4 d5 2.exd5 ♗xf5 that's obviously losing (chuckles). Not much other possibilities for moving the queen — others drop the bishop on f5. Interesting. Well, let me think (silent). Back to 1.♕f7 ♕d8. The queen's attacked. Doesn't seem to be a way to... well. One more possibility. 1.♕e5 attacks the queen on c7 then 1...♕ moves 2.♕xf4 So 1.♕e5 either 1...♘e6 or 1...♕xe5. 1...♕xe5 2.♖xe5 d6. What else? OK. 3.♘h4 dxe5 4.♘f4 covers g6. 1.♕e5 ♕xe5 Ha ha ha. Other moves. Is Black really threatening 1...♖xf5? Can I lure him into that? Maybe 1.♕d4 is interesting [15 minutes]. 1...♖xf5 2.♖e8+ ♔h7 and now 3.♕e4 pins the rook and threatens g4. Kind of artificial. Well. Hmm. This is my normal thing — this position will suck up a lot of my clock [short interlude to discuss time management]. 1.♕f7 ♕d8 White may be in trouble. Come up with all the fancy moves 1.♕f7; 1.♕e5. 1.♕e5 ♕xe5 2.♖xe5 d6 is annoying — it attacks both the rook and the bishop:

de Groot Ernie
White to play after 1.♕e5 ♕xe5 2.♖xe5 d6
Correctly finding the exchange sacrifice

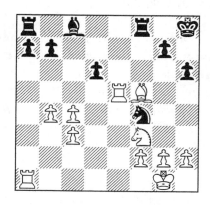

Probably forced to play 3.♗xc8 dxe5 4.♗xb7 ♖b8 5.♖xa7. White does get quite a bit of compensation for the exchange — light-squared bishop is a strong piece. [Subject did not realize he was ahead a pawn to begin with, and thus underestimates the result.] 1.♕e5 ♕xe5 2.♖xe5 d6 3.♗xc8 dxe5 4.♗xb7 maybe 4...♖ad8 5.♘xe5. White is OK — has passed queenside pawns. 5...♖d2 ♘d6 OK. 1.♕e5 ♕xe5 d6 3.♗xc8 dxe5 4.♗xb7 ♖ad8 Umm. Want to play 5.♘xe5 — eliminate Black possibility to put rooks on the second rank — probably good for White. Difficult for Black to manage pieces to stop White's queenside pawns. Now that I found that continuation — good for White — double-check: is there anything better? 1.♕d4. If 1...♖xf5 2.♖e8+ ♔h7 3.♕e4 attacks the rook and threatens g4 — now can Black play ...g6 to defend the rook? Then 4.♕e7+ with at least a draw. Any line where you have at least a perpetual is worth looking at [!]. 1.♕d4 ♖xf5 2.♖e8+ ♔h7 3.♕e4 d5 same situation but missed it — have 4.cxd5 and the threat for g4 is still on. Now 4...g6 loses to 5.♖e7+. Wow! Seems like a pretty good continuation. Also ♘h4. Hmm. All kinds of stuff — variation gets pretty complicated there. Black can take on c3 and threaten ...♕xa1 — then ♖e1. Very complicated. Break pin with ♘g6? Let's see there. Is h4 and h5 a possibility? Also ♘d4 with h4 — ...h4 what happens? (silent). Yeah, 'cause 1.♕d4 ♖xf5 2.♖e8+ ♔h7 3.♕e4 d5 4.cxd5 ♘g6 5.h4 with the idea of pushing g4, h5. But g4 then ...♖f4 so that does not work: ...♖f4-xg4 so h4 is not effective. I take that back — 6.h5 ♖xh5 7.♖ae1 with the idea of ♘e5. The whole thing is that Black's queenside can't get developed. Time consuming. 5.h4 — like to get my queen to g8 and c8. 1.♕d4 ♖xf5 2.♖e8+ ♔h7 3.♕e4 d5 4.cxd5 ♘g6 —

don't see anything else for Black. 4...♘g6 5.d6 with the idea of 5...♕xd6 6.♕c4 threatening c8+, ♕g8#. What can Black do? Anything? 6...♘e7 holds both. Also 6...♖f8 that doesn't work. 5.d6 ♕xd6 this variation does not seem enough for White — check one last time [30+ minute warning]. Last variation somewhat good for White. 1.♕e5 ♕xe5 2.♖xe5 d6 3.♗xc8 dxe5 — can Black take on c8? — 4.♗xb7 ♖ad8 5.♘xe5. I really like 5...♖d2 6.f3 ♗f8 and my minor pieces are good. Can't get checkmated. Then push c-pawn with bishop on b7 controlling the c-pawn march c4-c5-c6. So that variation is good. 1.♕e5 hit clock.

This is a good example of "long analysis — wrong analysis." It is not so much that Subject A-5 made many mistakes in his longer lines (although everyone makes some!), it is that he overlooks that he is trying to find the best move, not figure out everything that is going to happen. The subject would be much more time-efficient if he would hone in on 1.♕e5 and 1.♕d4 and then simply ask himself, "Based on the main lines of each, which do I think is better for me?" and then just play that move. (See the discussion on "progressive deepening" in Section 9.3.) For too long he tries to get into the intricacies of 1.♕d4, when much of that information may not be needed. Although for 1.♕d4 quite a bit of information is needed, there is always a practical point of *diminishing returns,* especially with the clock running. Either the main lines generate sufficient pressure to make that candidate more promising than the exchange sacrifice of 1.♕e5, or they don't. That's really the main issue. When World Champion Dr. Max Euwe finds 1.♗xd5 (see Appendix A) he doesn't look more than two (!) moves ahead in the principal variation and decides he has enough pressure. Right before moving, Euwe states, "Much is still up in the air..." and then quickly moves. Instead of deciding *what* is up in the air, he properly leaves this for future moves. *Euwe understood that his goal is to find the best move possible, not to figure out exactly how good it is. Once you determine the best move, you are done. Any further analysis is just a waste of time.* Of course, sometimes you have to look very deeply to see if a move is good, but that is not always the case. See Protocol A-7 for more discussion on this concern.

Protocol A-6 (de Groot A; age 16; 1800; 8 minutes)

1.♘xd5 ♗xd5 2.♗xd5 exd5 3.♖xc8 ♖xc8 no good. 1.♗xf6 ♗xf6 2.f4 ♗d7 [?]. 1.b4 I don't like it. 1.f4 ♘xc3 2.♖xc3 ♖fd8 3.♖fe1. No. 1.♗xd5 ♘xd5 2.♗xe7 ♘xe7. Hmm. 1.♗xf6 ♗xf6 2.♘e4 ♗g7 Hmm. 1.b4 ♘xc3 2.♖xc3 ♖fd8 3.♖fe1 ♗e4. No, that works: good for Black. 1.♘xc6 ♕xc6 — never mind — no good for Black. 1.f4[?] ♘xc3 2.♖xc3. 1.f4 ♕xb2 2.♗xd5 ♘xd5 3.♗xe7 ♘xe7 no good for White. 1.♘xd5 ♘xd5 2.♗xe7 ♘xe7 kinda like it for White. 1.♘xd5. Push clock [PV 1.♘xd5 ♗xd5 2.♗xf6].

There are two general ways to arrive at a move: by principle and by analysis. Most positions require a little of both, but some require one approach much more than the other. Obviously Subject A-6 believes de Groot A is a completely analytical position, and he is mostly correct. He gave almost no descriptive clues as to why he was analyzing specific candidates or why he thought certain replies were forced or best. He just went into lines as if they were obvious or forced. The evaluations are there, but not explained — good players do that sometimes in their hurry to beat the clock.

Subject A-6 initially rejects 1.♘xd5 when only considering the reply 1...♗xd5, but later decides he likes 1.♘xd5 if Black replies 1...♘xd5. Then he concludes that he will play 1.♘xd5 based on the latter! Where's the logic in that? If 1.♘xd5 ♗xd5 was not good for White, that why would Black choose 1...♘xd5 — and why would White choose to play 1.♘xd5? Subject A-6 did not even consider 1.♘xd5 exd5, which may be bad for Black, but you would not know it from this protocol. While it is far better to use 100% analysis on positions like this than 100% principles and Hand-waving (which would never work), this protocol is an excellent example of how just examining moves without thinking about objectives, principles, or descriptive evaluations can be dangerous, especially if you are not a top-notch analyst. The subject also failed to assume the opponent will play his best move.

Another interesting point is that, after 1.♘xc6 ♕xc6, Subject A-6 states "never mind — no good for Black" and never considers it further. But since he is White, did he mean "— no good for White"? If it were truly no good for Black, that would certainly merit further investigation!

The next protocol is one of my favorites because it is very instructive. It represents a unique type of problem exhibited by players at this level.

Protocol A-7 (de Groot A; adult; FIDE 1800; time unknown)
The position is about equal; White has the initiative but a potentially bad endgame. After 1.♗xd5 I think 1...♘xd5 is OK. 1.♗xd5 ♘xd5 2.♘xd5 (takes a while and then realizes White is winning a piece). 2...♖xc1 [sic]. I think 1.♗xd5 is winning but no, Black can play 1...exd5:

de Groot A
White to play after 1.♗xd5 exd5
Correctly realizing this recapture is forced

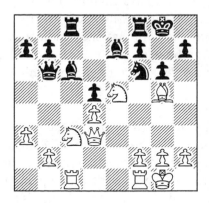

When you see a good move, look for a better one. Now 1.♗xd5 exd5 is forced. Then I can play 2.♕f3. Then 2...♗g7 is forced [Can the bishop on c6 move?]. 3.♗xf6 ♗xf6 4.♘xd5 ♗xd5 and I can win the d-pawn... [The subject spent additional time examining the continuation 1.♗xd5 and then played it; I am not sure if I have the entire protocol.]

I will never forget the conversation after this protocol. I suggested to the student that he could improve by keeping in mind that his goal was to find the *best* move and it is not always necessary to spend a lot of time figuring out exactly *how good* a candidate is. I read him the Euwe protocol (see Appendix A) and emphasized the final paragraph, where Euwe mentioned that "much was up in the air" but played the move immediately thereafter anyway. There was a stark contrast between this Subject A-7 and Euwe. Subject A-7 had correctly pinpointed 1.♗xd5 as the key move – and for the right reasons – but had continued exploring it as no student has, before or since. After I explained how keeping in mind the idea of "finding the best move" would help him, my student protested that without extensive analysis of 1.♗xd5 he would not be able to find out how good it was. Thus he could not determine whether it was the best move without extensive analysis. I replied that extensive analysis is sometimes necessary, but not in this case. Even if extensive analysis were needed, that would require the player to periodically go back and compare how good the positions were after the 1.♗xd5 lines to other lines to see if indeed it were the best. *Only if you have*

a choice between two (or more) strong candidates would it make sense to ana-
lyze extensively before playing one.

For example, suppose you have examined all the reasonable candidates and know that the best you can possibly do with any of them, except one, is to get a slight advantage. But with that one candidate you get at least a bigger advantage; it might even be winning. You can confidently make that move because it is the best possible, even though you don't know exactly how good it is.

I pointed out to my student that none of the grandmasters in de Groot's book felt it was necessary to look so deeply into what might happen after 1.♗xd5. It wasn't necessary. But instead of helping him, this made my student defensive (something I never want to happen). He became indignant and refused to accept my advice. I felt bad about his reaction, but to this day I also feel like I did try my best to help him. The pain is all the more since this student obviously had impressive talent for an 1800 player: to identify the key line so quickly and so well. Yet something was retarding his progress...

Protocol A-8 (de Groot A; adult; FIDE 1800; 5.5 minutes)
The pieces and pawns are equal. The knight on e5 can take the bishop on c6.
...g6 weakens Black's kingside. 1.♘e4 ♘xe4 2.♗xe7 then 2...♘xe7 protects the knight at e4, so no good.

de Groot A
White to play after 1.♘e4 ♘xe4 2.♗xe7 ♘xe7
The bishop on c6 guards the knight, although 3.♘xc6,
removing the guard, is worth investigation

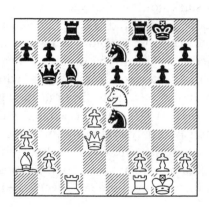

The c-file is blocked. Maybe 1.♘xc6 followed by 2.♘e4 to stop Black from guarding the knight at e4. 1.♘xc6 then 1...bxc6 or 1...♖xc6 or 1...♕xb2 attacks the rook at c1 and the bishop at a2. I could play 1.♗h6 to attack the rook at f8. Then 1...♖fd8 attacks d4. b2 is loose in some variations. So I can play 1.b4 — that strengthens the outpost on e5. If I don't do anything what would he do? 1...♖fd8 anyway. 1.b4 ♖fd8. How does that do? I can do 2.♘f3 to protect my d4 if I have to. 1.♘c4 allows 1...♕a6 so I think my move is 1.b4 to threaten 1.b5 or... 1.b4. Push clock.

This is quite a bit of Hope Chess from a player rated so highly. Subject A-8 does not consider whether Black has any forcing move (such as 1...♘xc3) which might be difficult to meet after his chosen move, 1.b4. Subject A-8's overall feel for the position was not bad. After seeing that 1.♘e4 probably wasn't safe (few players who considered 1.♘e4 were able to see that Black's 2...♘xe7 recapture would allow the bishop on c6 to guard e4), he deduced that 1.♘xc6 would make a later 2.♘e4 safer. This type of good deductive analysis is not usually found in players rated under 1700. The player had been close to FIDE 2000 but had semi-retired from chess during his middle age. Subsequent play on the ICC will probably show this player's strength to be somewhat below 1800 FIDE.

Protocol A-9 (de Groot A; adult; USCF 1830; 15 minutes)

Lots of interaction — the material is equal. There's an isolated queen's pawn. The c-file is open; all the pieces are on the board. There are weak dark squares around the black king. Look at Black's captures: 1...♕xd4 is not safe — there is a discovered attack on the bishop on g5 — can he take advantage of that? 1...♘xc3 uncovers the bishop on c6 to attack g2. 1...♘xc3 ♖xc3 and White can double rooks on the c-file. Can he make a threat with the f6-knight to hit g5? 1...♘d5 [sic] 1...♘e4 capture OK, 1...♘g4 so no major discovery on the bishop on g5.

Look at 1.♘xd5 or 1.♗xd5. Don't see why I should fork 1.♘xd5 ♘xd5 hits the bishop on g5; I don't want to initiate trades [!]. 1.♖c2 to double rooks on the c-file — there's a skewer on b5. 1...♘xc3 2.bxc3 ♗b5 gotta deal with that. Taking on d5 first doesn't help that. 1...♘xc3 2.♕xc3 but then he has a discovery — not good. 1.♘xd5 ♘xd5 uncovers on the bishop on g5 and keeps the skewer threat alive — got to deal with that somehow. 1.♖fd1 ♘xc3 2.♖xc3 ♗b5 3.move the queen but rather move the knight. If I move the queen he can go to d5 anyway. Another is 1.a4 ♘xc3 anyway. 1.♗c4 is a stupid place for a bishop.

What to do about 1...♘xc3 2.♕xc3 no good. 2.bxa3 no good. 2.♖xc3 no good. Gotta deal with that for sure. Move the queen out of the line of fire. Where can I place it? 1.♕h3 no longer guards d4. So 1.♕e3 is not safe. 1.♕e4 not safe. 1.♕d2 is the most reasonable — overworked piece on d4 or g5. 1.♘xd5 doesn't work. 1.♗xd5 ♘xd5 2.♗xe7 ♘xe7 just seems like it helps him more than it helps me. Strategically, what do I want to do? Get rid of the blockade. Against the isolated queen's pawn one wants to get rid of minor pieces [!]. So 1.♕d2 ♘e4 hits the bishop and the queen. 2.♘xe4 leaves me a piece up. Ah! Let's see. Sorry — another thought. 1.♘xc6 is an obvious option: 1.♘xc6 bxc6; if 1...♕xc6 there's a discovery. 1.♘xc6 ♖xc6 then I could simply double on the c-file — he gets a tempo, too.

de Groot A
White to play after 1.♘xc6 ♖xc6

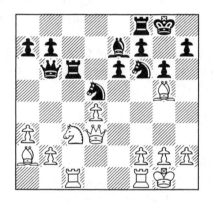

A whole bunch of trades on the c-file. That's a much better option than 1.♕d2. 1.♘xc6 rids a good knight but that's a secondary consideration. 1.♘xc6 ♖xc6 2.♘a4 hits the queen. 1.♘xc6 ♖xc6 2.♘a4 with the idea of 3.♖xc6 bxc6 is good for me, so 2...♕a6 could get lots of trades, maybe fix up my pawns, or 2...♕c6. I guess that's OK. Nothing horribly wrong with that. In a king-and-pawn endgame he would be better. I can figure that out later. 1.♘xc6 what does he have? 1.♘xc6 ♘b4 2.♕xb4. 1...♘f4 also OK — no intermezzo. 1.♘xc6 ♖xc6 2.♖c2 — what else? 1.♗h6 then he moves the rook or plays the skewer idea ...♗b5. OK, not seeing anything else. Play 1.♘xc6. Push clock.

Subject A-9 becomes convinced that 1...♘xc3 followed by 2...♗b5 is a threat, even though White has the c4 square firmly under control. For example, after 1...♘xc3 2.bxc3 ♗b5 White can play 3.c4 (or even 3.♗c4), while if 2...♗xa3 then 3.♗xf6. Or if 1...♘xc3 2.♖xc3 ♗b5, then 3.♗c4 is safe. In any case, he eventually finds that getting rid of the bishop with 1.♘xc6 is the "only defense" — a move that is reasonable not for the purpose of stopping ...♗b5, but to win the bishop pair, an idea he never recognizes! Interesting that he worries about 1...♘xc3 and 2...♗b5 but never even mentions 1...♛xb2 (!). Early on in the protocol he mentions that he does not wish to trade, probably because he has the isolated pawn, but then later he states, "Against the isolated queen's pawn want to trade minor pieces," so I assume he was looking at Black's point of view then. Ironic that he plays 1.♘xc6 — and the best move is 1.♗xd5 (see Appendix B), so this clearly shows that *players strong enough to understand that you don't trade off minor pieces when you have the isolated queen's pawn are also hopefully strong enough to also understand they should ignore that generalization if the specifics of the position call for it!* In this case, the best move is a trade of minor pieces.

Protocol A-10 (de Groot Ernie; adult; USCF 1900; 16 minutes)

The queen is attacked by the knight on f4, which has checks on e2 and h3. I'm looking at moving the queen somewhere [no eval]. 1.♛a5, 1.♛e5, 1.♛d2, 1.♛d4. Is there any intermediate move? 1.♛e4 is a possibility. 1.♛f7 is potential as well — mate on the back rank. Looks fairly strong: 1.♛f7 ♖xf7 2.♖e8+ ♖f8 3.♖xf8# (silent). If 1...♖g8 then 2.♖e8 looks strong. 1.♛f7 anything obvious I am missing? 1.♛f7 ♛d8 or 1...♛d6 nullifies a lot of the threats. 1...♛d8 is probably better. 1.♛f7 ♛d8 hmm. The queen's now hanging and blocked — there's no escape square. 2.♛e7 drops the bishop to 2...♛xe7 3.♖xe7 ♖xf5 (silent). Still looking at 1.♛f7 then 1...♛d8. I need some kind of continuation — the queen is trapped. 2.♛e7 ♛xe7 3.♖xe7 ♖xf5 is not so good. Are there other queen moves? 1.♛e5 ♛xe5 2.♖xe5 ♘d3 — knight forks don't amount to anything. 1.♛e5 d6 attacks the bishop twice and b5 still defends. 2.♛a5 b6 I think the bishop is dropping. 1.♛e5 ♛xe5 2.♖xe5 d6 — the rook needs to guard f5: 3.♖a5 b6 4.♖b5 a6 removes the guard, so 1.♛e5 does not work. 1.♛e5 d6 does that just win? No, 2.♛xf4 is an awkward pin, so 1...♛xe5 is better. 2.♛c5 drops a piece. Got to keep the contact with the bishop on f5. 1.♛e4 he can play 1...d5 which drops a piece — need to make a move to combine threats on the back rank. 1.♛e4 d5 2.♛e7 doesn't work (silent). 1.♛c5 ♛xc5 2.bxc5 ♖xf5 hmm. 1.♘e5 is interesting but the queen is still under attack. 1.♛f7 ♛d8 2.♘e5 doesn't work, does it? If 2...♖xf7 3.♘xf7+ wins the exchange. 1.♛f7 coming back to the same variation 1.♛f7 ♛d8 2.♘e5 does it work? 2...♖xf7+ 3.♘xf7+ picks up the queen on d8. The knight may be trapped — maybe I can

*save it [sic: he is ahead a rook]. 1.♕f7 ♕d8 2.♘e5 ♖xf7+ 3.♘xf7+ ♔g8
4.♘xd8 with the threat of 5.♖e8#. Is there a way out for Black? Pretty crazy.
So 1.♕f7. Push clock.*

As previously discussed, GM Lev Alburt and Al Lawrence write in *Chess
Rules of Thumb* that if you see a move that seems to win, it's a critical move,
so be careful and take your time. Subject A-10 gets caught up in the unforced
line 1.♕f7? ♕d8 2.♘e5 ♖xf7?? 3.♘xf7+ ♔g8 4.♘xd8 which he first said
wins the exchange — actually it wins a rook. But if you think you have found a
line that is winning, then ask whether all the opponent's moves are forced. In
this case Subject A-10 does not find (or almost seems to not wish to find) the
proper defense 2...d6!, which wins for *Black*. For a much better analysis of
these lines, see protocols M-7 and M-8. Another key line missed by Subject
A-10 was 1.♕e5 ♕xe5 2.♖xe5 d6 3.♗xc8 (instead of his lines moving the
rook, when Black tries to remove the guard on the bishop although 3.♖a5 b6
4.♗e4! is a move I missed when first shown this position) 3...dxe5 4.♗xb7,
when White ends up with more than enough material for the exchange. Part
of the problem may have arisen because Subject A-10 did not begin with an
assessment of the position, starting with counting the material. Had he begun
with the realization that White started already ahead a pawn, then a move
like 3.♗xc8 would have been much easier to find.

Summary of Class A

Characteristics of the thought process at this level:

• While B is the class where the "Real Chess" thinking process first appears, at the A level it is more prevalent, although not universal.

• It is clear that players at this level, on the average, put a lot more thought
into their moves. The reason is not just because they know to take more
time, but also because they understand how to use that time to proper
effect. *It is one thing to play slowly. It is another to be able to use that time
wisely, analyzing lines that have a high probability of affecting the quality
of the move.* For example, unless one can move purely by eliminating
all the other moves via deductive logic (sometimes possible in certain
endgames or when facing a check or other severe threat), then *it is im-
perative to spend a certain amount of your thinking time on the move you*

actually end up playing. This key trait is seen more and more as the players approach expert and master level.

- As each higher level is reached, the players become better and better at seeing what the opponent will do. This creates a side benefit in that they analyze lines that are more likely to occur — and thus are more likely to accurately evaluate the position. Weaker players are not as proficient at deducing what is forced, and thus their final evaluation also suffers.

Improvements to the thought process that would help in getting to the next level:

- It was once said to me that, "experts think to get out of trouble; masters think to avoid trouble." Yet this also applies to Class A players trying to become experts.

- I think experts and masters question themselves and their conclusions more honestly than do class players. As GM Jonathan Rowson wrote in his book *Chess for Zebras,* when he analyzes with a grandmaster, the grandmaster often mentions several possible ideas and plans, while his 1700-level students are often sure there is only one idea in the exact same position. This conclusion apparently applies to A players as well.

- I think A-level players seem to spend less time on their final decision than do higher-rated players. In this chapter's protocols, the subjects often consider several ideas but, when they switch back to the final candidate, it is often for a short time. I think stronger players return to their final move and try to do the de Groot Phase 4 "proof" (see Section 9.3) that it is indeed the best move they can find.

Chapter 8

Expert and Above

I. Expert

This chapter includes players rated expert (2000-2199 USCF, or roughly 2150-2350 ICC standard), national master (USCF 2200-2399), and above.

For each protocol, I list the de Groot position (for example, de Groot A, de Groot B, de Groot C, etc.; see Chapter 1 for those positions); the age of the subject; the subject's rating; and the time the subject spent to choose his move.

Comments in parentheses indicate outside actions or comments that reflect the action of the player, such as (silent) if he paused for a long time. Comments in brackets are my thoughts. My frequent use of [*sic*] means that the subject is making a clear mistake in analysis or visualization. In contrast, [!] indicates that the player has made a comment that is very insightful for their level of ability or a surprising error. A frequent note is [no eval], meaning that the subject did not try to evaluate which side stood better, by how much, and why.

Protocol X-1 (de Groot Ernie; adult; 2150; 19 minutes)
Don't recognize the opening — backward d-pawn. His knight is attacking the queen. Must move the queen. Tactics to delay it? 1.♕f7 is interesting! He can't take the queen because 2.♖e8+ leads to mate. 1.♕f7 is a candidate. Others? 1.♕c5 ♕xc5 bxc5 nothing. Material? Up a pawn to boot! Don't have to go in for major tactics?! 1.♕e5 is worth a look: 1.♕e5 ♕xe5 2.♖xe5. The rook attacks the bishop at f5 — that narrows the candidates. 1.♕b5 a6 — yeah, that's the case. Not 1.♕a5 maybe 1.♕a5 b6 same problem 2.♕e5 ♕xe5 3.♖xe5 d6 attacks the rook and bishop — doesn't look like it works. 1.♕e4 looks playable. If 1.♕f7 does not work can bail out with 1.♕e4 — look at 1...d5. Maybe I can't bail out with 1.♕e4. So 1.♕f7 is the candidate move. 1.♕f7 then he moves 1... ♖g8 or 1...♖d8 or protect with 1...♕d6 or 1...♘e6. No, 2.♖xe6 and he can't

take back. So 1...♘g6 is ridiculous – 2.♗xg6. 1.♕f7 ♕d6 or 1...♕d6; 1...♕d6 2.♖e8 is good – sufficient to win. 2...♘e6 at worst I exchange the pieces and I am up a pawn – OK. 1.♕f7 ♕d6 2.♖e8 ♘e6. Yeah, forced. 3.♗xf8 White is ahead in development with a much better game. ...♘e2+? 1.♕f7 ♕d8 looks best – rule out 1...♖d8 2.♖e8+ ♖xe8 3.♕xe8#. 1...♖g8 again: 2.♖e8 my best – not as certain. 2...♘e6? No. Maybe 2...g6. 1.♕f7 ♖g8 2.♖e8 same problem. Same threat; in most positions it (the defense) does not work. So 1.♕f7 ♕d8 only. Problem: both my queen and bishop are attacked. The queen has no good squares (groan). This does not look very good now. 2.♕e7 no. It all looks bad. Starting to think I may be in trouble here. Any tricks? 1.♖e8? Doesn't look very good. Re-evaluate. Anything tactical I missed somehow? 1.♕e4 d5. Maybe I should be looking at something else altogether. 1.♕f7 ♕d8 2.♕e7 ♕xe7 3.♖xe7 ♖xf5. Down a piece. 4.♘d4? Can I take advantage of the bishop being undeveloped? If 1.♕e5 d6 no good. 2.♕xf4. 1...♕xe5 2.♖xe5 d6 3.♗xc8 dxe5 4.♗xb7 doesn't look so bad – picking up the bishop on c8 and the pawn on d7. Pretty sure I have to play 1.♕e5. Only used 12 minutes (equivalent to six at a two to one ratio for thinking out loud). 1.♕e5 ♕xc4 is annoying but I am not in danger of losing a piece. 1.♕f7 was so pretty, too! But not against 1...♕d8. 1.♕a5 ♕xa5 2.♖xa5 b6 Oh! I have 3.♗e4:

de Groot Ernie
Black to play after 1.♕a5 ♕xa5 2.♖xa5 b6 3.♗e4
Subject X-1 spotted this key idea but I didn't!

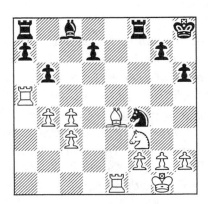

1.♕a5 b6 anything worth...? So I can induce ...b6 – is that helpful? It allows ♗e4 with tempo or allows him to develop the bishop. 1.♕a5 b6 2.♕e5 ♕xe5 3.♖xe5 not that concerned. Oh, I do – it hits the bishop on f5. Looks like ...b6 is

not helpful (to me). 1.♕e5 ♕xe5 2.♖xe5 d6 3.♗xc8 exd5 4.♗xb7 rook moves. Maybe then 5.♖xa7 – starting to look very promising. 1.♕e5 ♕xc4 2.♖e4 ♘e2+ doesn't win the knight. 3.♔f1 ♘g3++ hits rook, so 3.♔h1 then maybe nothing. Still it looks promising. 1.♕e5 ♕xc4 ♖e4 ♘e2+ 3.♔h1 – no, 3... ♕xc3 4.♖xe2 so 1.♕e5 ♕xc4 others? No, maybe 2...d6 but I'm certainly not worse. He might get equality but I should be OK. No alternatives to 1.♕e5. 1... ♕xc4 or 1...♕xe5. 1...♘e6? No, 2.♗xe6. 1...move queen then 2.♕xf4. Gotta move the queen unless 1.♖e8 ♖xe8 cute but nothing. Alright, 1.♕e5, 1.♘h4, 1.♘e5. Sort of Philidor's Legacy – not enough tempi. Almost ready to play 1.♕e5 ♕xe5 2.♖xe5 d6 3.♗xc8 dxe5 4.♗xb7 rook moves. I can't play 5.♖xa7 if he threatens a back-rank mate, but I have sufficient compensation for the exchange. OK, 1.♕e5.

Subject X-1 got off to a rough start, taking quite a long time for a player of his caliber to notice that 1.♕f7 is refuted by 1...♕d8. However, the remainder of his protocol is a model of good analysis which would be acceptable to many master-level players. In the diagram he spotted a key idea which I had missed when I was shown this position: luring the pawn to b6 allows a counterattack with ♗e4. Moreover, Subject X-1 fully weighed the various possibilities and chose a line where an exchange sacrifice gives excellent winning chances. While he missed the computer's best line, it was not that he saw a good move and did not look for a better one. After 19 minutes he found a line which seemed to win, and Trigger 2 (see Chapter 11) indicated that result was about as efficient as he was going to get.

Protocol X-2 (de Groot A; adult; 2000; 12 minutes)
Material even, White has an isolated queen's pawn. The knight at e5 is a decent outpost. Black blockades the isolated queen's pawn well. Threats: 1... ♕xb2. White can't actually win a piece: 1.♗xd5 ♗xd5 does not win a piece. Feels good to get a knight to e4, e.g. 1.♗xf6 ♗xf6 2.♘e4 but 1.♗xf6 ♘xf6 stops that. Like in most isolated queen's pawn games, White should play for a kingside attack – in the middlegame. How do I do that? Got to open things up on the kingside. A pawn advance? 1.g4. I want to get in f4 and f5. Need the pawn at g4 – may need a buildup to make that happen: g4, f4, double rooks on the f-file. 1.g4 weakens f3 and h3. Can Black take advantage? What would Black do if I played 1.g4?

de Groot A
Black to play after 1.g4?!

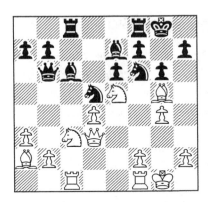

1...♕xb2? Suppose 1.g4 ♖fd8. Are there any other Black candidates? Don't see [!]. Black threatens 1...♘xc3 followed by ...♕xb2 and is a piece up [?]. 1.g4 ♕xb2 2.♖f2 or 2.f4 ♘xc3 3.♖xc3. So g4 is premature or not good at all, so I need to deal with b2 (silent). 1.♖c2 – I have more active pieces or 1.b3 or 1.b4 possible; ♗b1 is possible if b3 but not likely. 1.b4 or 1.♖c2 possible. 1.b4 weakens c3 badly – don't believe he can take advantage of that: 1.b4 ♘xc3 2.♖xc3 ♘e4 big problem. So, no 1.b4. How about 1.♖c2? It guards the b2 square – tidy and tight – no major threats that will kill me here. 1.♖c2 ♘xc3 with the idea of ...♗a4. What other possibilities for Black? 1.♖c2 ♖fd8 2.♖fc1 issue: 2...♘xc3 – never mind – it's OK. Would I lose the d-pawn? No. 1.♖c2 ♖fd8 2.♖fc1 and my development is completed with a typical isolated queen's pawn game. I rate the position dynamically equal [good]. How do I move forward after that? 1.♖c2 ♖fd8 2.♖1c1...? (silent). I don't see any major threats for Black or for White – I can move forward. White moves 1.♖c2. Blunder check and make 1.♖c2. Push clock. (PV = 1.♖c2 ♖fd8 2.♖1c1 with approximate equality).

A very strange protocol for a 2000 player. Subject X-2 hardly considered any of his forcing moves, not 1.♘xd5 or even 1.♘xc6 winning the bishop pair. To spend so much time on the very strange 1.g4?! without investigating the more forcing captures is original, but not indicative of what most players at this level would do. The best way to meet 1.♖c2 is 1...♘xc3 when White needs to find 2.♘xc6! to stay in the game (although Black is still slightly better). Instead, if 2.bxc3 then 2...♗e4 is a winning skewer. If 2.♖xc3 then 2...♕xb2 is very good for Black and, finally, if 2.♕xc3 then 2...♘e4 wins, but not 2...♗xg2?? 3.♕xc8 — a line missed by several players who assumed the discovery on the queen would automatically win.

The next subject woke up early to provide a protocol.

Protocol X-3 (de Groot Ernie; adult; 2040; 8 minutes)

White is better — on general principles: Black is not developed much. Black is attacking my queen. Unless I have a check or threat. 1.♖e8 flashed in my mind: 1.♖e8 ♘xd5 2.♖xf8#. Maybe he has 1...♘e6: 1.♖e8 ♘e6 — let's see: three attacking, one defending. 1.♖e8 ♘e6 2.♗xe6 ♖xe8 — so I can't do 2.♗xe6. 1.♖e8 ♖e6 2.♖xf8+ ♘xf8 and... Well, let's see. I'm a pawn up. He's got a crummy position. What would I do? Fun then after 2...♘xf8; can play something like — looking at 3.♘e5 and then ♘f7+ with general havoc — he could play ... ♘e6 again. I would go with 1.♖e8... 1.♖e8 is a total disaster. 1.♖e8 ♖xe8. It is too early in the morning! So I can't play 1.♖e8 — I like spectacular moves. So I have to move my queen. What about 1.♕f7 using the ♖e8 idea? 1.♕f7 threatening 2.♕xf8+. He has no checks to discombobulate that. Defend the rook or move it. 1...♖d8 2.♖e8+ finishes that. So he would have to play 1...♕d6 2.♖e8 attacking the rook twice — not a bloody thing he can do about that — that's about it. It looks like 1...♘e6 ♖xe6 pretty much finished off the knight. Yeah, I am going to play 1.♕f7. Push clock.

Unfortunately, it was probably too early for Subject X-3. As an expert you would not expect him to miss both 1.♖e8?? ♖xe8 — which he eventually did find — and also **1.♕f7? ♕d8!** which he did not find, but Subject X-1 did:

de Groot Ernie
White to play after 1.♕f7? ♕d8!

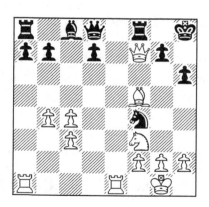

Surprisingly, 1...♛d8! is not just a defense — it's a winner. For example, the best try **2.♘e5!?** still loses to **2...d6! 3.♗xc8 dxe5!,** winning a piece as the queen and bishop are both attacked, and 2.♕e7 ♕xe7 2.♖xe7 ♖xf5 3.♖e8+ ♚h7 is not nearly sufficient compensation for the piece for White. I told Subject X-3 to keep in mind that if he thinks he has found a winning move, slam on the brakes and take extra time to make sure it is really winning: if so, then the extra time spent will not hurt him; if not, then the reason why (in this case 1...♛d8!) might turn out to be so important that the seemingly winning move might not even be good. Even though he thought 1.♕f7 won, Subject X-3 did not follow that advice, or Lasker's Rule to look for a better move. If you have time and don't do either, you had better be correct that the win is there! After the exercise, Subject X-3 felt a little sheepish at not doing so well (partly from not getting enough sleep), and asked to do it again:

Protocol X-4 (de Groot Shafritz; adult; 2040; 38 minutes)
Reminds me of a position I played as Black in Canada in the 1970s — some kid took me to school. I thought Black was threatening but he nullified it with e3 and f4. Wow! So I go back to things I remember. Funny how you do that. First move I think of... no pawn on e2! I consider myself to have some problems. Black has a kingside demonstration. He has ...e4 and ...f4. Oddly enough, my first impression is a defensive one. Let's see. I don't like... look at pawn moves. Don't see anything too great. If 1.f4 then 1...e4 and that might not be too bad — stops all the crap. Then something like 2.♘b5 with the idea of 3.♗c3 to get rid of his pesky bishop. That's something. Oh, my, I could try 1.f3 to stop that altogether. Just pawn moves — what are the other candidate moves? Pretend to "Think Like A Grandmaster" (laughs). 1.f3 or 1.f4. What if I do 1.♘b5 first? He can't chase it. If 1...e4 then f4 is available to the other knight. If 1...f4 then I just win a pawn. Sometimes I just see ghosts. 1.♘b5 f4 then 2.gxf4 and then... oh boy, he would not take on f4. 1.♘b5 f4 2.gxf4... If I were Black — White can't take on e5 to give that square to the bishop and knight. Maybe 2...♕f6 with the idea of getting the bishop to h3 or to get the rook to f5 — he has all sorts of things. Seems like a very good position [for Black then]. I can bring the knight back to c3 to get into the e4 square. He can play ♘ef6 to discourage that, or 1.♘b5 f4 2.gxf4 ♕g6 3.♘c3 ♘df6 then 4.fxe5 dxe5. Oh, my! I can play 5.♘g3 and I am happy as a clam — a pawn up. So 1...f4 is not playable and so 1.♘b5 f4 2.gxf4 ♕g6 3.♘bc3 ♘ef6 then instead of 3... ♘df6 to stop White from exchanging on e5. He wants to keep e5 open. Now White can't take on e5, so 4.♚h1 with the idea of 5.♖g1 with my own little

counterattack. Pretty happy with that − don't want to see Black start to attack, so I don't think 1.♘b5 f4 is so hot for Black. After 1.♘b5 if 1...♕h5 − very "Dutch-like" − trying to figure out what to do (short break) 1.♘b5 ♕h5, so I look at the reason ♘b5 is to get ♗c3 to oppose the diagonal and stop pawn attacks: 2.f4 e4 3.♗c3 − he doesn't want to exchange. So 3...♘df6 and I don't want to allow ...♘g4 so I have to play h3: too many weaknesses for White: ... ♔h8 and ...♖g8 to attack the g-pawn. So maybe we consider 1.♘b5 or 1.f4. Pawn moves create weaknesses. I can move the queen and he can move to the kingside − good spot. I can put the knight on e2 somewhere.

Maybe 1.♘c1 looks ...Then if 1...f4 − umm. I have three defenders ... f3. 1...f4 2.f3 ♕g6 then 3.♘e2 right back where I started however 3...fxg3. Would almost rather be Black here; White is holding on here. Then ...♘df6 to open the bishop. Then...♘h5. So I have to come up with something. Might want to play the bishop from e3 to f2 and be OK., e.g. ...♘h5 ♗f2. Then White is kinda OK. Don't care for this position − I would rather be Black here. Umm (silent) I don't know.

It's kind of a closed position but I prefer the [1.f4 e4 2.♘d1] 2...♘df6 3.♘e3 have a nice blockade:

de Groot Shafritz
Black to play after 1.f4 e4 2.♘d1 ♘df6 3.♘e3

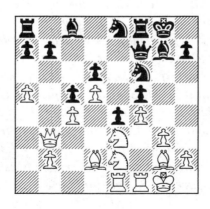

Then ♕a4 or ♕a3 and then b4 and do that. I don't know. He has to play...1. f4 e4 2.♘d1 ♘df6 3.♘e3 h5. I can hold that position with 4.♕a3. If he plays 4...♘g4 then 5.b4 and I feel like I am doing something − he can't take me. He

can play 5...♗d4. Having... Umm — trying hard to imagine the position (silent). Well, I'm looking at the other alternatives — they were too fluid and helped Black. Here I may have a chance and block the attack: 4.♕a3 ♗d4 — two pieces attacking e3, two defending — can't take the c-pawn because of the bishop on d4. Then I've got to get rid of the bishop with 5.♘xd4 cxd4 then got to move the knight somewhere like 6.♘c2. Then he has those pawns — I can blockade and try stuff like c5. He has to defend the d-pawn and can't do that. I think I am OK here.

Go back to 1.f4. I think I would play 1.f4 then 1...♘df6. No, he can't — then 2.fxe5 so maybe 1...♘ef6 (silent). The d-pawn is not doing anything so 2.♘b5. If he goes something like 2...♕e7 that is bad — the knight can get to c7, so 1...♘ef6 2.♘b5 ♘e8 to protect c7 and d6 so ♘b5 is good against ... ♘8f6. 1.f4 ♘ef6 2.♘g5 ♘e8 3.fxe5 ♘xe5 then 4.♘f4 both sides have nice posts for their knights. My knights are well placed — that's good for White — the knights have good squares. Try to get b4 in — neither White nor Black can be successful [in this line] on the kingside. The plan is that after 4.♘f4 the idea is to tie up the kingside — since he [Black] is stronger than I am there. Then I have the idea of ♕a3 and b4, exchanging pawns — I am making some queenside movement there. 1.f4 — he can't move the knights. 1.f4 ♕h5 2.fxe5, now I can get squares for my knight if 2...dxe5: if he plays ...f4 then I get ♘e4 and if he gets ...e4 then ♘f4. So those pawns are just hanging there on e5 and f5. 1.f4 ♗h6 — can't take him [pin on bishop on d2]. Hmm. So he has to go back to 2.♕c2. [At this point I gave a 35-minute warning.] Don't know. What would he play here? So many moves. Comfortable blocking the f-pawn — to be honest, I don't see. 1.♘b5 seems good, but I can always go ♘b5 so I would play 1.f4. Push clock.

Well, perhaps feeling chastised by playing a little too superficially in X-3, the expert more than made up for it in X-4. I think Protocol X-4 is somewhat a case where a player was trying too hard to look deep in some lines analyzing how good a move was, without keeping in mind that he only has to find the best move (as was discussed in the comment for Protocol A-5). True, sometimes you need to look deeply to know exactly how good a move is. But other times you don't really have to know to that degree, and the extra depth of search wastes time. This admonition is especially true when the moves you are considering are not forced. Many of the lines that Subject X-4 considered for Black were "tries" rather than forcing sequences that were immediately dangerous. It may be enough to see that they are not dangerous and save the time for later in the game, when truly dangerous lines appear on the horizon.

Protocol X-5 (de Groot A; adult; 2030; 24 minutes)

Material even — all pieces on the board. Black's kingside has weaknesses on the dark squares. All pieces are defended — especially ♗e7 guarded by the ♘d5, which can be removed: ♗a2, ♘c3 attacking ♘d5. Most of tactical play — weakness on the dark squares — tactical play around the Siamese two knights. Variations: White has quite a few captures: two on d5, ♗xf6 not primary, ♘xc6.

What variation to do first? 1.♘xd5 — two ways to take back. 1.♘xd5 ♘xd5 is reasonable — 2.♗xd5. 1.♘xd5 ♘xd5 2.♗xd5 and if 2...♖xd5 3.♗xe7, so Black should play 2...♗xg5 attacking the rook on c1 — the piece ♗d5 is hanging. If 3.♗xc6 ♗xc1 worse for White. 1.♘xd5 ♘xd5 ♗xd5 ♗xg5 3.f4 hits the bishop but then there are captures on d5, e.g. 3...♗xd5 4.fxg5 is roughly even:

de Groot A
White to play after 1.♘xd5 ♘xd5 2.♗xd5 ♗xg5
A key position

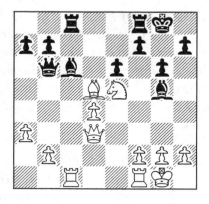

Have a sense for a White tactic with White's pieces more aggressively placed. 1.♗xd5 doesn't seem to do much: say 1...♘xd5 2.♗xe7 ♘xe7 roughly even. 1.♗xf6 then two ways to recapture — both appear to be OK. Don't see any clear advantage to White — captures don't seem to give a clear advantage to White.

There's a knight fork on d7 — but two pieces guarding it. (silent) Not seeing any clear way to get rid of both pieces: 1.♘xd5 ♘xd5 seems like Black holds there; the bishop on c6 guards d7. I can play 1.♗h6 but 1...♖fd8 is OK. Any other ideas? Looking at quieter moves to set up tactics. What does Black have? White's pieces are all protected except the bishop on g5; not a big worry.

Looking at quieter ideas. 1.♘a4 attacks the queen — I don't like putting pieces on the side of the board. The black queen can go to a5, c7, or d8. 1.♘a4 ♕a5 then the knight hangs. So no 2.b4 but 2.♘c5 ♗xc5 3.♖xc5 hits the queen, a small advantage to White. 1.♘a4 ♕a5 2.♘x5 b6 but then... the bishop on c6 is weakened. 1.♘a4 ♕a5 2.♘c5 b6. Where does the knight go? 3.♘b3 hangs a3. 1.♘a4 ♕a5 2.♘c5 b6 — the knight needs a square, or 3.♗xf6 ♗xf6 (silent). Also looking to see if the black queen is getting trapped. 1.♘a4 ♕a5 2.♘c5 b6 3.b4 — he can take with the knight. Complicated. Where can the knight go? 1.♘a4 ♕a5 2.♘c5 b6 — not a lot of places to go. 3.♘e4 ♘xe4 4.♗e7 ♘xd5 5.♕xe4 pretty long line, might be reasonable but the bishop on c6 hits the queen. 1.♘a4 ♕a5 2.♘c5 b6. Should be a simpler move there. 3.♗xf6 ♘xf6. 1.♘a4 ♕a5 2.♘c5 b6 3.♗xd5 — the bishop is no longer hanging, so b4 is possible: 3...♗xd5 4.b4 — the queen has some squares. Any other reasonable moves there? 2...b6 is ugly but no good place to put the knight. After 1...♕a5 the knight is hanging. No good ways to defend. Strange line. I like the idea of getting the knight to c5.

All right, 1.b4 first with the idea of ♘a4-c5. Then 1...♘xc3 ♖xc3 probable; reasonable for White. Not exactly a clear advantage — pressure on the c-file. Other ideas here? (silent) Toy with 1.f4 — don't like the black queen on the same diagonal with the king — too loose. I might just play 1.b4. Tactical check: 1.b4 h6 no good. 1.b4 a5 possible but then 2.b5 is good. Kind of like that. Not worried about 1...a5 2.b5. 1...♖fd8 still 2.b5 possible. 1...a6: 1.♘a4 ♗xa4 so that was a waste [finally!]. 1.b4 a6 — still 2.b5 axb5 3.♘xb5 no good — loses pawn 1.b4 a6 not accomplish that much there (silent). Simple — double rooks with 1.♖c2. 1.b4 a6 not accomplish that much. 1.♖c2 ♗a4 2.♘xa4 so 1.♖c2 (silent). What is Black's long-term plan here?...♖fd8 attacks d4 (silent). What does it accomplish to play 1.♖c2? 1.♖fd1 with the idea of ♕g3-h4. So I would play 1.♖fd1 — no way to get a clear advantage for White. Worried about d4 long-term. 1.♖fd1. Push clock.

After the exercise, I suggested to Subject X-5 that he should at least have considered 1...♕xb2 in some lines. It may not be good, but it at least has to be considered. So, like a good expert, he went home and analyzed 1.♖fd1 ♕xb2 and showed that was not the best line for Black after 2.♘c4!. However, my point wasn't that 1.♖fd1 ♕xb2 was good for Black; it was that if you don't consider a capture like 1...♕xb2 then if it turns out to be good for White you are lucky rather than good, and in the long run you want to be good! It was also curious that Subject X-5 took so long considering 1.♘a4 and not until much later realized that it is not safe after 1...♗xa4. In fact, he took about ten times as much time on 1.♘a4 as he did after the move he actually played, 1.♖fd1. That's always dangerous. I once wrote an article on the theme of, "Spend Time on the Move Chosen" — the idea that no matter how much you analyze other moves, once you play a particular one that's the only one that matters and the one the opponent will be trying to refute, so a minimal amount of time on the move actually chosen is usually necessary. Notice that Subject X-5 did arrive at the key position in the diagram above after 1.♘xd5 ♘xd5 2.♗xd5 ♗xg5, which Euwe spent so much time studying. In my experience, almost no player below 1800 gets to this position during analysis, while most players over 2000 do; if nothing else, this shows both the better deductive logic of the higher-rated players and also their ability to find and analyze in detail specific key lines, and not Hand-wave.

Protocol X-6 (de Groot Shafritz; adult; 2070; 5 minutes)
Early middlegame; probably a King's Indian except the bishop's pawn is on c5 instead of c7, with exf5 gxf5. Without a bishop on g2 in a Classical King's Indian Defense that f4 is common but with ♗g2 it's a candidate. Any other defensive-type moves?

**de Groot Shafritz
Black to play after 1.f4**

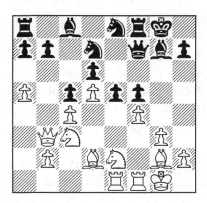

Probably not. 1.h3? No. Only defensive moves. 1.f4 e4 closes things up and makes things slower for Black. If 1...exf4 White can capture many ways — one of them White is OK, perhaps better, for example 2.♘xf4 with the idea of ♘e6.

Yes, 1.f4 is a candidate. If I ignore 1.f4 what is an idea? Not sure what White would do. 1.♘b5 or 1.♘a4? A queen move? Not sure b4 may or may not be desirable with a black knight on d7. 1.♘b5 puts pressure on the d-pawn. What's his plan if not 1.f4? 1.♗g5 I can look at; does that have any value? Maybe. If it's kicked, then 1.♗g5 h6 2.♗h4 something to consider. Don't see how White will make progress on the queenside; need to know more about the King's Indian Defense. 1.f4 stops Black's play cold. Gives time to do something on the kingside. I will make my decision now — I will play 1.f4. Push clock.

Follow-up question: "What if 1.f4 e4?" — *Answer: Then maybe ♗e3 with the idea of ♕a3 or something.*

Subject X-6, like all strong players, immediately gravitates toward 1.f4. Positionally, it's the only logical choice, but that doesn't mean it is the best move. Just because a move is positionally desirable, doesn't mean it is tactically safe. And strong players understand that even though 1.f4 e4 gives Black a protected passed pawn, that is not enough to overcome the other benefits of 1.f4. On the other hand, it's the continuation 1.f4 e4 2.g4! that gives the move its real power, and thus my follow-up question. That's not to say that Subject X-6 would not have played 2.g4, but that clearly was not his reason for playing 1.f4 — and it shouldn't be the only one.

Summary of Expert

Characteristics of the thought process at this level:

- I once read about an experiment where researchers performed EEGs on players of different strengths to determine which rating levels used which amounts of analysis vs. memory to determine their moves. The researchers made the distinction by the activity in various parts of the brain. Their conclusion? *The players who do the most analysis are experts!* Players below expert tended to do less and less analysis. Players above expert relied more and more on their memory. In other words, experts know how to analyze and do it quite intensely. As they get more expertise and rise in rating, they recognize similar positions that they have either analyzed before or seen in the literature. Then they play those ideas more from memory. GM Michael Rohde once wrote in *Chess Life* that there are about five moves per game where grandmasters don't know what to

Researchers performed EEGs on players of different strengths to determine which rating levels used which amounts of analysis vs. memory to determine their moves. The researchers made the distinction by the activity in various parts of the brain. Their conclusion? *The players who do the most analysis are experts!* Players below expert tended to do less and less analysis. Players above expert relied more and more on their memory.

do and have to think, eight moves per game for international masters, ten for FIDE masters, and fifteen for national masters.

- As shown by the expert protocols, sometimes within all that analysis resides the one big error that one could drive the proverbial truck through. That's why it is so important to at least double-check the analysis on the move you are going to play before playing it — especially if the position is complicated and the move is critical! Interestingly, this same type of error happened in a World Championship game on the same day I edited these lines:

Kramnik–Anand
World Championship (5)
Bonn (Germany) 2008
White to play

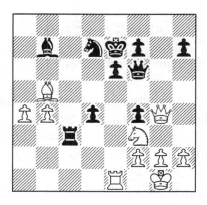

Kramnik had 23+ minutes remaining until the first time control and had spent several minutes on this move (the unofficial Internet Chess Club clock went down from 23:45 to 16:11 for this move) before deciding on the critical line of sacrificing a piece with **29.♘xd4?**. Anand thought for only about 2½ minutes before seeing the hole in Kramnik's play and, af-

ter **29...♛xd4!,** both players rattled off the remaining moves very quickly:
30.♖d1 ♞f6 31.♖xd4 ♞xg4 32.♖d7+ (not best, but already too late) **32...
♚f6 33.♖xb7 ♖c1+ 34.♗f1 ♞e3!** (the fly in the ointment) **35.fxe3 fxe3,**
and Kramnik **resigned:**

White resigns

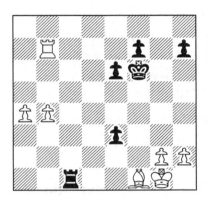

This shows that, although these type of "big" analysis errors occur less
and less as the level of play increases, they never disappear entirely.

- Experts are usually more thorough and accurate than Class A players.
  They know where to extend their analysis and have a better feel for which
  replies are critical. While this is true for any set of levels, the lack of consistency and thoroughness for levels below A makes the contrast more
  clear between expert and A, since both know to take their time to look for
  the meaningful lines and do it fairly consistently.

- For the reasons stated in the previous bullet, experts are less prone to "quiescence" errors than class players. They are much better at figuring out
  when the analysis should be terminated and evaluated, and much less likely
  to stop prematurely (i.e. make the quiescence error) when further checks,
  captures, or threats could affect the analysis and resultant evaluation.

Improvements to the thought process that would help in getting to the
next level:

- Expert is the level where aspects such as opening knowledge and evaluation start to matter much more. By doing whatever it takes to improve

their evaluation function (such as analyzing with strong players, comparing their evaluations of positions to those of computer chess engines, reading appropriate books, etc), experts would be able to take some of that extensive analysis and provide more meaningful conclusions. Result: improved playing strength.

- Experts often get into time trouble due to their intense analysis, so practicing good time management would help many at this level.

- The observed difference in planning and judgment between expert and master is high. Therefore, one of the best things an expert can do is to study many annotated master games or, even better, hang out with masters, play chess with them and, best of all, analyze games with them.

- Getting to the next level becomes much more difficult once you are above 2000!

II. Master, FIDE Master, and International Master

Protocol M-1 (de Groot A; adult; 2300; 5 minutes)

♘d7 is possible. Tons of trades you can do. No real mate threat. That's not what I would look at. 1.♘xd5 ♗xd5 then 2.♗xf6 ♗xf6 3.♘d7 wins something. 1.♘xd5 then Black must play 1...♘xd5 2.♗xd5 threatens 3.♗xe7 so 2...♗xg5:

de Groot A
Black to play after 1.♘xd5 ♘xd5 2.♗xd5
The master easily deduces that 2...♗xg5 is forced

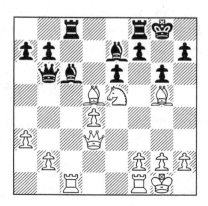

— then ♘d7 is possible. So then the knight is trapped and ...♗xf1 is possible. So 1.♘xd5 ♘xd5 2.♗xd5 ♗xg5 3.♖xc6 gives the d7 square. I sort of like that idea. 1.♘xd5 exd5. I guess he would take back with the pawn if I took 1.♘xd5. Ah! Then maybe 2.♕f3 and he has trouble holding the knight on f6. So the only other trade is 1.♗xf6. I don't see how that leads to a whole lot. So I would probably do 1.♘xd5. Push clock. [PV = 1.♘xd5 and I didn't see a good continuation for Black].

Around the same time he performed this protocol, Subject M-1 beat GM Hikaru Nakamura in a tournament game — a huge upset! In this protocol he easily finds 2...♗xg5 after 1.♘xd5 ♘xd5 2.♗xd5 — in my experience almost no player rated under 1800, out of a total of hundreds of subjects, has ever calculated this critical move. However, after that sharp find his analysis is a little vague. Somehow he reaches the conclusion (maybe a visualization error, not seeing that the bishop on c6 is still guarding d7) that this line is good for White, possibly after 3.♖xc6. He likes the idea so much that he never looks for a better move, erroneously saying the only other trade is 1.♗xf6 when, in fact, there is also 1.♗xd5, which happens to be the best move. For a 2300 player, not considering a major capture is a big oversight, probably explained by his satisfaction with finding 1.♘xd5 to be better than it actually is.

Subject M-1 did not verbalize an evaluation, but it's a good bet he could tell you the material count, which side he felt was better, and why. When a player gets to that level, board vision becomes so proficient that this base information is usually quickly assimilated and escapes the necessity for conscious verbalization.

A friendly FM did three protocols (M-2, M-3, and M-4):

Protocol M-2 (de Groot C; adult; 2300; 14 minutes)
Material equal. Queen in a funny spot. Strange squares. White knight on f3 a target. Behind in development but my king is safer. I can put a piece on e4 or play ...♗d7. Umm. I see various things not worth comment. 1...♗d7 loses a pawn but compensation: 1...♗d7 2.♗xe6+ ♗xe6 3.♕xe6+ ♔h8 with compensation. ♘g5 a worry — rather annoying. 4...♖e8 5.♘f7+ ♔g8. 1...♘e4 but 2.♖he1 but 2... ♘c3. I suppose he would have to play 2.♔b2 with the idea of ♖he1. Doesn't look all that useful. 1...♕e4 leaves me weak on c7 — only good if it was something. 2.♖he1. If no follow-up, then it only helps White. 1...♕e4 2.♖he1 ♕g6 3.♘xc7 good for White. Love to do something to ♘f3, but doesn't seem possible. I am more drawn to 1...♗d7 or 1...♘h5 but 2.♘g5 makes it look silly. Oh! 1...e5 I had not noted.

de Groot C
White to play after 1...e5

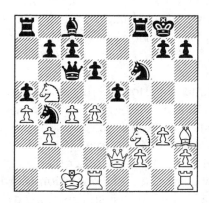

Would take advantage of king position and pin. Looks like a good move.
1...e5 2.♗xc8 ♖acx8 3.♘a7 I want to work: 2...♖fxc8 3.dxe5 ♘e4 with the
idea of ♘c3. No, wait a second. Is 4.♘fd4 a winning move there? I don't see
it if 3...dxe5 4.♘xe5. Hmm. If it gets my queen out of the tangle I am not too
optimistic. Can I prepare ...e5? Something like 1...♔h8. Now 2.♗xe6 is im-
possible. So maybe 2.♗g2 but ♘f3 has no place to go. 2.♗g2 ♛e4. No, the
c-pawn still hangs. Hmm. Strange position (silent). 1...♗d7 weird because it
runs the queen out of places to go. If 1...♔h8 2.♖he1 what did that do? Sort
of cramped. Back to 1...♘e4. Wait! 1...♘e4 2.♔b2 ♘xf2 could make a huge
difference. What does he do? Oh wait! ♘b5 defends c3 — embarrassing with
♘c3. 1...♘e4 just looks silly. Hmm. Now I like the position less and less. I
want to play 1...e5 — positively I almost have to do it. 1...e5 2.♗xc8 ♖fxc8
3.dxe5 does not look so good. Is the position so bad as to be worth sacrificing
a pawn? Yeah, frustrating — no way out of it. But I have to make a move.
1...♔h8 probably wastes time and does not make it better. How about 1...
h6? Probably a decent waiting move. 1...e5 2.♗xc8 ♖fxc8 3.dxe5 and I see
no move for Black so I return to general principles so I play 1...♗d7. Push
clock.

The de Groot C position gave even the grandmasters difficulties. After I
gave this position to the computer (Appendix B) I had a difficult time determining why its best lines were superior. Therefore, congratulations to Dr. de
Groot for finding such an unclear position and kudos to those subjects who
successfully waded through the murky lines.

In the X-4 protocol, the subject begins by stating that the position reminds him of something he has seen before, and Subject M-2 begins by noting that some pieces are placed strangely. For strong players this capability to "compare notes" with previous situations is a powerful tool. Another similarity is criticality assessment — good players recognize that they have to be very careful to take their time in positions where they are not sure what they are doing — their sense of the "red light of danger," based on their criticality analysis (see Section 12.1), gets very keen as they improve to this level.

Let's list the candidate moves in protocol M-2: 1...♕e4, 1...♘e4, 1...♗d7, 1...♘h5, 1...e5, 1...♔h8, and 1...h6. Subject M-2 was working hard trying to find something he felt satisfactory. Good players are not satisfied to play "just something" and see what happens. They are chess "control freaks" who wish to find something where the continuation will be comfortable, and doing the work to find that comfortable line is often fun for them.

Protocol M-3 (de Groot B; adult; 2300; 14 minutes)
Count material: two bishops for a rook and three pawns — ordinarily not enough. Second set of rooks helps Black. Vague kingside attacking chances:

de Groot B
Black to play
Advanced knowledge. FM knows: 1) If there are two rooks vs. one,
the side with one does not usually want to trade off;
2) When behind in material, look to attack, especially the king

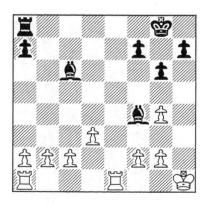

Can we open the h-file? Give rook... So 1...h5 or 1...♔g7. Hard for White to organize his position. 1...h5 most dynamic. Hard for White to ignore that. Can I

recapture with the pawn and go to h3? 1...h5 2.gxh5 ♔g7 3.hxg6 ♖h8+ 4.♔g1 not too impressed by that for Black. Hmm. Strange position. 4...♗h2+ 5.♔f1 ♗f4 and it's hard for White to do anything. 4...♗h2+ 5.♔f1 ♗f4 what does White do? He can just push pawns in the absence of a follow-up. My guess is that White is faster: 1...h5 2.gxh5 gxh5. Incredibly hard to stop the bishops. Hmm. Hard for White to find anything to do at all. 1...h5 2.gxh5 gxh5 3.c4 ♖d8 so 4.♖ad1. Doesn't look that great: 4...♖d4. White can play ♔g1 and meet ...h3 with g3. Another idea 1...♖b8 White guards and then lift rook to kingside: 1...♖b8 2.b3 ♖b5. Even there, doesn't seem I am going to get anything concrete. 1...♖b8 2.b3 ♖b5 complicated. 3.c4 ♖g5 4.d4 ♖xg4 5.d5 – quite awkward, actually. If I can't get a concession on the attack on the g-file. If White gets in d5 things will be bad for Black. 1...♖b8 2.b3 ♖b5 3.c4 ♖g5 4.d4 does not look good for Black. Not so easy for White either. If pawns advance, they can be blockaded more easily. I do win a pawn after all. ...♔g7. White has to commit himself to a plan. Best case ...♖g5 ♔h1 ♖h2. Then White has a problem. Then g3. Not so easy: ♖g2+ and ♔f1 so what? Oh, the idea is ...♖h1#. ...♖h2 f3. What have I gained from this venture? I can push the g-pawn down. This takes 1-2-3-4. One free move for White without captures and two more to push pawn to g4. Implies he will play c4, d4, and d5 plan and bishop is dead. With the h-file attack rather do 1...♔g7. Only other thing is 1...♖b8 2.b3 ♖b5. Doesn't matter – can't stop 1...♖b5-g5. Threats to a7 not relevant since I can play ...a5. ...♗d7? ...♗xg4 ♖e4 wins bishop. I get the feeling White is slightly better overall:

de Groot B
White to play after 1...♖b8 2.b3 ♖b5

High-level players are careful to make evaluations and let this information
guide their planning

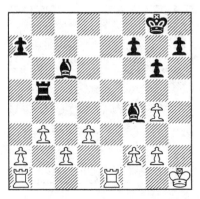

1.♖b8 b3 ♖b5 3.c4 ♖g5 4.d4 I can at least cause some trouble – dangerous for Black to abandon the back rank away from the queenside. Well, I think I

prefer White here, but so far it looks like 1...♖b8. I might start and wait for some en passant *play. Another weird idea: march the king to grab g4. 1...♖b8 makes things worse there, so 1...♔g7. It's a nice idea; it's not so easy. White would love to sac the exchange but he can't afford to do it. 2.c4 ♖d8 3.♖ad1 ♖d4 4.♔g1 unravels the king. 4...♗d6 5.f3 ♗c5. Hmm. ...h5 still presses upon the kingside. So 1...♔g7 gives both ideas ...h5 or ...♔f6, ...♔g5 so more flexible than 1...♖b8. Choosing between 1...♔g7 and 1...♖b8. Well, ah — this is basically a race. Eventually White will mobilize the pawns so I would play 1...♔g7. Last check: 1...♔g7 no other hot ideas. Sharpest is 1...h5 2.gxh5 gxh5 3.c4 ♖ad8 4.♖ad1 ♖d4 maybe that's better than I thought. 1...h5 2.gxh5 gives up d4. Maybe equally or more significant. ...h4 d4 ♖d8 c4 h3 d5 and I'm out of commission. Hmm. 1...♔g7 I guess 2.d4 is White's move. 2...h5 3.gxh5 ♖h8 4.c4 ♖xh5+ 5.♔g1 with the idea of d5. Black is the tiniest bit too slow. So still 1...♔g7 or 1...♖b8 so 1...♔g7. Push clock.*

One error I noticed in the FM's analysis was that he often became fascinated with his apparent main line and looked really wide and deep within it, at the expense of looking wider earlier. Interestingly, in GM Andrew Soltis's book *The Wisest Things Ever Said About Chess,* entry #112 is, "It is more important to look around than to look ahead."

Notice that Subject M-3 feels that he is worse in de Groot B and thus knows to try to use his bishop pair for a kingside attack. This type of general knowledge, when used properly, will create a "mini-plan" which will drive the analysis. In other words, he is first figuring out what Black needs to do and then trying to find moves to meet those needs.

Protocol M-4 (de Groot Ernie; adult; 2300; 25 minutes)

The queen is attacked. 1.♕f7 — mate if he takes. 1...♕d8 2.♕g6 no good — the knight guards. 1.♕f7 ♕d8 anything else? Umm. Don't see much. 2.♕e7 interesting. White's a pawn ahead, so even exchanging queens is a good result. Should just be a good position for White; don't need to do anything fancy but would be nice to win quickly. 1.♕f7 ♕d6 2.♖e8 is devastating. 1.♕f7 ♕d8 2.♕e7 ♕xe7 3.♖xe7 ♖xf5 is no good. 1.♕f7 ♕d8 starting to look silly. Where else can I go? This is surprisingly awkward.

1.♕e5 ♕xe5 2.♖xe5 d6 then 3.♗xc8 dxe5 4.♗xb7 then presumably 4...♖b8 — lost my focus. 1.♕e5 ♕xe5 2.♖xe5 d6 3.♗xc8 dxe5 4.♗xb7 is a good position for White — the e5-pawn is weak; the knight guards g6. Preliminary conclusion: 1.♕e5 is a promising line for White. 1.♕e5 d6 2.♕xf4 ♗xf5 — how do I evaluate that? Nice to be a pawn up, but now Black's pieces are activated, but White still is better. Anything else after 1.♕e5? 1...♕xc4 gets pain – a little murky – some tactical possibilities: 2.♕e7 ♖xf5 3.♕d8+ ♔h7 4.♖e8 is interesting. How did I get there? 1.♕e5 ♕xc4 hmm (silent) – very tricky position. Could be something there. 1.♕e5 ♕xc4 2.♕e7. I'm rusty. 1.♕e5 ♕xc4 2.♖e4 d6 that's... 1.♕e5 ♕xc4 2.♖e4 d6 I can play 3.♕xf4, 3.♖xc4, or 3.♕xd6 is also important. 3.♖xf4. If 3.♕xd6 that's terrible for Black – everything's under attack. 1.♕e5 ♕xc4 2.♖e4 is just good for Black; can't play that way, so 2...♕xe5 3.♖xe5 d6 4.♗xc8 is good for White, not necessarily winning – can choose between 1.♕e5 and 1.♕f7 ♕d8 can't play.

Other option is... fantasy 1.♘e5 can't play, can I? 1...d6 ♘f7+ weird. 1.♘e5 ♘xd5 2.♘g6+ ♔g8 or 2.♘f7+ ♔g8, nothing there. So 1.♕f7 rejected due to 1...♕d8 2.♕e7 ♕xe7 3.♖xe7 ♖xf5 4.♖e8+ ♔h7 can't be good. Frustrating when you see 1.♕f7 ♕d8 – I can play 2.♘e5 or 2.♘h4: 2.♘h4 no good but 2.♘e5 is weird – he can't take the queen. If he goes 2...d6 have I looked at this before? 3.♘g6+ ♘xg6 and the queen and bishop are hanging. So I keep being rejected after 1.♕f7. If 1.♕e4 d5 powerful counterattack. I lose a piece – that's winning for Black. 1.♕f7, 1.♕e4, 1.♕c5 can't play – running out of ideas.

1.♕b5 unaesthetic – usually a bad place to put a queen; better than it looks. 1.♕b5 a6 to exploit the loose bishop; 2.♕a5 or 2.♕e5 is an improvement!

de Groot Ernie
Black to play after 1.♕b5 a6 2.♕e5

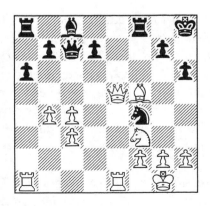

1.♕b5 a6 2.♕e5 then 2...♕xe5 3.♖xe5 d6 – the other line is 2...♕xc4. So 1.♕b5 a6 2.♕e5 ♕xe5 3.♖xe5 d6 this is even worse for Black than 1.♕e5 –

both are good for White. What else can Black do after 1.♕b5? OK — 1.♕b5 a6 2.♕a5 b6 3.♕e5 (laughs) 3...♕xe5 4.♖xd5 but now Black is better off because the pawn is not at b7. Consider 1.♕a5 — if I'm going to interpolate on the queenside I want 1.♕b5 a6 2.♕e5 to put all of Black's queenside pawns on light squares. 1.♕e5 not many possibilities 1...d6 2.♕xf4 is the main one — he takes 2...♗xf5. Most complex is 1.♕e5 ♕xc4 2.♖e4 d6 pretty much it. 3.♕xd6; 4.♕xf8 is a huge threat. 3...♕f7 4.♖xf4 — different position — still a pawn ahead. White is still doing very well. I'm about ready to play 1.♕b5 with the idea that after 1...a6 2.♕e5 then 2...♕xe5 3.♖xe5 d6 4.♗xc8 is good for White. OK 1.♕b5 Push clock.

The next master-level subject was already familiar with de Groot A, so I started him with de Groot Ernie.

Protocol M-5 (de Groot Ernie; adult; 2300; 5 minutes)

A tactical moment back-rank mate: 1.♕f7 ♖xf7 2.♖e8+ and mate. So 1... ♕d8 or 1...♕d6 possible. 1...♘e6 2.♖xe6 OK. So 1.♕f7 ♕d8 more solid. What can I do then? 2.♖e7 doesn't work — want to take on g7 and mate. ♕g6 doesn't work — the knight protects g6. All right, 1.♕f7 ♕d8 2.♘g5 doesn't work. So I don't see a mate on 1.♕f7. Other moves: 1.♘e5 ♖xf5 2.♘g6+ ♘xg6 3.♕xf5. 1.♘e5 ♖xf5 2.♘g6+ ♘xg5 3.♖xf5 — ...♕d6 is also possible. No forced win for now. The queen on d5 is attacked, so I need to stop the queen capture — the endgame gives Black a chance to recover — keep the queens on the board. 1.♕f7 ♕d8 — retreat ♗f5 (silent). Getting hard to think and talk. 1.♕a5 ♕xa5 2.♖xa5 b6 develops the bishop and he is OK. 1.♕e4 hit clock:

de Groot Ernie
White to play after 1.♕e4? d5!

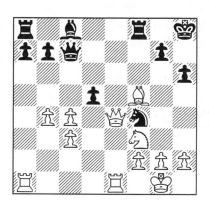

161

English is not the first language of Subject M-5, so he was a little flustered by this first attempt. Later, when I pointed out that 1.♕e4 loses to the simple 1...d5 hitting both the queen and the bishop a second time, he was a little embarrassed at committing two errors more commonly seen in class players: 1) what I call "Hope Chess" (not looking to see if his candidate move could be defeated by an reply that cannot be met), and 2) not "Spending time on the move chosen" — he played 1.♕e4 almost without thinking as a safety fallback (which it clearly isn't), although his total time was five minutes. So he was eager to make amends with a second chance:

Protocol M-6 (de Groot Shafritz; adult; 2300; 17 minutes)
A closed position — more strategy than tactics. Let's come up with an evaluation of the position — do I push for the initiative or come up with a defensive plan? If I evaluate the position as worse then I may take it sharper to get chances. It's similar to a King's Indian with a pawn on c5. Black got in ...f5, pretty good. At first sight I actually like Black; I don't control central squares nor outposts for knights; the bishop on g2 looks at the d5-pawn. Black may push ...f5-f4 so arriving more and more to the conclusion that White is worse. I'm worried about ...f5-f4 but I can capture the pawn so it's not yet dangerous for me. So 1.f4 challenges the center. If fxe5 and a black piece recaptures, then the pawn on f5 becomes isolated and weak — that's good for White. If Black plays ...dxe5 then d5 is a passer and d6 becomes possible. 1.f4 is a decent move so far. Petrosian did 1.f4 in a similar position. If nothing else the consequence of 1.f4...

1.♘b5 allows 1...a6 and the b-pawn is backward but ...♖b8 and then push the b-pawn is OK; then ♘a4-♘b6. 1.♘b5 a6 2.♘c3 ♖b8 — can sacrifice ...b6 — the b-pawn will eventually fall, or Black can ignore ♘b5 and it's not doing much there; then ...e5-e4 and ...f5-f4 with some preparation. OK. 1.♗h3 activating the light-squared bishop. 1...f4? 2.♗e6 wins the queen but 1...♕h5 hits the bishop and loses a tempo because 2.♗g2 e4 — too cheap to be anything serious. Concentrate on 1.f4. Looks like his pieces are too far away on the back rank — he can prevent capture with 1...♗h6 pinning the f-pawn to the bishop on d2, then 2.♗c1 gets rid of the pin. More serious is 1...e4 with a passer in the center, a possible advantage in the endgame but then e3 is good for blockade with ♘d1-e3. .....♗g7-♗d4 can pin the knight on e3, so can't play g3-g4 right away, but ♔h1 with an eventual g4 to break the base of the pawn chain. In many games e4 can become with a break like g3-g4.

Do I need to play 1.f4 right away or can I play a useful positional move first? If no immediate attack, I have time for more positional development of pieces: "If you don't know what to do, improve your worst piece" — probably ♗g2 here. The queenside already has space with a5; ...b7-b6 is probably an option for him — it should be OK for me because the b5 outpost for me. All right, what other improving positional moves are possible? Plans with b4 to create weaknesses by trading on c5. So 1.♕a3 say 1...b6 2.axb6 ♘xb6 attacks c4, but a7 is isolated with some complications to follow. If I do nothing what would Black do? He can improve his position. If ...e5-e4 then I can play ♘d4-♘e6. So he moves his knight on d7 — ♘e6 dxe6 is a pawn sac with nice squares. Black would prepare ...f5-f4 so the knight on the d-file would go to the kingside. So if White "passes," then ...♘df6-♘h5, preparing ...f5-f4. OK. What can I do? Not much. 1.♗f3 just gives him a tempo. So some play with ...♘df6-h5 doesn't look like White can do nothing. Pretty much convinced. Did I miss something really stupid? 1.♘c1 no. 1.♗d2 no. Other pawn breakthroughs? 1.h4 too brave and dangerous. After 1.f4 no tactics coming with no exchanges. 1...exf4 2.♘xf4 OK for White — the f4 outpost is so nice. What else is possible? If 1.f4 b6 2.fxe5 so 1...e4 is the most principled response:

de Groot Shafritz
White to play after 1.f4 e4

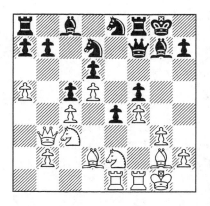

1.f4 e4 protected passer. 2.♘d1 or 2.♗e3 and ♘f2. So 1.f4. Push clock.

Like almost all players rated over 2000, the master chose 1.f4 in de Groot Shafritz. It's pretty much the only logical move. From my standpoint I was always watching to see if they did it because 2.g4! is strong or for some other reason. Here the master did not find 2.g4 but instead left the decision to the next move. He did briefly mention that if 1...e4 he could get in ♘d4-e6, but not sure if he was missing 2.♘d4? exd4 or just musing in general.

The next protocol was by a local FM:

Protocol M-7 (de Groot Ernie; adult; 2400; 37 minutes)
White is up a pawn and better developed; Black is weak on the light squares. White has a better structure on the queenside – he is probably winning! 1.♕f7 and if 1...♖xf7 2.♖e8 and mate. 1.♕f7 – the queen is hit by the knight; 1...♖d8 2.♕e8+ or 2.♖e8+ mates. 1...♖g8 2.♖e8 is mate. His checks: 1...♘e2+ and 1...♘h3+ I can ignore. 1.♕f7 ♕d8 2.♖e7 then White's queen hangs. So 1...♕d8 is the only move.

So let's see, what else can we do? 1.♕f7 skip 1.♕e4 d5 hits the queen and the bishop on f5. 1.♕e5 ♕xe5 2.♖xe5 1...d6 is possible: 2.♕xf4 ♖xf5 and Black is better than before. 1.♕e5 ♕xe5 2.♖xe5 d6 hits rook and bishop so 3.♗xc8 dxe5 4.♗xb7 ♖ad8 or 4...♖ab8 – the bishop moves or 5.♖xa7 ♖f7 pins the bishop to the rook – so that's a blunder, so instead White would play 5.♗e4 with two pawns for the exchange – better for White but I don't think White should trade queens. Does the queen need to guard the bishop or not? 1.♕f7 ♕d8 is nothing special. Look for 1.♘h4 ♘xd5 2.♘g6+ ♚g8 doesn't work. What else? Don't know. Let me think. 1.♕f7 ♕d8 (silent). Let's see here 1.♕e5 I guess.

1.♕d2 ♖xf5 2.♖e8+ ♚h7 3.♕c2 d6 defending f5, then 4.g4 so 3...g6 is better. 1.♕d2 ♖xf5 2.♖e8+ ♚h7 3.♕c2 g6 4.♖e7+ ♚g8 again 5.♖ae1 threatening unpleasant stuff. 5.♖f7 might not be enough. What else? The queen is hanging – what else can I do?

1.♕d4 ♖xf5 2.♖e8+ ♚h7 3.♖e7 ♖e5 is bad – hangs material:

de Groot Ernie
Black to play after 1.♕d4 ♖xf5 2.♖e8+ ♚h7 3.♖e7
Masters rightly consider sacrificing the bishop for the attack

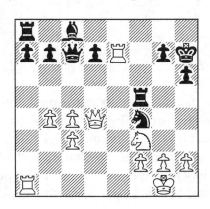

Same on 3...Rg5 3...Nh5 then what? 4.g4 Rf4 5.Qd3+ then gxh5 but the knight hangs on f3. If 4...Rxf3, 5.gxh5 wins material. 1.Qd4 Rxf5 2.Re8+ Kh7 3.Re7 Nh5 4.g4 and Black has these moves: 4...Qf4, 4...Rf4, 4...Rxf3, 4...Nf6, and 4...Rg5. If 4...Nf6, 5.gxf5. If 4...Rg5, 5.Nxg5 so 4...Qf4 — the knight's defended, 5.gxh5 threatens mate 5...Qxd4 6.Nxd4 Rxh5 equality in material but White should be winning with Nb5-d6, no good for Black. 4...Qf4 5.gxf5 may also be good — up the exchange. 5...Qxf3 Black has two pawns for a rook with the threat 6...Nf4 but has to defend g7. 6.Rxa7 Rb8 or 6.Rxa7 Rxa7 7.Qxa7 now White is ahead in material but 7...Nf4 no good. So 6.Rae1 and now ...Nf4 allows mate on g7. The pawn on f5 is hanging: 6...Qxf5 7.R1e5 hits the queen. If not Qb1 and then take on h5 and then mate on g7. White can play 7.R5e5 hits the knight on g5. ...Qb1 is not forced; ...Rg6+ should be better for White but it's not over yet. 1.Qd4 he doesn't have to take 1...Rxf5 2.Re8+ Kh7 3.Re7 Ne6 [good that he considers this line] 4.Qe4 pins the rook to the king — also threatens Qxe6 with the pin. If 4...Kg6 5.Nh4 and wins the rook. If 4...g6 that's illegal — that eliminates 3...Ne6.

1.Qd4 d6 2.Qxf4 Bxf5 up a pawn — should be winning. 1.Qd4 d6 2.Bxc8 Raxc8 3.Rxa7 Qxc4 then 4.Qxd6 or 4.Rxb7 Black threatens ...Ne2+ but g7 is hanging with checkmate. 4...Qxc3 defends g7. 1.Qd4 d6 2.Qxf4 Rxf5 3.Re8+ Kh7 4.Qe4 so 2...Bxf5 is correct, then 3.Nd4 Bd3 with the idea of ...Bxc4 later. 1.Qd4 d6 and the bishop is hanging twice, so 2.Bxc8. 1.Qd4 threatens 2.Re7. 1.Qd4 Ne6 2.Bxe6 dxe6 3.Ne5 dominates with the idea of Ng6+, that's lost for Black. 1.Qd4 b6 2.Re7 hits g7 is similar, but Black is not up a piece. 1.Qd4 b6 2.Re7 Rg8 3.Ne5 Ne2+ 4.Kh1. 1.Qd4 Rxf5 pretty forced. 1.Qf7 Qd8 don't see anything — what can I do? 2.Qxg7+ no — what else? 1.Qd4 Rxf5 2.Re8+ Kh7 what else? 3.Re7 best — what other moves? 3...Nh5 (3...Ne6 was already checked). Anything better than 4.g4? Maybe 4.Qe4 Qf4 OK; 4.Qd3 Kg6 5.Nh4+ Kg5 6.Qxf5 and mate in a few moves. 4...Nf6 5.Qxf5 Ke7 6.Qxh5+ or 6.Re1 is probably mate — yes it is. That's it. 1.Qd4 don't see anything else. 1.Qd4 Rxf5 2.Re7 first — no 2.Re8+ Kh7 3.Re7 Nh5 4.Qe4 or 4.Qd3 — if not, ...Kg6, then 4...Qf4 5.Rf7 Nf6. So 5.Nh4 Qxf2+ (or 5...Qxh4) 6.Kh1 no back-rank mates. f5 is hit but now 6...d6. So 1.Qd4. Push clock.

Subject M-7 took a long time but, like all subjects, was under the instruction that thinking out loud in a "cold" position is worth roughly 2-1 in time compared to a game. That means if you take N minutes for the exercise, that is roughly the equivalent of taking N/2 minutes in a real game. Would an FM take almost 20 minutes in a position like this, especially when considering a piece sacrifice like 1.♕d4 ♖xf5 ? Of course! That is a reasonable time to take in such a critical position. That makes this a good model protocol for how to approach the position de Groot Ernie. Note that at the end Subject M-7 clearly did what de Groot, in *Thought and Choice in Chess,* called Striving for Proof. That is the last phase, where a strong player tries to prove that his move is the best, or at least as good as any other. You can see throughout this book that inexperienced players rarely attempt this aspect of the thought process. In fact, the final Striving for Proof phase of strong players is often longer than the entire thought process phase of most players who play too fast!

Finally, we have a local IM who also tackled de Groot Ernie and Shafritz with similar interesting, but entertaining, results. Note that the IM quickly finds the interesting (but ultimately unworkable) line 1.♕f7 ♕d8 2.♘e5 which the FM did not consider:

Protocol M-8 (de Groot Ernie; adult; 2540; 32 minutes)

1.♕f7 jumps in my head. 1.♕c5 decent — up a pawn, loses a bishop — I don't want to do that! 1.♕f7 is natural, then 1...♕d6 White wins on 2.♖e8 so 1.♕f7 ♕d8 — Agh! 2.♘e5 should be good somehow with the idea of ♘g6+. 1.♕f7 with the idea of ♘e5 — what else? Does 1.♘e5 make sense? No. Other moves? 1.♕f7 might win; look closer; look for every legal move. 1.♕f7 ♕d6 2.♖e8 forced win. Ah, 1...♕d8 only; if 1...♖g8 then 2.♖e8. 1.♕f7 ♕d8 2.♘e5 d6 hmm. Something looks annoying. Ah-huh, it's hard to say everything; maybe White's winning but look for other moves, e.g. 2.♘g5 with the idea of 3.♘e7. No, 2...hxg5. All right, almost wins. Quickly look for other possibilities: 1.♘h4 ♘xd5. If 1.♕e5 then he can take and 1...d6 might win a pawn. 1.♕e4 is pathetic — 1...d5 wins. 1.♕f7 ♕d8 now what? The big question. 2.♘e5 d6 is annoying. Hold on — hold on! Jeez. Every move I look at loses a piece. Only threat to take the knight. If 1.♕f7 ♕d8 2.♘e5 d6 3.♗xc8 dxe5 and I don't know what's going on — doesn't look so good for us. What's happening here? The position is starting to annoy me. 1.♕f7 ♕d8 2.♘e5 d6 — hard to stop looking at those moves 3.♘g6+ ♘xg6 4.♕xg6 loses. 3.♗d7 no; 3.♕g6 takes 3...♗xf5. Umm. In a game I might spend 5-10 minutes on this. 1.♕f7 ♕d8 2.♘e5 I feel like there should be some move there. After 2...d6 looking for weird moves. Can't seem to find a good move. 1.♕f7 ♕d8 another move 2.♘g5 hxg5 no — don't see another move that makes sense. 1.♕f7 ♕d8 2.♘e5 only try.

What first move doesn't lose? 1.♕c5 ♕xc5 and then 2...♖xf5. 1.♕e4 d5 annoying. Hmm. Weird. Gotta figure out something, though. 1.♕a5 doesn't lose —

maybe 1...b6. We can go 1.♕a5 ♕xa5 2.♖xa5 b6 3.♗e4 saves the day — doesn't lose. 1.♕a5 b6 2.♕e5 ♕xe5 3.♖xe5 d6 4.♗e4. Want to make sure I have a move that doesn't lose immediately. 1.♕f7 ♕d8 2.♗g6 ♖xf7 3.♘xf7+; 1.♕f7 ♕d8 2.♘e5 d6 — don't look at the board. 1.♕b5 doesn't lose probably but 1...a6 then 2.♕a5. 1.♕f7 ♕d8. How can this be? 2.♘e5 d6 3.? 3.♖ad1 ♗xf5 I think. Trying to make something work. It's tough. 1.♕f7 ♕d8 2.♘e5 d6 — hard to pull yourself away — waste a lot of time thinking about it. Maybe there's nothing.

Other ideas: 1.♕d2 ♖xf5 2.♖e8+ ♔h7 3.♕c2 g6 — he's down a bishop and a rook: 3...g6 4.♖ae1. Maybe ignore the bishop with 1.♕d2 or 1.♕d4. Say 1.♕d2 ♖xf5 2.♖e8+ ♔h7 3.♕c2:

de Groot Ernie
Black to play after 1.♕d2 ♖xf5 2.♖e8+ ♔h7 3.♕c2

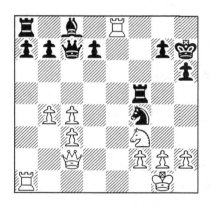

...threatens 4.g4 — if 3...g6 4.♖ae1 with the idea of ♖1e7. So I'm leaning toward 1.♕d2 — lots of positions where ♗c8, ♖a8 stuck — they're usually bad. 1.♕d2 ♖xf5 2.♖e8+ ♔h7 3.♘d4 may be OK — I can play down a piece with the idea of ♘b5-d6. 1.♕d2 ♖xf5 2.♖e8+ ♔h7 3.♕c2 is the most direct threat. If 3... d6 or 3...d5 I have 4.g4 — I may win a rook — threatening ♖xc8 and ♕c5 wins a pawn. 1.♕d2 ♖xf5 2.♖e8+ ♔h7 3.♕c2 and now how many moves don't lose for Black? I have 4.g4 or 4.♘d4. If 3...g6 4.♖ae1 ♘h5. This position...hmm. All right, one second — my gut tells me I want to do that: 3.♕c2 g6.

I can go 1.♕d4 instead — try to see if that helps — it might. Hope I'm not missing something obvious. 1.♕d2 ♖xf5 2.♖e8+ ♔h7 3.♕c2 g6 — hmm. Don't see how to end things. One line is 1.♕d4 ♖xf5 2.♖e8+ ♔h7 — 1.♕e4 d5 bad, I think; otherwise 1.♕e4 great but 1...d5 attacks the queen. Wait a second ...umm — position is interesting. 1.♕d2 ♖xf5 2.♖e8+ ♔h7 3.♕c2 g6 4.♖e7; no 4.♖ae1 ♘h5 must be good for White; ♘d4 with the idea of ♖e7, ♘e6. 5.♘d4 ♖f6 is bad — looking at 6.♖8e7 or 6.♖1e7 ♘g7 7.♕e4. Don't ***[illegible] too complicated.

Got to make a decision soon [I note to Subject M-8 that he has taken about 30 minutes, the equivalent of 15 in a real game, assuming 2-1 ratio for the exercise]. 15 minutes is not so much for a position like this. Can't bear to go 1.♕a5. 1.♕a5 ♕xa5 2.♖xa5 b6 3.♗e4 as far as I can tell 3...bxa5 4.♗xa8 maybe White is better but 1.♕d2 gives up an entire piece. I keep chasing 1.♕d2 or 1.♕d4 — not sure why.

1.♕d2 with the idea of going to c2, but 1.♕d4 hits g7. 1.♕d4 ♖xf5 2.♖e8+ ♔h7 3.♘h4 looks pretty good. 3...♖g5 4.♕e4+ ♘g6 5.♘xg6 ♖xg6 6.♕d5 with the idea of ♕g8+. Looks like something good is happening. Don't like 1.♕d4 because ...♘f4-e2+ in some lines but never seems to come up. Any weird move to take advantage of ...♘e2+, i.e., distract the rook? 3.♘h4 ♖f7 4.♕e4+ ♘g6 5.♕d5 ♘f8 look at that: ♘xg6 — I don't know — pick between 1.♕d4 and 1.♕d2. Is there any difference? I can go ♘d4 in some lines. I kinda like 1.♕d4. I can't sit here all day. At least it draws somehow. 1.♕f7 ♕d8 2.♘e5 d6 OK. So 1.♕d4 hit clock.

A fascinating and entertaining protocol. If you combine protocols M7 and M8, they form a pretty good set of examples of how strong players take their time in critical positions, visualize far if they need to, and then slowly try to find their way to the best solution they can. Contrast this with class-player protocols which include a lot more Hand-waving (as opposed to careful analysis), the inability to recognize a critical position, and the corresponding inability to give it a great amount of careful thought, including the failure to compare various candidate moves at sufficient depth.

Protocol M-9 (de Groot Shafritz; adult; 2540; 6 minutes)
Never do good at these positions. It's even in material — a King's Indian — weird. Getting my bearing. ...e4 gives White f4 — to threaten ...e3. I don't know. A lot of times you can go 1.f4. I don't play positions like this. 1.f4 e4 then you can get your knight to e3 is standard: ♘d1-♘e3. 1.f4 is very committal — you can't make it unless you know. Does 1.♘b5 do anything?

This is different — more positional. I can try the weird-looking 1.g4 to control e4 — worth mentioning. 1.g4 fxg4 2.♘e4, nah! 1.f4 always trying to do things right away. 1.f4 e4 2.♘d1 with the idea of ♘e3:

de Groot Shafritz
Black to play after 1.f4 e4 2.♘d1
The solid idea of blockading with ♘d1-♘e3

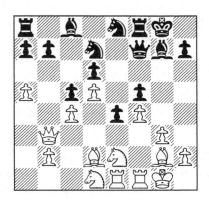

If he doesn't take — this opens up for me — his pawns can be targeted. Definitely what I want to spend time upon. 1.a6 don't see it. Don't know — what to do... Umm, other moves? What's Black doing? 1...e4 with the idea of ...♘d7-♘e5. If ...f5-f4 2.♘e4. 1.f4 I'm not scared of 1...e4 then 2.♘d1 — I really want to do it. I want to play 1.f4 — with this structure I can think about the knight blockading it. 1.f4 looks good. 1.f4 exf4 how can he do that? The knight gets ...♘e5 and then ...♘d3 — his f-pawn is bad. Pretty sure 1.f4. Push clock.

After the exercise, I asked Subject M8/9 if he had considered 1.f4 e4 2.g4! and he admitted he had not but, like many strong players, he logically suggested that, if that position *had* arisen on the next move, he is pretty sure he would have considered it! Then he said that he was so happy with the standard blockading maneuver 2.♘d1-e3 that he might have played that anyway. We'll never know...

Summary of Master

Characteristics of the thought process at this level:

- As noted in the study first mentioned in the Expert Summary, masters sometimes need to think less than experts and can rely more on memory. The de Groot exercises given to the masters were not "trick" positions; they were just relatively unfamiliar and needed to be carefully analyzed. Therefore, in the protocols given in this section, the masters thought at least as long as, if not longer than, the experts. Notice that the median length of the protocols of the players rated over 1900 was much longer than the length of lower-rated players. This is consistent with the observation that at multi-class tournaments like the World Open, the top sections have almost all their games still going when the lower sections become half or more empty.

- More than any other class in the book, the masters were willing to give up material if they believed that a long-term attack or initiative worth the material might be forthcoming. In particular, in de Groot Ernie they were the main class willing to accept ideas like 1.♕d4 or 1.♕d2, simply giving up the bishop with 1...♖xf5 (on purpose!) so that they could infiltrate the position with 2.♖e8+. It takes experience to realize when such sacrifices are realistic and worth investigation and when they are just a waste of time. That's one reason why I suggest to my students that if they have a choice between an even line and an unclear one, they should almost always choose the unclear one to learn something — making it less unclear when a similar situation occurs in the future (unless it's the final round of the World Open and they need a draw to win money!).

- The masters show many superb skills, none more so here than "chess" deductive logic ("If I do A, then he pretty much has to respond either B or C") and visualization. Almost all the masters were able to look 8+ ply if necessary and still analyze the position almost as well as if it were right in front of them.

Chapter 9

Thought Process Basics

This chapter introduces a simplified process for finding a move.

9.1 Thought process considerations

Unlike a problem, where the subject has a defined goal, in a de Groot exercise the goal is (or should be) the same as in a game: *to find the best move possible in a reasonable amount of time.*

The "best move possible" is often not "the best move." If the goal were to find *the* best move, then human limitations would often prevent this from happening in any reasonable amount of time (if ever). So the chess clock makes the goal much more practical. *In some quiet positions there are many moves that end up being close to the best move. To play any of those is acceptable. However, in sharper positions, to play quickly and settle for what turns out to be a vastly inferior move is a terrible mistake. Never make a bad move fast.* If you do decide to play more quickly than you should, you should be almost certain that a much better move is not available.

There is no single standard thinking process for how to correctly find the best move possible in all possible positions. Even if we had a systematic process, we would find that this process would not be followed exactly by any strong player. A player rigidly following such a process at one time control would be forced to modify it for a faster or slower time control.

Moreover, any single thinking process would, at the very least, include a high-level decision on which sub-process to apply, depending upon whether

> The "best move possible" is often not "the best move." If the goal were to find *the* best move, then human limitations would often prevent this from happening in any reasonable amount of time (if ever).

the position were analytical, purely positional/judgmental, or a combination of the two. For example, even if you subscribe to Kotov's *Think Like a Grandmaster* "tree of analysis" process, you would use it for analytical positions (e.g., most of those in this book) but not to figure out where to develop a bishop on move 6. Making fun of Kotov's overly structured approach, GM Soltis, in his book *How to Choose a Chess Move,* playfully labeled one of his sections, "Think Like a Kotov" (!).

However, there are common threads to a good thought process. These threads represent the basis for a simplified version of this process. How does one play "simple" chess? Here are ideas that should be contained in any simplified process:

- Look at your opponent's move and try to determine *all* the reasons that move was made. This includes asking yourself, "Is my opponent's move safe?" and, "What are all my opponent's threats?" Don't forget to look for discoveries, squares your opponent is no longer guarding, and so on. Often, an overlooked idea from one's opponent is a consideration not directly involving the moved piece.

- Look at what moves you might play (candidates), see what might happen after those moves, and determine which move leads to the position you like the best. Always assume the best or most dangerous moves from your opponent. When picking candidates, start with the forcing moves: checks, captures, and threats for both sides.

- Look for the Seeds of Tactical Destruction (aspects of a position that might allow an opponent's tactic) for *both* sides; if you have a tactic, consider playing it. If your opponent has a tactic, strongly consider stopping it. If there is no tactic, what are you trying to do? If you don't know, consider identifying your least active piece and making it better. Always try to use all of your pieces all of the time! Similarly, try to minimize the activity of your opponent's pieces.

- If you see a good move, look for a better one — you are trying to find the best one you can in an amount of time that's reasonable for your situation. Obviously, if your move clearly wins easily, looking for a better one may not be necessary.

- Manage your clock time so that you spend much less than the average amount of time on non-critical moves (use general principles). By doing so, you will have more than the average amount of time for critical moves (use precise calculation). Try to use almost all your time each game, unless someone blunders quickly and resigns. For more on time management, see Chapter 12.

Thus we can summarize good, simple chess: *"First, see if there is a tactic for either side; if so, address it; if not, maximize the activity of your pieces and minimize your opponent's."* You can play pretty well if you just follow that advice! A similar statement is: *"Take your time to do the best you can at keeping your pieces as safe and active as possible — and your opponent's pieces the opposite."*

What can go wrong in trying to follow this "simple" advice? The following are common errors involving these "simple" concepts. For a more complete discussion of thought process errors, refer to Chapter 11, "The Most Common Thought Process Mistakes."

1.   You don't consistently look at the dangerous moves ("checks, captures, and threats") that your opponent could make *after* your candidate moves. *Result:* You make a move. Then your opponent replies with a threat that you can't meet. I have dubbed this problem "Hope Chess." Almost every player rated under 1500 plays Hope Chess at least one move per game and, as a result, blunders.

2.   You make analytical moves based on general considerations, such as principles, instead of careful analysis — what I have termed Hand-waving. *Result:* You make moves that superficially seem good, but often can be easily refuted by an opponent willing to analyze. Besides Hope Chess, Hand-waving is the other big "process error."

3.   You see a good move and don't look for a better one. *Result:* You end up playing too fast and making a series of second-rate moves which throw away the game unnecessarily.

4.   You constantly play too fast for the situation (see Chapter 12, "The Basics of Time Management"). *Result:* Even if you have lots of time, you overlook simple ideas, often squandering big leads, and missing completely what is going on for both sides. Consider the following: Suppose you play your clone in a match in which you take 5 minutes for each game and your

clone takes 60. What percent of the games would you win? You can play much better if you consistently take your time and play carefully.

5.   You consistently play too slowly during non-critical stages of the game, agonizing over whether your bishop belongs on e2 or d3, even though your opponent has no tactics at that point, and a chess engine evaluates ♗e2 as +0.17 pawns and ♗d3 as +0.19. In other words, you are spending too much time on a decision that makes little or no difference to the outcome of the game. *Result:* When the game finally does become tense, you find yourself running short on time and have to make a critical move quickly. For the critical move, the engine finds that if you had played the right move you would be +2.4. But the move you played hastily is -3.6. You should save time for when you most need it.

6.   You don't repetitively study basic tactics. So instead of recognizing tactical situations when they occur for either side, you count on your re-nowned ability to "figure them out." *Result:* You are eventually able to calculate tactical situations correctly, but it takes a lot more time than it should. And sometimes, after looking in vain for a tactic for yourself, you overlook a basic tactic for your opponent that nets him a piece. Another annoying loss! A second result is that your ability to recognize danger ("criticality assess-ment") is impaired, causing you to both look for tactics when they are not there and to fail to look for tactics when they are.

7.   You cut off analysis of your candidate moves without trying to deter-mine what your opponent can do to you, or stop your analysis premature-ly when there are further checks, captures, or threats that would affect the evaluation ("quiescence error"). *Result:* Your evaluation of the situation is superficial and based upon incomplete information. You will likely come to the wrong conclusions and make the wrong move.

8.   You *calculate* the position well, but *misevaluate* it. "Misevaluation" means you come to incorrect conclusions about how good is the position at the end of your analysis. Thus, even if your analysis is plausible, you may end up choosing a move which leads to an inferior position. *Result:* Another wrong, possibly disastrous, move chosen.

9.   You find a reason why your opponent made a move and then stop looking for additional reasons, instead of asking what are *all* the things the

opponent's move does. *Result:* After you move, your opponent's reply reveals another reason he made his previous move. Oops! This oversight is enough to lose another game. I devoted the chapter, "Just Because It Is Forced," to this concept in my earlier work, *Everyone's 2ⁿᵈ Chess Book*.

10. When you consider a move, you don't assume that your opponent will make the best (or most dangerous) reply. *Result:* You play bad moves and hope your opponent plays worse ones. When he makes a good reply you think, "Whoops!" or "Darn!" Cousin problem: When your opponent moves, you assume it is a good or safe move without any analysis. *Result:* You are giving your opponent too much credit! By assuming your opponent has played a good move, you never analyze that your opponent's move allows you to mate, win material, or gain advantage in some other way. *While analyzing your move, assume that your opponent will make the best move against it. When your opponent actually makes a move, assume it might be a mistake* and check to see if you can take advantage of it.

11. You don't play enough chess to be able to recognize common patterns and gain experience. *Result:* Both the probability and the effect of many of the previously noted problems are increased.

12. You spend adequate time looking at one or more moves but, when they fail, you quickly switch and make a seemingly "safe" move without adequate analysis on that move. *Result:* The "safe" move turns out not to be that safe. *Spend time on the move selected.*

If you find yourself a victim of one or more of the above problems, you are not alone! There are plenty of other players out there who are nowhere close to master – or even expert – strength. There is likely some reason for this besides just raw talent. You may think the reason you are not as good as players in the classes above you is that they know the Caro-Kann better. But your problems are more likely one of the above.

By not properly implementing thinking-process basics, many players end up making the game of chess much harder than it is. For example, they might avoid piece trades because an advanced positional text tells them not to trade when they have an isolated pawn. Yet by blindly following that advice they overlook a simple trade that would win material. Sound familiar? I see these "penny-wise and pound-foolish" decisions quite frequently. It would be better for many players to avoid extensive study of positional weaknesses until their ratings got above 1400.

None of the above means that chess is an easy game. Some things in chess are extremely difficult. Let's list a few of the more difficult tasks:

1. Finding a combination which would make Shirov or Kasparov proud. It may be 15 ply deep in the critical line and would take a grandmaster 20 minutes to find, if they could find it at all. These are the kinds of tactics featured in the advanced text *The Magic of Chess Tactics* by Meyer and Müller or even *Nunn's Chess Puzzle Book*. There is practically no limit to the difficulty of this part of chess.

White to play after 31...♗e2

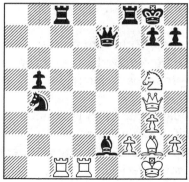

I am playing White and have just allowed Black to double-attack my queen and rook with 31...♗e2. My opponent is a good tactician and believes he has found a hole in my analysis. However, I found a very pretty combination which for many players would fall under the category of "difficult":

32.♕xc8! ♗xd1

This is forced, as 32...♖xc8? 33.♖xc8+ ♕f8 would lose to 34.♖1d8! (stronger than 34.♖xf8+, which also wins easily).

33.♕e6+

Always consider checks, captures, and threats, usually in that order of descending force.

33...♛xe6

Black's moves are all forced, which is good!

34.♞xe6 ♜e8

Black might have also tried 34...♜xf2, hoping for the unnecessarily complicated 35.♚xf2 ♞d3+, though 35.♜xd1 instead wins cleanly.

35.♜xd1 ♜xe6 36.♜b1

Removal of the guard is probably the most underrated tactical motif; here White removes the guard to the square d5.

Black resigns, as the perfect geometry continues: 36...♜e4 is not safe, and a knight move is met by 37.♝d5 winning the exchange and a pawn.

2. Deciding between two subtle but consequential evaluations. Spot the small but important difference between the two similar-looking positions in the diagrams below.

Black to play #1

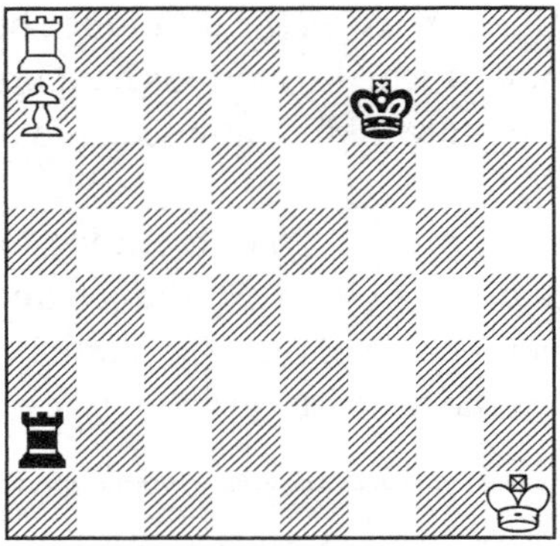

Black to play #2

In the first diagram, Black can eventually draw with the subtle **1...♔g7!**.

However, in the second diagram Black has no reasonable defense to the threat of **2.♖h8** followed by either promotion on a8 or a skewer on h7, e.g. 1...♔d7 2.♖h8 ♖xa7 3.♖h7+ winning the rook, or 1...♔f6 2.♖f8+ promoting. If instead 1...♖a1+ 2.♔g2, eventually Black will be faced with the same unstoppable threat.

Many are under the impression that playing well is almost entirely knowledge, including pattern recognition. Knowledge is extremely important, but analysis and evaluation skills are probably even more so.

It is not often easy to spot subtle details, but sometimes it is critical. A little difference can sometimes make all the difference between a winning and a losing position. Subtle but critical distinctions happen quite frequently in the endgame. To get it right requires skill, patience, and a good eye.

3. Deciding on the right plan when either none look promising or many look equally so. It takes quite a bit of experience and judgment to find the right plan a reasonable percentage of the time. And, if you go down the wrong track, it could prove to be the decisive mistake. Not easy at all.

Many are under the impression that playing well is almost entirely knowledge, including pattern recognition. Knowledge is extremely important, but analysis and evaluation skills are probably even more so.

4. Winning a won game when the margin for victory is razor-thin and the opposition is putting up optimum resistance. This is sometimes the equivalent of finding a needle in a haystack. The ability to win a not-so-easy-to-win won game is called *technique*. This is different from the less-often discussed (because it is supposed to be "easy") ability to win an *easily* won game.

So there are many difficult challenges in chess which give the game its deserved reputation as mental challenge requiring skill. Players who play too slowly think these critical situations come up almost every move and, when facing easy decisions, treat these as way too difficult. Don't make all chess play so hard. Sometimes playing reasonable chess, especially in non-analytical positions, is relatively easy. Of course, *if you are not sure that your move is non-critical, you must assume that it may be critical — and play slowly and carefully.*

Moreover, for every reader who plays too slowly there are likely two who play too quickly and carelessly. Those who play fast are especially vulnerable when faced with a move that *is* critical. In those situations, one loses immense strength unless time is taken and the analysis is done carefully. For those who cry, "I didn't see it!" afterwards — of course you didn't see it. One misses a lot when playing too quickly!

The moral of the story is clear. There are two main goals most players should work toward:

1. Becoming a *better* analyst, a strong component of which is in one's tactical recognition and solving; and

2. Learning to recognize *how much* analysis is needed in each position. Improve at recognizing when your decision is critical. Critical positions include not only the difficult situations illustrated by the diagrams, moves, and commentary above, but also key strategic decisions such as where to place your king or whether to trade queens. There is a reasonable amount of time you should take on each move. There are often dire consequences if you play too fast or too slow.

If the position is critical, take your time and try to analyze carefully. If you have a non-analytical position where tactics and analysis are not required, it is probably best to use general principles and play relatively quickly.

9.2 A simplified thought process

Based on the considerations developed in Section 9.1, the sidebar shows a simplified and high-level five-step process that could be used in most analytical positions.

How to Approach Analytical Positions

1. *What are all the things my opponent is trying to do?* This includes, "What are all the things my opponent's move does?" This also includes, "What are all the moves he can do now that he could not do before?"; "What are his threats?"; and "How did did his move parry my previous threat?" Don't forget the important step of asking about his move, *"Is it safe?"* Also, don't stop when you find one reason for your opponent's move, because the ones you miss may cost you the game.

2. *What are all the positive things I want to do?* This is the main goal of planning, and your decisions should be based on both sides' threats, strengths, and weaknesses. This step also includes identifying potential tactics. After considering tactics, other positive moves/ideas are those which restrict your opponent's plans and pieces, in addition to those that enhance yours.

3. *What are all the candidate moves which might accomplish one or more of those goals?* I once read the advice, "Don't look for the best move; look for the best plan and the moves which accomplish that plan." This advice describes a combination of Steps 2 and 3. The moves identified in this step are initial candidates.

4. *Which of those initial candidates can I reject immediately because they are not safe?* In other words, does my opponent have any checks, captures, or threats which can quickly defeat an initial candidate? Once you have eliminated these "unsafe" candidates, the remaining candidate moves are final candidates. Doing this step consistently I call, "Real Chess." As stated in our 12-point list on page 173, not doing it is Hope Chess. In the lower-class protocols, the majority of players made their moves without checking to see if their opponent could reply with a decisive, forcing move.

5. *Of the final candidate moves, which is the best one I can find in a reasonable amount of time?*

The final step in the sidebar is by far the most difficult one; if you can perform this step perfectly then you can play world championship-level chess. On the other hand, as we saw in Chapters 2-6, weaker players don't usually compare final candidates. They often just latch onto one idea and play a move they think meets Step 2, ignoring Lasker's Rule: *If you see a good move, look for a better one.* For analytical moves, Step 5 involves both finding best-move sequences (searching for the Principal Variation; PV) and comparison of possible positions to see which one is the best. *Assuming the opponent plays his best moves, the move which leads to the best position is the best move.*

Interestingly, strong players usually perform Steps 1-4 in a very short period and then spend the overwhelming majority of their time on Step 5. In a sense, many "improvement" chess books (except those on planning) are about performing Step 5. However, most weak players omit one or more crucial steps in performing Steps 1-4, or, conversely, spend way too much time on them! Consistently being able to complete all the steps at least moderately well in a reasonable amount of time usually means that you are on your way toward becoming a good player.

As a matter of "safety-first" priority and efficiency, strong players often perform steps 3 and 4 in parallel rather than serially. That is, they generate a move and then ask, "Is it safe?" for each move, rather than generating a list of moves and then going down the list to ask if each one is safe (in a sequence 3-4, 3-4, 3-4... as opposed to 3-3-3...4-4-4...). However, this does *not* mean that they extensively analyze each move as they find it; that would be very inefficient and possibly lead to lengthy analysis of moves that may otherwise be easily overshadowed by other candidates. Instead, strong players simply check to see if a candidate is safe, *if it is possible to quickly and easily determine this.* The extensive analysis is all contained later in Step 5. Moreover, as discussed in the next section, strong players do not isolate each move and exhaustively analyze it; that would be inefficient. Instead, their desire to compare moves and search for the best one is done by what de Groot calls *progressive deepening* (see next section).

9.3 De Groot's four phases

The following are the four phases of the thought process proposed by de Groot as a result of his study:

Phase 1: **Orientation** (problem formation) — the subject assesses and evaluates the position and tries to postulate what he is trying to achieve.

Phase 2: **Exploration** — the subject tries out a couple of lines in various moves to see what is out there as possibilities.

Phase 3: **Investigation** — deeper searches are made to try to strengthen the case for one move or another. Here the analysis (for stronger players) is more sharp and precise and oriented toward the goals set in Phase 1.

Phase 4: **Proof** — the subject attempts to prove either that the move found is the best available to meet the objectives, or at least that it is better than the others he has been able to find in a reasonable amount of time. (In his work, de Groot does not mention time, so this is my spin since the best move cannot always be proven or found in a reasonable amount of time.)

Part of de Groot Phase 2 and all of Phases 3 and 4 occur during what I called "Step 5" in Section 9.2. The reason is that de Groot worked primarily with very strong players, and players at those levels do Section 9.2's first four steps very quickly and accurately, so that those four steps are almost entirely contained within his "Orientation" phase.

However, I work with players of all classes, and have found that the further players are rated below 2000, the more difficulty they have in performing Steps 1-4 accurately or consistently, so these "basic" steps become a much bigger part of the observed process for players at all levels.

Therefore, players who use a Hope Chess thought process (and those who use "Flip-Coin Chess" — see Chapter 10 for more on this) — that is, players rated under about 1600 USCF/FIDE — should concentrate more on improving the first four steps of the process in Section 9.2. Stronger players looking to improve their processes should concentrate mostly on Step 5: determining which of the final candidate moves is the best they can find within a reasonable amount of time.

For example, in Step 5, when examining multiple moves in depth, players should use progressive deepening. That means a player should not spend all his time on one final candidate, but instead look around and examine all the candidates at increasingly deeper levels. This is a much more efficient way of trying to either eliminate candidates or identify one as clearly best.

Let's illustrate this benefit of progressive deepening. Suppose there are three final candidates "A," "B," and "C." If a player initially spends all of his analysis time considering just A, then he has no information as to how good "A" is compared to "B" or "C." There may be information he can derive from quickly examining "B" and "C" that could either:

- eliminate "A" – by making it clear that "B" or "C" is superior – and spend the rest of his time examining only "B" and "C"; or

- eliminate both "B" and "C" – in which case once "A" is established as remaining safe, it could be played.

In each of those cases, a player would save an enormous amount of time because he would not have to examine "A" nearly as deeply. *Keep in mind that the goal is to find the best move possible, not to identify exactly how good "A" is.* Therefore, progressive deepening by examining each move a little deeper in turn is much more efficient than completely examining candidate "A" first.

9.4 Performing a de Groot exercise

When performing a de Groot exercise, the subject is faced with three primary differences between the exercise and a real game: the requirement for verbalization, lack of familiarity with the position, and lack of knowledge of the opponent's last move. While verbalization primarily slows down the process, it should not fundamentally change it. However, lack of familiarity does change the process by requiring players to first undergo the "Phase 1" step identified by de Groot: orientation.

The primary part of orientation involves static evaluation. The best way to begin is to count the material. The other primary static evaluation criteria I suggest are king safety, the activity of all the pieces on both sides, and pawn structure. The major dynamic, which can make all the difference, is whose move it is. In a de Groot experiment, it is always the subject's move. Using prior experience, these factors are weighed. Questions such as, "Who stands better, and by how much?" can then be answered.

This evaluation is important for two reasons:

1. It provides the basis for deciding on drawing maneuvers. A player who is otherwise worse would be happy to force or play for a draw, while the player who is better would almost never do so.

2. In accordance with Steinitz's laws, the static evaluation, if properly done, should be the optimum "goal" of the de Groot exercise! For example, if White stands a little better, then, theoretically, his best move should leave him a little better.

Very few subjects are aware of #2 and, among those, even fewer use this information. One subject, USCF Expert Jerry Kolker, as discussed in the introduction, proclaimed White to be better but could not find a line where that was the case. Using his evaluation as a reason, he refused to give up. Only after half an hour did he find a line to his satisfaction. I give great credit to Jerry for taking this approach, one that I have not seen duplicated in roughly five hundred de Groot exercises.

Before starting his exercise, Dr. de Groot did not provide the opponent's previous move, and I did not either — although, if asked, I postulated a reasonable one. Without this information, the subject has to be extra careful to look for the opponent's threats. Many weak players not only skip the evaluation, but also, without the cue of the prior move, forget to look for those threats.

Before the exercise, I did not cue any of the subjects as to how to find their moves, other than the instructions listed in Chapter 1. Thus each player — at least the first time they performed the exercise — used whatever process they normally applied during tournaments, resulting in a variety of methods and abilities.

Chapter 10

The Thinking Cap

10.1 Introduction

This chapter, based on a popular online series, addresses various aspects of the chess thought process:

1. What it is;
2. What are the component parts;
3. Why it is important;
4. How it varies from individual to individual;
5. How it is learned incorrectly by almost everyone;
6. How it can be re-learned to improve your chess play;
7. How it is measured;
8. How it relates to other important issues, like Time Management;
9. Exercises you can do to practice a good process, etc.

Let's start at the beginning. Chess is a thinking game, so obviously your thought *process* is an extremely important part of your proficiency at the game. Yet almost no one is initially taught a good thinking process, so almost all beginners develop bad habits that must be overcome if they want to become stronger players.

Normally, when someone learns chess, all they are taught is:

*   How to set up the pieces;

*   How the pieces move;

*   Basic rules such as checkmate and some draws (like stalemate or insufficient mating material);

*   Some tips, like "Keep all your pieces safe;" "In the opening, don't move your queen out too early;" and "If you see a good move, look for a better one."

This is all good and adequate to help a beginner start playing and enjoying the game. However, it does postpone the important question: "Once your opponent makes his move and it is your turn, what is the process you should use to efficiently and effectively find and make your move?"

Great players do not all use the same process. For example, GM Victor Korchnoi is known as a meticulous calculator, while World Champion Mikhail Tal would play the same positions primarily on instinct and judgment. But all good processes possess common basic elements, such as not allowing one's opponent to make a one-move threat which could not be parried. If they did not have this element, then you or I could occasionally beat a Korchnoi or Tal just by threatening a checkmate that they could not defend against. However, they would never allow us to make such an unstoppable threat unless they were in severe time pressure — and probably not even then!

Moreover, a good thought process must be subconscious, because if one has to think about how he is thinking, it interferes with the process! For example, when you first learned how to walk, your brain spent a lot of processing time trying to figure out how to prevent you from falling. But once you got the hang of it, you no longer consciously thought about keeping your balance. Now, when you walk across the room, you don't think about which foot to move next or which muscles need to be used in order to do so.

But when you develop bad habits in your chess thinking process and become aware of them, for a time you need to adjust your process. This requires conscious effort. At first this intrusion into your chess thinking is awkward and possibly counterproductive. However, once you play many slow games and have a more effective and efficient process down pat, you think about the improved process less and less until you just do it, with markedly improved results. More on this as we continue.

Before we go any further, let's introduce some definitions, since there are no standard ones and chess authors tend to use some of these terms differently:

Analysis — The part of the thinking process in which you say to yourself, "If I go there, what is he going to do and then what I am going to do in reply?" It is the part of the process that creates the mental "tree of moves," so to speak. Some players call this *calculation,* but I rarely use that term. If pressed for a definition, I would say that calculation is the part of analysis that deals with forced sequences, such as tactics.

Evaluation — Looking at a position and deciding who is better, by how much, and why. *Static evaluation* is when you evaluate a given position without analyzing any moves. *Dynamic evaluation* is done at the end of each line of analysis, after you have determined a potential sequence of moves. Note: When someone says, "Evaluate this move," what they are really saying is, "Evaluate the positions that would result from this move — assuming each player is trying to make his best move."

Planning — What you do with the information of why someone is better (evaluation of strengths and weaknesses) and what might be done about that in future moves. It is how you will try to exploit opponent weaknesses, negate yours, use your strengths, and negate his. It is the way you are going to try to achieve some general short- and long-term goals.

Threat — A move which, if left unmet, could do something harmful (win material, checkmate, damage the position) *on the next move.*

White to play

1.♕c5 *threatens* checkmate with 2.♕c8#.

Attack — To move a piece so that it can capture a piece on the next move. An attack on the king is called a check. (Another definition of "to attack" is to play aggressively, keeping the initiative.) Note that not all threats are attacks (a threat to checkmate is not an attack, nor is a threat to control an open file), and many attacks are not threats. A queen move which attacks a guarded pawn is not usually a threat since taking the pawn next move usually results in loss of material.

White to play

White is *attacking* the pawn on g6, but not threatening it

Candidate move — a reasonable move a player might/should consider.

Killer move — a reply by the opponent which would refute most of your potential moves and prevent them from becoming candidate moves.

White to play

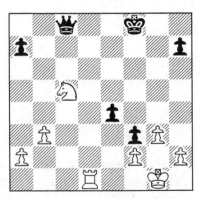

For example, in the diagram above White is considering his possible moves, but any move that would allow Black to play **1...♕h3** followed by the unstoppable **2...♕g2#** is refuted. Therefore, **1...♕h3** becomes a *killer move*.

Time Management − The process of managing one's clock time so as to find the best moves possible in the given time limit. (For more on time management, see Chapter 12.)

10.2 King of the Hill

There is a children's game called "King of the Hill." The idea is to find a mound of dirt and all the kids try to climb to the top. The one who gets there first is the "King of the Hill" and the others try to knock him off and take his place.

Computer programmers have something similar. It is called the first pass of a "straight sort." Assume there exists a set of numbers and one needs to find the largest (or smallest) one. Programmers start by assigning the value of negative infinity to the King of the Hill and then proceed to look at each number in the set. Each time they find a number larger than the King of the Hill, it becomes the new King of the Hill and they continue examining the next number. Once they have examined all the numbers, the one left as the King of the Hill is the largest number of the set.

In chess we have a saying, "If you see a good move, look for a better one − you are trying to find the *best* one you can!" When it is your move, the best move you have found so far is the King of the Hill. When you are finished analyzing, the move you should play is the "final" King of the Hill. Every chessplayer should have something similar in his thought process when considering moves during slow games, but many don't for various reasons.

Take the following diagram from a recent event. A student of mine, rated 1680 USCF, had White and was on the move:

White to play

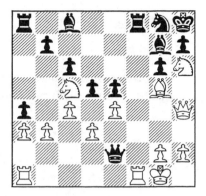

White was sorely tempted by the smothering move **1.♘f7+** winning the exchange, and played it. However, after **1...♖xf7 2.♖xf7 axb3** he soon ran into some trouble (if 3.♘xb3 ♕b2) and was losing at one point, although he later pulled out the win.

When I reviewed the game with him, we reached the diagram position and I did not know which move he had chosen. I said,

"Well, you can win the exchange with 1.♘f7+, but when you see a good move, look for a better one... Suppose you play **1.♖xf8**, what then? If Black plays **1...♗xf8** then **2.♗f6+ ♘xf6 3.♕xf6+ ♗g7 4.♕d8+ ♗f8 5.♕xf8#**, and if **2...♗g7** then (I paused for a second or two) **3.♘f7** is a smothered mate! So yes, I would play 1.♖xf8."

Jumping on desirable moves like 1.♘f7+ without fully analyzing the consequences and looking for better alternatives is a common mistake among weaker players. A player gets enamored with an idea or a type of attack and pursues it without regard to other, possibly better, options.

Therefore, a good thought process needs to contain an efficient way to search for the best move possible in a reasonable amount of time. There are many ways to do this, but they mostly boil down to picking out the reasonable moves (perhaps the moves which implement your most plausible and effective plans), analyzing each, assuming the opponent will make the best responses to each, finding the resulting positions, and then evaluating those positions. There is no way around it — in most positions this takes time, which is why the best players are usually the last ones to finish at open tournaments.

Suppose the first move you look at is OK, but you feel the position promises more. Then you should feel that a further search is worthwhile and that you might be able to find a better move than your King of the Hill. If the first move you consider results in a *bad* position and you feel your position is not bad to begin with, then you might not even assign that move as King of the Hill, knowing that a reasonable candidate is sure to emerge.

Suppose you find a move that exceeds all expectations. The temptation might be great to play the move immediately, but maybe you have underestimated your position and can get even more. Our example above covers this case: White thought he would be better with 1.♘f7+ and stopped his search, but if his King of the Hill expectations had been higher, he might have kept looking.

A computer chess program will show one or more analysis lines that look something like this:

11 ply (1/42) +0.83 19.♖he1 d5 20.cxd5 exd5 21.♗h4.

If there is more than one line of sequences (the default setting for the *Fritz* engine is to show the expected variations of the top three moves), then the top line contains the King of the Hill – in this case 19.♖he1 – and the line of expected moves on that first line (the best moves for each side) is called the Principal Variation (PV). The "11 ply" on the left indicates how many half-moves deep the computer is currently searching, the "(1/42)" means that it is analyzing its best current move out of the 42 legal possibilities, and the "+0.83" means the computer thinks White is better by about 0.83 pawns in the PV.

But once the engine finds a move it considers better, the first move of the sequence changes:

11 ply (7/42) +0.98 19.♖ad1 d5 20.cxd5 ♖xd5 21.♗f2

...and that means the new King of the Hill is 19.♖ad1. Note that the new evaluation (in this case 0.98) must be higher than 0.83 or it would not have changed its King of the Hill.

Humans don't think in this manner, but their intent should be similar: consider reasonable moves, assume the opponent's best replies, evaluate what will happen, and then compare this evaluation with the one you estimated with your current King of the Hill. Replace your King of the Hill if the new move results in a superior position. Given the situation and the time-control restraints, continue for a reasonable amount of time and then play your King of the Hill. (For more, see the discussion about "Trigger 2" in Chapter 12.)

10.3 Is it safe?

While a good thought process is flexible, there are common elements. A checklist you might use after your opponent makes a move is:

1.　Is his move legal?

2.　Am I in check?

3.　Can I checkmate him by a series of forced moves? (If so, nothing else usually matters...!)

4.　Is his move safe (for him)?

5.　What are all the things his move does? (In other words, how does his move change the position, and what can he do now that he could not do before? What are his threats for next move?)

6.　What are my candidate moves?

...and so on.

For now we are just going to consider the fourth item on this list: "Is his move safe for him?"

While reviewing my students' games, after some moves I blurt out, "He can't do that — it's not safe!"

That means the move leaves the piece in immediate jeopardy. It is not usually subject to a combination, but rather one of three simple possibilities:

1.　The piece is *en prise* — that is, it is attacked and not defended;

2.　The piece is subject to capture and there is a sequence of captures on that square that loses material; or

3.   The piece is instantly trappable — usually that means it can be attacked by a piece of lesser value and has no safe way to retreat.

As an example, take the sequence **1.e4 c5 2.♘f3 ♘c6 3.♗b5 a6 4.♗a4??**:

Black to play

The bishop is not safe because Black can perform a simplified "Noah's Ark" pattern, trapping the bishop with **4...b5 5.♗b3 c4.**

In many cases where a clearly unsafe move was made in my students' games, neither my student nor his opponent realized that the piece was not safe! They were too busy asking themselves other questions like, "What does that move do?" or "What are his threats?" or "What are my candidate moves?" When I show a position to a student and ask, "Black has just moved X. What should you do as White?", the first thing they usually do is look for candidate moves. This may work if it is a "White to play and win" problem but, in a game, looking for candidate moves before you check for the safety and purpose of your opponent's move can be disastrous. If a piece has just been made unsafe, I almost always spot that first, but my student sometimes sees the problem only *after* I bring the issue to his attention. The fact that sometimes they do see it immediately means that their thought process is faulty, because they obviously *can* see the move was unsafe; they just don't always consider the possibility. Therefore, the immediate safety issue is automatic — and important — to me, but not automatic for them.

Many students are almost as likely to spot an unsafe move by their opponent in a speed game as they are in a slow game! The reason is simple: in a speed game they expect their opponents to make silly, material-losing moves and are alert for those kinds of mistakes. In a slow game, they assume their opponents will *not* make such bad mistakes, and so they just skip that safety check, even though their opponents might be weak or playing fast and may just be giving them material.

A common, related mistake is for a player to remove his own piece's guard! He takes a piece that is defending another and moves it, leaving unsafe the one that was adequately defended. For example, consider the position after **1.e4 c5 2.c3 ♘c6 3.d4 cxd4 4.cxd4 d6 5.♘f3 g6 6.♗c4 ♗g7 7.0-0 ♘f6 8.♘bd2 0-0 9.♘g5?**:

Black to play after 9.♘g5?

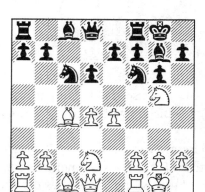

After this error, *Black* often becomes so fixated on the new "threat" to f7 that he fails to notice that the knight that moved to g5 was is no longer guarding d4. Since f7 is adequately guarded and **9.♘g5** has made the pawn on d4 unsafe, Black should just calmly capture it with **9...♘xd4.** But instead he often plays an unnecessarily passive move like 9...e6?. From this example, you can see that *you should not only ask yourself if the moving piece is safe, but also whether the moving piece is leaving something else unsafe.*

Another mistake many players make is to break off analysis in the middle of a forcing sequence (captures, checks, threats) and to evaluate the position before reaching the end of the sequence. This is called a *quiescence* error because they think the position where they stop and evaluate is quiet when it is not. Consider the following example:

White to play

Black has just played **1...♖d8-e8.** White might calculate the sequence of captures on d5 and think that Black has removed his own guard as in the previous example, but the d5-pawn is still safe because if **2.♘xd5?? ♘xd5 3.♖xd5? ♖e1#.** For White to stop his analysis after **3.♖xd5** and conclude that he is up a pawn is a quiescence error because he is not searching one move further to see the checkmate on e1.

Sometimes players assume an opponent's piece is safe, but they don't consider all the key lines and see that the entire capturing sequence is good for them. An excellent example of this occurs in the Ruy López after **1.e4 e5 2.♘f3 ♘c6 3.♗b5 a6 4.♗a4 ♘f6 5.0-0 ♗e7 6.♖e1 0-0? 7.♗xc6 dxc6 8.♘xe5 ♕d4 9.♘f3 ♗g4??:**

White to play after 9...♗g4??

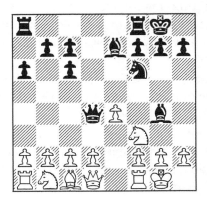

I have shown this position to students of many levels, even letting them know that **9...♗g4??** is a mistake and that it is now White to play and win. Yet even after they are aware that White can win, many continue to make the error of assuming that their knight is pinned and cannot move, and so look to just preserve their extra pawn with a move like 10.d3?. But when you see a good move, look for a better one. White has a much better one by moving that pinned knight with **10.♘xd4 ♗xd1 11.♖xd1**. This wins a bishop since Black's queen was unguarded and White's queen was not. Therefore Black's move **9...♗g4??** did *not* make his queen safe, as one should readily find if asking the right question: "What happens if I still capture the black queen?" If White misses 10.♘xd4, this *type* of error is similar to a quiescence error because White wrongfully assumes the position is quiet — and bad for him — if he ever moves his knight and allows his queen to be captured. The "tactic" that wins material after 10.♘xd4 I simply call *counting*. Counting is the ability to determine if any sequence of captures can win material; becoming proficient at it is one of the most important parts of learning to play well.

None of the above mistakes involve difficult combinations; all are basic safety issues. Even good players can make these kinds of simple mistakes occasionally — especially in time trouble. Therefore, unless you are playing a computer or a very high level of competition, *don't assume that your opponent's move is safe*. Even if your opponent's move *is* safe on 99% of his moves, that means once every 2-3 games you are going to be given a gift! Asking "Is it safe?" about each move is an important part of the thought process.

10.4 Three levels of chess thinking

I have studied players' thinking for about 45 years. I am convinced that one way to differentiate levels of chess play is to separate players into three categories, depending on how they deal with threats when playing slow chess:

1. Does not pay attention to all (or sometimes even any!) of the threats generated by the opponent's *previous* move.

2. Does pay attention to all the threats generated by the opponent's *previous* move, but, before making their current move, does not check to make sure that all checks, captures, and threats *by the opponent on the next move* (in reply to the player's move) can be safely met.

3. Not only deals with the opponent's threats from the previous move but, before making their move, also makes sure that the opponent will not have any checks, captures, or threats that cannot be met after that move, and does this check on every move possible/necessary.

Several years ago I published this thesis and dubbed these three levels of thinking *Flip-Coin Chess*, *Hope Chess*, and *Real Chess*, respectively. Defining these levels in relation to threats was published in my book *Looking for Trouble*.

Let's take the "killer move" example from 10.1 and apply it to the thought process definitions.

White to play

Suppose White sees that Black is threatening his knight. That means he is not playing Flip-Coin Chess since he did see Black's threat. But now suppose he is playing Hope Chess and decides to save the knight with **1.♘xe4?**. Then after **1...♕h3** White would be unable to stop the threatened checkmate on g2. If White were playing Real Chess, he would see that Black is not only threatening his knight, but also **1...♕h3**, and would try to find all the moves which would stop both. As the reader may already have seen, the best way to do that is **1.♖d8+ ♕xd8 2.♘e6+** with a good king-and-pawn ending. To reject **1.♖d8+** because it is not safe would be a quiescence error.

Perhaps Hope Chess was a bad label for the middle level, because many readers confuse Hope Chess with the common "hope" problem of making a threat and hoping that your opponent will not see that threat, or, similarly, making a bad move and hoping the opponent makes a worse one. I have dubbed these mistakes (they are not thought processes as much as they are bad habits within a process) as just *Bad Chess* or perhaps even *Hopeful Chess*, but not Hope Chess, as defined in #2 above.

Flip-Coin Chess describes the thought process used by most youngsters right after you teach them how to play. They haven't developed the ability to anticipate their opponents' moves, and the winner is usually the one who makes more, or larger, threats that are duly ignored. At this level of play, threatening checkmate, no matter how bad the move is otherwise, is often rewarded — which of course leads to bad habits.

Hope Chess is practiced by 99%+ of the adults who do not play in tournaments, and by almost all tournament players rated under ~1600 USCF. I have run into several players rated ~1300 who tell me that they have read my material on Real Chess and are now happy to announce they no longer play Hope Chess. Unfortunately, upon testing them, it turns out they *still* play Hope Chess (else their rating would not remain at 1300). When I find evidence of Hope Chess in their play and explain the concept of Hope Chess to them, their most common answer is, "Oh! So that is what Hope Chess is! I thought it was..." and then they go on to describe something else, often Hopeful Chess.

I have had a few strong players tell me that my theory is wrong because they do not use what I describe as a Real Chess thought process. But upon inspection it almost always turns out that they actually do, or at least they incorporate the minimum criteria for Real Chess. For example, if you don't play Real Chess, then you often allow unstoppable threats by your opponent. Strong players rarely allow such threats and, therefore, must use this aspect of Real Chess to reject candidate moves that allow them. However, they may not realize they are using this process because they have been doing it so automatically for a long time and are not *consciously* looking for all upcoming checks, captures, and threats. Otherwise, any 1300 player could occasionally beat a very strong player (say an IM or NM) who allows such an unstoppable threat. Unless the strong player is in severe time trouble, this happens so rarely that we can easily conclude that strong players avoid unstoppable threats, consciously or not.

It becomes natural for strong players to think, "Suppose I make move X, then what will he do? Suppose he then plays Y, threatening Z, what can I do?" If the answer is, "I have no defense against Z, so I would lose," then they discard X as a candidate. Of course it takes good board vision and analysis skills to quickly recognize all of the forcing Y's that the opponent can do to you, and, further, to figure out whether the resulting threat Z is stoppable or can be allowed. There is a great amount of skill involved, which is one small reason why the range of Real Chess players is so very large (approximately 1600 to 2800).

Bottom line: if you don't use a Real Chess thought process, you probably will never be a strong player. However, even if you do practice Real Chess, there is no guarantee that you will be a strong player, either! You still have to learn about all the other important concepts that most players study: openings, endgames, pawn structures, planning, tactical patterns, and so on.

One key to graduating from Hope Chess to Real Chess is checking for upcoming danger *on every move, and not just most of the time*. For example, suppose you "only" play Real Chess on 95% of your moves but on the other 5% allow unstoppable threats. Assuming the average game is 40 moves, twice each game (5% x 40) you open yourself up to immediate defeat. If you allow these two oversights each game, your rating will be *much* lower than if you play Real Chess on every move. After all, it only takes *one* bad move to lose a game! If you play at 1700 strength for 38 moves but on two moves play at only a 500 level, what do you think your average playing strength will be for the entire 40 moves?

It is not a mystery that players who read many books and accumulate decent chess knowledge often lose to players with much less knowledge. The "well-read losers" can attribute their losses to talent or luck (usually the latter!), but often they are simply not playing Real Chess. This also explains why 1900-level players with relatively little chess experience (but who are "good game players") can easily beat 1500-1600 players with far more experience — the two main reasons are tactical ability and a better thought process.

What does it take to graduate from Hope Chess to Real Chess?

• The knowledge of what Real Chess requires;

• The desire to do it (if it is fun, you will);

199

- The opportunity to practice it (slow games at 90 minutes or more per side are helpful);

- Practicing it until you don't have to think about it — this is actually one of the easier parts, since at first you *will* think about your process and it will be distracting, but if you play enough, checking for danger becomes subconscious, like walking;

- Practicing Real Chess consistently, persevering move after move, game after game. There is a fine line between desire and being careful — no doubt, naturally careful players have an advantage, just as players who are naturally good with any chess skill also have an edge.

Implementing a good thought process — combined with having the opportunity to hone this process through many slow games against strong opposition — is a key to unlocking that "barrier" that separates weaker players from those at the next level (or two!).

10.5 Checks, captures, and threats

Chess players use *analysis* primarily to determine what might happen if a certain move is played. This creates a "tree" of analysis with moves branching at each ply. However, the number of legal possibilities is very large, so humans "prune" their tree of moves to include only those they think might be (at least at first glance) reasonable. If this is not done, then the tree can grow astronomically! For example, if each side has 30 legal moves, then to look at even 2 moves deep (4 ply) would require 30 x 30 x 30 x 30 sequences, or 810,000! Hardly possible for a human in a year, much less in a game requiring 40 moves in two hours. Similarly, pruning the tree is necessary even for computers, which use "full-width" searching to examine all moves, but alpha-beta (and other) cutoffs to avoid looking at the entire tree.

One way to help categorize what happens when a human prunes his analysis tree is to break the types of moves into different categories:

- Checks;
- Captures;
- Threats;

- Moves that increase your pieces' activity or decrease the opponent's pieces' activity;

- Forced moves, like "the only legal" move, or necessary recaptures (note that *forced* moves are almost the opposite of *forcing* moves like #1-3, although it is possible for a forced move to be a forcing move!);

- Other moves.

One way to control the tree — and, happily, to find the best move — is to try and maximize the situations where the opponent's moves are forced. In other words, if your opponent has to play a forced move and does not have the flexibility to do whatever he wishes, then the tree is not only smaller, but more under your control. If you can consistently force your opponent to reply to your forcing moves, we call this pleasant situation *having the initiative*.

For this reason, when you are searching for your best move or considering your opponent's best reply, you want to start with (or assume) the most *forcing* moves, which are almost always checks, captures, and threats. Although most checks are more forcing than most captures and most captures are more forcing than most threats, this is not always the correct ranking of how forcing your potential moves may be. For example, a mate-in-one threat is often more forcing than any capture and even than some checks. Therefore, when searching for forcing moves, always consider mate threats near the top.

The Real Chess thinking process requires a player to see if his candidate move can be refuted before considering it further, much less playing it. At a minimum, this usually means asking:

"Suppose I make this move. Then what are all my opponent's forcing moves in response, and can I safely meet all of them?"

At this point you consider each of your opponent's checks, captures, and threats, making sure you have an adequate answer to each. If you do, then the move is plausible and it may remain a candidate move.

However, not all forcing moves are good moves, and some bad-looking moves are often actually good moves because of their forcing nature. Let us consider two examples. The first is problem #225 in the first edition of John Bain's excellent book on beginning tactical motifs, *Chess Tactics for Students:*

White to play and win

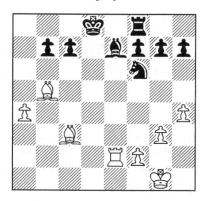

The answer is **1.♖xe7 ♚xe7 2.♗b4+** winning a piece. But let's ask a different question: excluding checks and captures (which sometimes can also produce threats), how many of White's possible moves are threats? This includes only immediate threats, not long-term threats such as to create an outside passed pawn. Hint: not all threats are good moves; they just have to be able to do something harmful next move. To find a threat, consider a move, *skip the opponent's reply,* and then see if the next move can gain something.

The answer is 5: **1.♗a6** and **1.♗c6** (they both threaten 2.♗xb7), **1.♗b4** (threatens to capture on e7), and **1.♗a5** and **1.♗e5** which threaten the removal-of-the-guard tactic 2.♗xc7+ ♚xc7 3.♖xe7+. On the other hand, 1.g4 does not threaten 2.g5 since, after 2.g5. 2...♘h5 holds g7. Notice that 1.♗a6, 1.♗c6, and 1.♗b4 are terrible moves that allow a capture, but are legitimate threats.

The Real Chess thinking process requires a player to see if his candidate move can be refuted before considering it further, much less playing it. At a minimum, this usually means asking:

"Suppose I make this move. Then what are all my opponent's forcing moves in response, and can I safely meet all of them?"

At this point you consider each of your opponent's checks, captures, and threats, making sure you have an adequate answer to each. If you do, then the move is plausible and it may remain a candidate move.

However, not all bad-looking threats are actually unplayable, and a good player needs to keep an open mind and investigate. The second example is this famous position from Bernstein–Capablanca, Moscow 1914:

Black to play

Black's move **1...♛b2!** at first glance looks like a typographical error. However, it not only contains two strong threats, 2...♛xe2 and 2...♛xc3, but the combination of both is unstoppable. **White resigned.** White clearly cannot play 2.♛xb2 due to 2...♖d1#. If White had played the tricky 2.♖c8, Black would have replied 2...♛a1+ 3.♛f1 ♛xf1+ 4.♔xf1 ♖xc8. Of course not 2...♛xe2?? 3.♖xc8#, nor 2...♖xc8?? when 3.♛xb2 guards c1 and stops the mate. White can try 2.♖c2, but then 2...♛b1+ 3.♛f1 ♛xc2 wins. Or if White tries 2.♛e1 then 2...♛xc3!.

These examples show that it pays to consider all forcing moves, including all threats. These include any moves your opponent may be forcing you to consider by his previous move, your current forcing moves, plus (importantly) his possible forcing replies to your candidate moves. If you have the time, include the moves that may appear silly at first.

In summary, when analyzing, the candidates that should be of most concern are the forcing moves: checks, captures, and threats. On offense, if you can successfully continue to make forcing moves, you have the initiative. Defensively, if you can successfully identify and plan to meet forcing moves by your opponent (or avoid them altogether!), then you will not be surprised, can usually stay in the game, and will often have good chances to win — or at least to draw — against formidable opponents. Therefore, learning to identify and deal with forcing moves is an important part of becoming a proficient chess analyst!

10.6 Space: a means to an end

I am often asked questions about the criteria used to evaluate chess positions. This is a subject I find very interesting: my first book, *Elements of Positional Evaluation: How Chess Pieces Get Their Power* (written in 1974 on a typewriter), addressed this subject extensively.

One interesting criteria is "space." In order to discuss space, we should first attempt to define it:

Space is *the amount of area (roughly measured in squares) between your pawn chain and your first rank* (including the first rank, but excluding the squares of the pawns, which are inaccessible to your other pieces).

Let's test this definition: as the pawns disappear, the amount of space becomes more amorphous and, as seems reasonable, disappears entirely in a pawnless endgame. That intuitively makes sense; therefore so far, so good.

Having more space is usually good for all those advantages we desire:

- It allows more room for your pieces to maneuver;

- It allows less room for your opponent's pieces to maneuver; and

- It gets your pawns closer to promotion, which also makes sacrificial promotion combinations possible.

But now for the important part. Consider the following pawn structure:

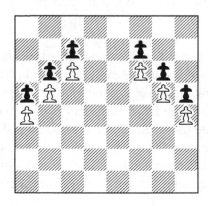

It is fairly safe to state that, by any measure, White has much more space. Further, if we place the pieces as follows (admittedly an extreme example!), White's pieces are dominating:

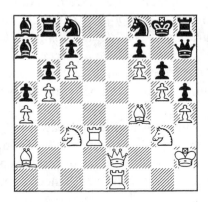

A great triumph for White's space advantage!

But suppose we leave the "space" unchanged (and even the king positions) and change the placement of the other pieces:

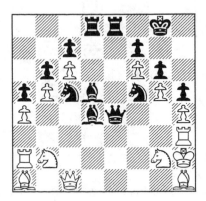

Now Black's pieces have managed to "get around" and penetrate "White's space," resulting in an enormous reversal of fortune.

You may think this example is far-fetched, but such penetration occurs fairly frequently. For example, consider an Open Sicilian where White castles kingside and correctly pushes his pawns for a kingside attack. But suppose that attack is misplayed, fizzles out, and Black breaks through in the center.

Then White's advanced pawns often leave him with an exposed king in the middlegame, and this infiltration can be the deciding factor in Black's favor.

Although the above diagrams are extreme examples, they help prove an important point! *Space in and of itself is not an inherent advantage; it is a means toward an advantage. The real advantage of having space is that, if utilized correctly, it allows your pieces to do more than your opponent's pieces ("better army activity").* No more, and no less. If a spatial advantage does not incur an activity advantage, then it can be — and likely is — meaningless.

Another common example is a king-and-pawn endgame with both kings centralized and the pawns locked, with one side having much more space (you can even use a similar pawn structure to the previous examples). Then the side having more space is often at a disadvantage since the enemy king has gotten "behind the lines" and can be used to "elbow out" the king whose side enjoys the space advantage. Take the following position with Black to play:

Black to play

Black, with the space advantage, *loses* because White has the opposition, but also in one sense because Black's pawns are so advanced and vulnerable.

So, on average, having more space *is* an advantage, but the advantage usually has to be in the form of more activity or the potential to promote pawns. The real objective is more active play, not space.

The same argument could be made about time/tempi as about space. For example, in a given position one side can be granted free extra tempi, but if those tempi are used unwisely to place pieces on less effective squares, then the "extra" time would not be helpful. Therefore, time, like space, takes a back seat to the real goal: having more — and better — things to do with your pieces.

In *Elements of Positional Evaluation,* I define the term *mobility* as the number of squares to which a piece can move. Mobility is extremely important since piece value is highly correlated with mobility — a queen is more valuable than a rook because it can also move like a bishop. But the value of mobility in a real position can, like space, also vary in that a piece can have many useless moves. Therefore the real goal is to have a "good" piece (or, in total, a good army) — that is, *activity.* No matter how you define "activity," when pieces have many good things to do — they are mobile, flexible, attack key points, and so on — that is the real advantage.

In the aforementioned book, I call space a *pseudo-element.* That means that space exists as an understandable and useful concept, but is not really an *elemental* basis to evaluate a position. So what are good measures of positional, *static* evaluation? *Total piece activity* covers the useful by-products of space and time. The four most important static evaluation criteria, in order of importance, are:

1. Material;
2. King Safety (you can make this #1 if the king is extremely unsafe!);
3. Total Piece Activity;
4. Pawn Structure.

The fifth, "non-board" consideration is the clock time factor, which can become the most important one during severe time pressure. Time remaining is always a big factor in games with faster time controls.

It is not that pawn structure is unimportant — it is, else it would not be on the list. For example, in common positions where the material is even, both kings are safe, and both armies equally mobile, pawn structure can easily be the deciding factor. Many weaker players greatly overrate pawn structure and think they are winning when their pawn structure is somewhat better, even in the face of clearly more active enemy forces! Similarly, sometimes players strive for more space and get it, only to find that the opponent's active and flexible pieces make their space advantage rather moot! This happens in many openings; Open Sicilians and the Modern Defense readily come to mind.

Arriving at the proper *dynamic* evaluation requires analysis to reach one of the types of positions that are worthy of evaluation: quiescent or speculative. These are covered in the next section.

In summary, next time you consider pushing pawns to make space, evaluate the likely result to make sure you are providing an advantage for your army. If so – and there is nothing better to do – go for it!

10.7 What makes one move better than another?

One question I ask chess students is, "What is your main goal each move?" Sometimes I get reasonable but erroneous answers like, "I am trying to win," or "I am trying to make my position better."

However, the correct answer is, "I am trying to play the best move" or, more accurately, "I am trying to play the best move I can find, given the time constraints."

The interesting follow-up question is:

"OK, but then *what makes one move better than another?*"

We touched upon this question in "The King of the Hill," but now we are going to focus on what exactly it encompasses. This is important, for *"What makes one move better than another?"* is at the very heart of what it means to play good chess!

First, let's eliminate the plausible but out-of-bounds answer, "The move that best follows the correct plan." While this may be an excellent way to help choose your candidate moves, it does not answer the question directly.

Let's list common (but incorrect) answers:

- "It leads to a win of something;"

- "It does more;"

- "The position after the one move is better than the position after the other."

The last answer is almost correct! In theory it *is* correct, but for humans it is usually impossible to apply (as will be shown below), so it won't do. However, this answer does address the fact that *we evaluate positions rather than moves,* so if one move is better than another, that means it must lead to a position that is better than another. However, which positions should we use?

The problem with using the position immediately after the candidate move is that the position may be clearly non-quiescent. For example, suppose you compare a "nothing" move like ♔h1 with a move like ♕xh7+, capturing the h-pawn. It may seem better to win a pawn with check than to just move the king, but what if your opponent's next move is ...♔xh7, winning the queen for the aforementioned pawn? So we must look further to see what happens after ♕xh7+, or else the evaluation that White is ahead a pawn is meaningless.

Generally, we stop our analysis at a point where we can evaluate as follows:

1. The position is quiescent. There are no more meaningful checks, captures, or threats which would change the evaluation. Most non-analytical positions are quiescent immediately after candidate moves;

2. The position is speculative. Then we use our judgment — for example, we sacrifice a piece to expose the enemy king, and even though *we cannot practically analyze to quiescence,* we judge whether or not the exposed king is worth the sacrifice;

3. A sacrifice fails since *the further possibilities cannot possibly give us a return equal to or greater than our sacrifice.* For example, if you sacrifice your queen and see that you might later win back a rook, there is no sense in analyzing further to see whether that is true, since the risk is greater than the reward in any case.

The first of these three is the most common.

However, knowing where to stop analyzing a line still leaves the question: With a large tree branching from each move, which positions are the ones we want to evaluate? In other words, which branches of the tree are meaningful? The answer is that we must assume — to the best of our ability to judge — the best moves for each side:

A move is only as good as the positions that will be reached from it, assuming best moves for both sides!

If you are not good at judging what the best moves are during analysis, you will arrive at the wrong positions and reach the wrong conclusions when you evaluate. This weakness, plus an inability to accurately evaluate positions with approximately equal material and the inability to recognize quickly and accurately the common tactical motifs, are three of the biggest "thinking" problems of weaker players!

So now we have our answer. Suppose we have analytical moves "A" and "B" and we want to know which one is better. First we attempt to determine the best sequence after A and B, only going as deep as necessary to evaluate, for example:

My move A followed by his best move A' followed by my best move A'' leads to quiescence (graphically):

A - A' - A''

versus:

My move B followed by his best move B' followed by my best move B'', his best move B''' and my B'''' leads to quiescence:

B - B' - B'' - B''' - B''''

This leaves a position after A'' that we feel we can evaluate. Let's call this position A* and the evaluation of this position E(A*).

The same holds for B: the position after B'''' we call B* and we evaluate it as E(B*).

Then we compare *these evaluations and decide which position we like better. If E(A*) is superior to E(B*) then we like move A better!*

Good players spend a great deal of time doing this when they are thinking!

Finally, we apply the King of the Hill method discussed in Section 10.2, and apply this to *all* our candidate moves in order to find the best one.

There are shortcuts to this method. Depending upon the position, non-analytical moves are made more on judgment than the above type of analysis. Good players don't *consciously* go through all this, but this is basically what should be happening when we think, or else we will end up with a less-than-optimum move. For example, many beginners don't even follow the guideline, *When you see a good move, look for a better one — you are trying to find the best move!*

Let's see how this comes out when a computer does it. From Section 10.2, we know an engine's analysis window displays something like:

11 ply (1/42) +0.83 19.♖he1 d5 20.cxd5 exd5 21.♗h4.

According to "game theory," your position cannot get better — or worse — if both you and your opponent make the best moves from a given point in a game like chess. Since playing the best move keeps the current evaluation from the previous ply, the engine assigns the value from the *final position* back to the *original move!* So if the position at 11 ply is evaluated at +0.83, then it judges 19.♖he1 to be "+0.83" as well and assigns it that value. The lines below the PV reach positions that are evaluated as not as good, and will be assigned lower values.

Next time you are trying to find the best move, keep in mind what you are really trying to do: to find the likely optimum position(s) that arise from this move and compare them to similar optimum positions that arise from each of the other candidate moves. Assume best play on both sides — don't expect that your opponent will make bad moves! The move that, in your judgment, leads by best play to the position you like the most is the move you should generally play.

Of course, analyzing in practice is difficult (and many books are filled with practical advice on doing so), but it helps to start by understanding what, in theory, should be happening. I hope that laying this groundwork helps!

10.8 Only part of the analysis tree changes on each move!

One fact that makes chess "easier" is that only two things change since the previous time you had to decide on a move:

1. Your previous move;
2. Your opponent's response.

That means that if you perfectly understood what was happening on the board last move — and that's a big "if" — then, unlike a problem in a book, you don't have to start from scratch to figure out what is happening this move — you only need take into account the consequences of the two moves that just occurred.

An easy example: suppose your rook on d1 was safe on the previous move, and no direct or indirect consequence of either new move affected d1. Then the rook must still be safe.

That forms the basis for guidelines such as, "Each time your opponent makes a move, ask yourself, *"Why did my opponent make that move? What are all the things my opponent can do now that he could not do before? What are all the legal moves my opponent can make now that he could not make before?"*

These guidelines often overlook the *other* consequence of the opponent's move, which is, *What was my opponent's piece doing before his move which it is not doing now?* This idea of checking to see what a piece is "no longer" doing is even more important when considering your own move: *If I move this piece, then what was it doing before that it will no longer be doing now?* I have many students who occasionally lose material because they are so interested in what a piece will be doing after their move that they forget that it was doing something important before, like guarding material or preventing checkmate.

Interestingly, the extra knowledge about only taking into account recent changes works better for stronger players. Why? Because stronger players have better board vision and more seasoned logic to account for the changes since the previous move. Weaker players, due to lack of board vision or even carelessness, often do not take into account all the aspects of a position and thus move hastily or with incomplete knowledge.

In addition to the changes since the previous move, there are "carryover" issues from the previous move. Carryover issues are primarily due to three factors: threats that had been purposely ignored, *Zwischenzugs* which left primary threats on the board, and blind spots/blunders which overlooked a threat on the previous move. For example, suppose a player does not notice an exploitable weakness in his position which his opponent mistakenly does not exploit. Since his opponent's move does not exploit the weakness but rather does something else, then if the player thinks, "What can he do now?" based solely upon the opponent's previous move, he will continue to overlook the leftover weakness and will again allow it to be exploited on his opponent's upcoming move. When this oversight happens to both players, it often leads to a "comedy of errors" where both sides continue to miss important issues that should have been addressed several moves ago.

This leftover problem does not occur nearly as much with stronger players, and not just because of their superior board vision. Stronger players also face stronger opponents, who do not often leave "unattended business" lying about the board. In other words, if a strong player overlooks something, then his opponent usually exploits this error, and the overlooked problem is resolved in the opponent's favor. But with weaker players, once both players have missed an idea, that leftover problem may remain around several moves until either one player "accidentally" notices it and either fixes it (if that player was the culprit) or takes advantage of it (if the noticing player is the opponent), or one of the players *unknowingly* makes a move which changes the position so that the leftover problem disappears.

An example from a slow game played recently on the Internet:

White to play after 33...♗xc4

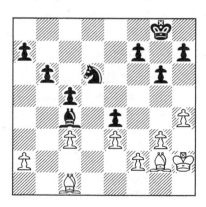

White, seeing the loss of his pawn on c4, completely overlooks that Black is also threatening the pawn on a2 and too quickly plays **34.f3,** allowing Black to win another pawn with 34...exf3 35.♗xf3 ♗xa2. Inexplicably, Black also misses this and plays **34...f5,** instead guarding the e-pawn. White finally real-izes the leftover problem on a2 and plays **35.fxe4 fxe4 36.a3** saving the pawn.

One interesting side effect of weaker players allowing leftover problems is the following: even if they are taught to look only for the differences in the position since the previous move, they often adjust their thought process to include a search for leftover problems. While this widening of their thought process is understandable, it is terribly inefficient; it causes a weaker player to approach positions more like a problem, in that he has to find and solve everything each move, and not just carry over from the previous move the pertinent safety information and only account for the differences. This extra work often becomes a burden for the weaker player who, probably correctly, does not fully trust his own analysis.

What can a weaker player who wishes to play efficiently, but is afraid of overlooking a "leftover" problem, do? There is no perfect answer, but here are some suggestions:

- Look for leftover problems during your opponent's move. But if you find one, don't slap your head and yell, "Oh, what did I miss?!" That tends to tip your opponent off, and he may use his move to identify and fix — or take advantage of — what you found. Some players make exclamations like this purposely as a ploy to lure their opponent into a trap. However, that ploy is also counterproductive because if your opponent is smart and you alert him — even as a ploy — he will be *less* likely to fall into the trap, since the main two possibilities are that you blundered or that you are trapping him, and he will figure out which one it is!

- Work on improving your board vision so you miss less in your analysis. This can be done by doing board-vision puzzles or just playing appropri-ately slowly in many slow games. Good sources of board-vision puzzles are Bruce Alberston's *Chess Mazes* or Jeff Coakley's *Winning Chess Puz-zles for Kids,* Vol. 2.

- Take your time and be careful on each move. If you are thorough, then you are likely missing less. That means you can be more efficient next move, and not have to worry about leftover problems nearly as much.

- Practice an efficient and consistent thought process. If you have a good thought process (such as one that includes the question, *"If I make this move, what are all the checks, captures, and threats he can make in reply, and can I safely meet them all?"),* then you will find most, if not all, of the key problems in the position.

There is one instance where a leftover threat is normal and must not be overlooked. This occurs when an opponent's threat is met with either a *Zwischenzug* (an in-between move) or a counterattack which temporarily ignores the threat. In that case one *purposely* allows the original threat to continue, so remember it next move or it could cost you the game!

Let's summarize what should occur during analysis:

A player creates a mental "analysis tree" of possible moves. Each time a move is made, he can trim that tree to include only the moves that were actually made. If the opponent makes a move that was not on the tree, he should see how that move affects the position, and generate new branches. If his opponent's move was already on the tree, he should verify previous analysis of that move and add new analysis. In general, any new analysis is most efficient when it focuses on the changes in the position made by the previous move, including both the creation of new possibilities and the elimination of old ones.

From a practical standpoint, using guidelines such as, "What are *all* the reasons my opponent made that move?"; "What are *all* the things he can do to me now that he could not do before (and can no longer do)?"; and "What are his new threats, if any?" are very helpful and powerful shortcuts for promoting thought efficiency. However, these shortcuts are much more effective once a player is strong enough to avoid most leftover problems. Therefore, play slow games and practice being thorough and careful.

10.9 Don't waste time on lines that won't happen!

The main principle to guide your analysis time:

Spend most of your time analyzing forcing moves in analytical positions. Don't spend as much time analyzing non-forcing moves; use your judgment in non-analytical positions.

However, from listening to hundreds of amateurs analyze, I have learned that they spend inordinate time analyzing lines that could never happen, primarily because:

- The player does not understand or attempt to deduce which moves are forced. Therefore he assumes moves that would never happen;

- The player wishfully thinks his opponent will not make the best move and assumes a bad reply, resulting in the overestimation of his own move;

- The player does not know when to stop analyzing a particular line. He reaches a position where he should stop and evaluate, but instead continues unnecessarily into lines that not only may not happen, but are irrelevant to the process of choosing the move. One common example is when a player proves that a move is not best (at any point in a line), but nevertheless continues because he does not realize that analyzing past such a move is irrelevant, since the analysis almost always will not be played.

There is no instant cure for wasting time analyzing moves that can't — or shouldn't — happen, and even strong players do this occasionally. But it is important to continually improve your ability to identify what is relevant and/or critical so you don't waste time on unnecessary lines.

What can be done? From a practical side, playing lots of slow games against stronger players and then analyzing with them afterward is a great step. Stronger players are better at weeding out what is irrelevant and, when they analyze with you, often show or state why. Even *watching* strong players analyzing their games can be quite an eye opener. If you cannot play stronger players, at least play reasonable competition. As you and your opponents improve, the moves you face will increasingly feed back to you whether you were anticipating something relevant or not, and your skill at differentiating relevant lines will slowly improve.

It is very helpful to first look for the forcing moves — *checks, captures, and threats* for both sides. An example of how to find one type of forcing reply would be to ask, *If I move the piece there and he simply attacks it with a piece of lesser value, would I have anywhere safe to move?* Looking for forcing moves is especially helpful if the reason you waste time analyzing lines that could never happen is because you have no idea which moves to analyze!

If in response to a candidate move there are *no* forcing replies by your opponent, then likely you can cease analysis of that line and evaluate the resulting position. If your opponent does have forcing moves, it can be wasteful to assume he won't play one and instead analyze a non-forcing move. If you are consistently surprised by opponents' tactics, then systematically considering your opponent's forcing moves as possible replies will likely be very helpful.

Another tip is to ask, "Would my opponent really do this?" or, "Why would my opponent make this move?" If the answer is that he would not make this move – because it is helpful to *your* cause or irrelevant to his – then it is likely he will not. Analyzing such moves just to see how good they are wastes valuable time. Remember that *your opponent is trying to find* his *best move,* so assume he will make his move with that in mind.

My students say they often consider opponent moves which are possible but, with a little analysis, can clearly be eliminated. If that is so, then your opponent will likely come to the same conclusion and, while he may also consider such lines, likely will not play them. You do need to analyze any plausible reply at least lightly to see if it really might be playable for the opponent. However, once you determine that a move is not playable, further analysis is not necessary.

You can also waste time by analyzing lines that are possible but not relevant. Suppose you determine the best move, but instead of making it, you continue to analyze to determine future possibilities. For example, suppose your opponent puts you in check and you have only one legal response, but afterward the game gets complicated. The reasonable choices are to make the move immediately or to resign. Looking ahead to see what will happen is not only unnecessary, but helpful to your opponent, because in that circumstance *he can think about his next move with perfect efficiency on your time.* While the "only one move to get out of check" is the most extreme case, the same problem can happen in less extreme cases: players often find the best move but don't make it right away out of curiosity. Even if a player delays playing the best move to triple-check whether it is really best, the time spent can get diminished returns, especially if the move is non-critical.

Even if you wanted to be as efficient as Dr. Euwe (see Appendix A), you would have to develop his superior board vision, analysis, and evaluation skills. Improving your skills – especially your thinking process – will also improve your efficiency so that more of your analysis will be relevant. Do too little analysis and you risk Hope Chess — your opponent will continually surprise you with moves. Do too much and you confuse yourself and get into time trouble. The goal is an efficient and happy medium.

Go "wide" in your analysis before you go "deep." There is no sense looking 10 ply (half-moves) down a line where the third or fourth reply is improbable. Instead consider:

- other candidate moves for yourself (first ply); or

- other reasonable replies for your opponent (second ply).

The deeper you analyze, the less likely that the line you are analyzing will occur. For example, suppose a line is not forcing and the chance that a specific move will be played at each ply is 40%. Then when searching three moves ahead (6 ply), the chances that this line will occur is only 0.4 to the sixth power, or about 1 in 250. It is more efficient to consider other moves at the first or second ply.

The bottom line: follow #322 in GM Alburt and Lawrence's *Chess Rules of Thumb*: "Think along the top of the variations. Before you go into a jungle of deep variations, search for different opportunities for yourself, and for your opponent, on the very first moves." Good advice!

In *The Seven Deadly Chess Sins,* GM Rowson advises always asking yourself, "What great things does this move do for my position?" If you can't find "great things," then it may be efficient to eliminate that move. Similarly, if you are considering an opponent's reply that does not do "great things for *his* position," then further analysis of that move is likely unnecessary. Analyzing lines that are likely to occur results in a better chance of finding the best move efficiently — and that's the goal.

10.10 Thinking on your opponent's time

Using your *opponent's* thinking time efficiently is an important part of managing a chess game. Your opponent's time is the best time to drink, eat, go to the restroom, and stretch your legs. It is beneficial to eat and drink during long games, and stretching your legs once in a while keeps your blood circulating and your body limber.

Although these activities take a certain percentage of your opponent's thinking time, you should keep these extraneous activities down to a moderate amount. For example, suppose you get up and stroll around after every move, checking your friends' games and so on, and return to your table only after noticing your opponent has moved. Even if you could be perfectly efficient and return each time just as he moved (in practice virtually impossible), then you'd still waste 10 seconds each move getting back to your board. In a 40-move game, this amounts to 400 seconds, or almost seven minutes! That wasted time can add up, *in addition to* the lost opportunities to use the opponent's thinking time more wisely. Therefore, wandering too much is wasteful. But if you are at the board, what should you be doing?

The classic suggestion is *to think specifics and tactics during your move, and generalities and strategy during your opponent's move* — and this is good advice. For example, on your move you might analyze specific lines such as "If I make move 'A', will he reply move 'B', and what is my evaluation of the position if he does?", while on his turn consider ideas such as, "With this pawn structure, should I push my queenside pawns and if so, which ones first?" or, "What would be the ideal square for this knight, and should it be the next piece that I need to reposition?" If you learn to do this efficiently, you will be making good use of your opponent's time, and that should result in better performances.

Another important part of general strategy that can be performed while your opponent's clock is ticking is time management. A great tip is:

While your opponent is thinking, try to determine whether you are playing too fast or too slow.

Base your consideration on such factors as:
- the complexity of the position;
- how many moves the game is likely to last;
- the time control;
- the current move number; and
- how much time remains on your clock.

A periodic adjustment is very helpful early in the time control, and adjustments should be made frequently as time becomes more of a factor.

Although considering general strategy is the most common activity that occurs on your opponent's time, it is not the only one. Deciding which activity is the most efficient depends on factors such as how much time is left on the clock and how efficiently you can predict your opponent's next move.

As discussed in Section 10.9, suppose your opponent only has one legal move, but for some reason he (erroneously) is waiting to make it. You can predict your opponent's move with perfect efficiency so, instead of thinking in generalities, assume that move will be made and begin to analyze your reply, just as if it were your turn.

With regard to your opponent's likely move, there is an enormous grey area between "forced" and "wide open," when his move is completely discretionary. *In this grey area, the more you can anticipate your opponent's move, the more you can think concretely on his time.* For example, suppose your opponent has two crucial replies and is taking some time to decide between them. You should also figure out that he has two choices, assume the one you believe more dangerous and then analyze what you would do if he made that move. If it turns out he makes the other move, you have lost very little — especially if you were correct that the one you were analyzing was better!

An example:

Yehl–Heisman
Liberty Bell 1968
Black to play after 16.♗b5+

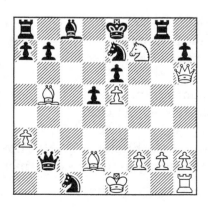

In this complex position, Black has four legal replies: 16...♕xb5, 16...♘c6, 16...♗d7, and 16...♔xf7. However, both sides quickly saw that 16...♕xb5?? fails to 17.♘d6+ winning the queen and that 16.♔xf7?? allows 16...♕f6#. So the real issue was whether Black should play 16...♘c6 or 16...♗d7, and I was taking a while to decide what to do.

White should take advantage of this by thinking along with Black. Since there are only two reasonable replies, White can efficiently assume the one he will calculate as best and start to work on his planned reply. Moreover, White may have already calculated that 16...♘c6 was bad due to 17.♗xc6+ bxc6 18.♘d6+ ♔d8 (18...♔d7 19.♕xh7+ wins) 19.♗a5+. If so, White could concentrate all his efforts efficiently on 16....♗d7. I, too, calculated that 16...♗d7 was best but in my inexperience decided to calculate whether it was winning for me or not (it was). I spent so long calculating 16...♗d7 that I forgot why **16...♔xf7??** was bad, changed my mind, played it, and was instantly mated! This example shows that the advice to *play the best move once you determine it* is very important!

A common practice among stronger players is to assume that your principal variation (PV) is going to be played. Since knowing the PV usually involves finding your opponent's best move, you can assume that move — at least initially — and see if your intended reply still holds. Quite often when using your PV it turns out that *although your opponent's next move may be optimal, your originally intended reply to it may only be sufficient.* For example, you might think "I will play X, which is clearly the best move, and if he plays move Y, then I can at least reply with move Z." But that usually only proves that your intended next move Z is *sufficient* to meet his expected move Y, not that Z is necessarily your best reply to Y. *Therefore, while finding such a sufficient Z is usually necessary to play X, it does not mean that Z is what you should play if Y is actually made.* Therefore, while your opponent's clock is running, you can think, "All right, I planned Z if he plays Y, but suppose he does plays Y — can I verify that Z is sufficient and possibly find a move better than Z?"

By cleverly using your opponent's time to determine if move Z would truly be best, then — if your opponent *does* play Y as expected — you won't have to rely on Z as simply a basis for new analysis, but will have much more information to start your turn.

While you are thinking during your opponent's turn, you may — unhappily — *refute* your intended move Z, and *need* to find another move that is at least playable. Hopefully that scenario won't happen too often, but when it does (especially when you are short on time and such analysis errors are occurring more frequently) starting your search for a sufficient move on your opponent's time rather than waiting and then finding out that Z is inadequate *on your time* may be the difference between winning or losing! It has happened to me more than once.

As it turns out, the next Yehl–Heisman game is an example!

Yehl–Heisman
Keystone State 1968
White to play after 13...♗xg4

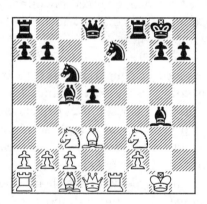

White has sacrificed his kingside pawns, intending 14.♗xh7+ ♚xh7 15. ♘g5+ ♚-any 16.♕xg4 with attack. However, if White had been thinking on the expected 13...♗xg4, he might have realized that 14.♗xh7+ is refuted by 14...♚h8! when Black wins the knight on f3. Unfortunately for White, this realization came too late and he took quite some time before admitting his mistake and playing **14.♗e2.**

After that I could have won prosaically with 14...♕e8!, but instead was bent on revenge and played the complicated **14...♗xf2+!?.** The game concluded in spectacular fashion: **15.♚xf2 ♘e5 16.♗g5! ♕b6+ 17.♗e3 ♕f6! 18.♖h1 ♗xf3 19.♗xf3 ♘g4+! 20.♚e1 ♘xe3 21.♘xd5 ♘7xd5 22.♗xd5+ ♚h8 23.♕d2 ♘xd5 24.♕xd5 ♕f2+ 25.♚d1 ♖ad8, White resigns.**

Sometimes when analyzing your opponent's possible reply Y, you realize that Y is not best (your PV was not correct) and that he would be making a mistake to play it. Then you should no longer worry about Z, but can spend your energies seeing which replies are more likely than Y and what you can do about them.

Sometimes time trouble prevents using sufficient time to find a PV. Then it is especially important to make optimum use of your opponent's time to calculate concrete variations in case they are played. Sometimes your opponent, if he has quite a bit more time, may move quickly to stop you from doing so. Ironically, this is usually a big mistake on his part, because he is negating his time advantage. During your opponent's thinking time, you can't think as efficiently about what your opponent is going to do as he can, so it would be a better strategy for him to play slowly — and for you to use that time as best as possible.

The major exception to playing slowly when your opponent is in time trouble is when a player is clearly winning but is very short on time. Then it is correct for the losing player to play quickly, even if he has adequate time.

I read that world-class GM Michael Adams had a habit of taking a stroll after almost every move. However, he became an even better player once he mastered the art of using his opponent's thinking time efficiently. Therefore, next time you play a slow game, see if you can implement some of these strategies to improve your results, too. Good luck!

Chapter 11

The Most Common Thought Process Mistakes

11.1 Thought process mistakes vs. other types of mistakes

Within the protocols of this book and the accompanying analysis, many different thought process errors were committed. This chapter will summarize and briefly discuss the most common such errors. However, there are many other types of chess mistakes, including psychological, physical, emotional, or knowledge mistakes. So it might be helpful to start by listing some typical mistakes which are *not* due to the thinking process:

- Not being familiar with a tactical pattern that causes you to lose material or to fail to win material;

- Not getting enough rest before a round;

- Offering a draw in a winning position because you are afraid of losing;

- Getting too nervous and moving before calming down;

- Playing with too much fear of losing;

- Being overconfident and thereby overlooking an opponent's resource;

- Allowing yourself to become dehydrated, hungry, or otherwise to experience physical discomfort;

- Being unnecessarily afraid of your opponent's rating;

- Forgetting a rule such as *en passant* or underpromotion;

- Failing to get the tournament director when something unusual happens; and

- ...many more.

Falling somewhere in-between are "vision" errors:

- *Board vision* — The ability to quickly and accurately recognize where all the pieces are and to assess what they are doing in the current chess position. Examples of board vision errors: miscounting the material, not seeing that a king is in check, or not noticing a bishop attack from across the board.

- *Tactical vision* — The ability to quickly and accurately recognize known tactical patterns and their likely consequences. Tactics includes not only winning material and checkmate, but also tactics for defense, such as preventing material loss or checkmate. Examples of tactical vision errors: missing that the opponent is threatening a back-rank mate or overlooking an easy removal-of-the-guard combination to win material.

- *Visualization* — The ability to keep track of where all the pieces are (and to "see" them as a position) as you move the pieces in your head while analyzing future possibilities. One common visualization error, as termed by GM Nikolai Krogius in *Chess Psychology,* is a "retained image" error where one visualizes a piece as remaining on a certain square even though that piece "moved" earlier in the envisioned analytical sequence.

Here are some examples:

White mates in 2

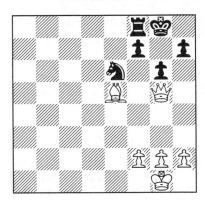

You may at first spot that 1.♕h6 does not work since the knight guards g7 and Black can always play 1...f6. However, the additional mating pattern with the queen going to h8 is "on" and so **1.♕f6** does the trick. This is an example of using *tactical vision.*

Now let's look at the same problem in a harder setting — harder because the tactical part is the same but the *board vision* is more difficult:

White to play and mate

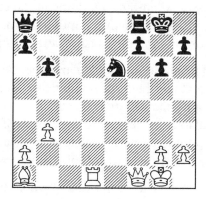

White has the exact same solution, **1.♕f6,** with the minor exception that this time the problem is not "mate in two" because the black knight can sacrifice itself on d4 and the queen on g2 before succumbing to the mate.

If these two problems are presented to intermediate players (but separated in time so they don't realize it's the same pattern), most will take longer on the second problem because there are extra, nonessential pieces on the board and because the bishop and queen are further away from the checkmating sector. These are board-vision issues — the tactical vision remains almost exactly the same.

Here is a position from one of my students' games:

Black to play

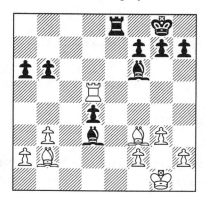

Fearful of back-rank mate problems, Black played 1...h5?. I asked him if he considered the forcing moves first (which always should begin by examining checks). His only check results in a mate: **1...♖e1+ 2.♔g2 ♗f1+ 3.♔h1** (or 3.♔g1) **3...♗h3#**. He replied that he did consider 1...♖e1+ ♔g2 but he did not "see" 2...♗f1+. If he were truly not able to visualize the bishop coming in from d3, this would be categorized as a visualization error. However, if he saw the bishop on d3 but did not recognize the checkmate pattern as meaningful and thus did not consider 2...♗f1+, then that would be a different error, a lack of tactical vision.

These vision errors are not process errors per se, but they obviously can highly affect the process. For example, inexperienced players who are not proficient at visualization often are inadequate at analysis because they can't see possible positions clearly enough to analyze them correctly. *You can't play what you don't see.*

Similarly, overconfidence is also not a process error but it can lead to process errors, most likely failing to take into account the possibilities an opponent with a bad or lost position still has. The more you are winning, the more you have to lose, so it's better to treat a winning position like having a lot of cash: the more you have, the more careful you should be because losing it will be all the more painful. *Always play with confidence, aggression, and respect for the opponent's moves and ideas.* And the more you are winning, the more you should *Think Defense First,* which doesn't mean playing passively, but rather giving priority to stopping the ways in which a losing opponent can get back into the game.

Other common errors that are similar to thought process errors, but don't really fall in this category, include:

- Selecting a bad "plan" which seemingly leads to future good (or equal) positions but which actually leads to less favorable positions than expected; and

- Misevaluating the position and thus selecting the wrong move. Evaluation is obviously a part of finding moves, but making an evaluation error is not an error in the process, per se (though obviously there is a "process" to evaluating a position).

When I bought *Thought and Choice in Chess,* I think my rating was about 1900. When I tried de Groot A, I analyzed the position fairly well and correctly came to the conclusion that, after 1.♗xd5, 1...exd5 was forced. But unlike Euwe, who immediately and correctly evaluated that position as good for White (see Appendix A), I misevaluated the position and thought, "Too bad, 1...♘xd5 and 1...♗xd5 lose but 1...exd5 holds and White is just losing the bishop pair." So, although my analysis was very good, my evaluation was terrible and I didn't choose the correct move!

An extensive discussion of all types of mistakes would take an entire book, such as GM Soltis's *Catalog of Chess Mistakes*.

But that still leaves many types of thought process mistakes, as we have seen throughout the protocols in earlier chapters. Here is a summary of the most common problems, each of which is addressed as a section in the remainder of this chapter:

- Playing too fast or too slow;

- Playing "Hope Chess";

- Hand-waving — using principles instead of analysis;

- Making quiescence errors;

- Not asking/seeing *all* the things the opponent's move does;

- Skipping the "Is it safe?" question;

- Not spending enough time on the move chosen;

- Stopping selection after finding what the subject thinks is a reasonable move, thus failing to attempt to find the best move;

- Using bad deductive logic and erroneously thinking a particular sequence is likely to occur, when in fact it likely would not;

- Overlooking an opponent's move, causing a tactical error.

11.2 Playing too fast or too slow

In this section, we will be addressing issues of playing tempo. It should be noted that these are relative problems — playing too hastily or too slowly for the situation (time and position). For example, a move made in 30 seconds with an hour left on the clock in a sudden-death time control situation might be entirely too fast, while the same move made in the same position taking the same 30 seconds might be too slow when there are two minutes left on the clock!

Although playing too fast or too slow are quite opposite problems, they can be addressed as a "pair." A player might suffer from one of these mainly for either psychological or process reasons.

For most players, the reason they play too fast has to do with psychological issues. For those who play too fast, this might be caused by problems such as anxiety, eagerness to get into the action, impatience, or even causes with a physical component such as ADD or ADHD. For those who play too slowly due to psychological issues, the causes might be fear of making a mistake, fear of losing, inability to make decisions, general apprehension, etc. For a more detailed discussion of these "slowness" problems, I would refer the reader to GM Rowson's book, *The Seven Deadly Chess Sins*.

But it is entirely possible that playing too fast or too slow can be caused by process errors. For those "lucky" individuals whose problems are purely process-related, once the process error is corrected, they can often quickly move toward a more desirable move rate.

Obviously, any omission of necessary process can cause someone to play too fast, but the two principal and basic omissions are:

- Failing to heed the basic principle, "When you see a good move, don't play it. Look for a better one. You are trying to find the best move you can in a reasonable amount of time." Having tested hundreds of inexperienced players by having them think "out loud" to find a move, I have found that many, if not most, are not interested in comparing moves to see which one leads to the best position; they are more interested in finding a move they like which they think will lead to a favorable outcome.

- Not checking to see if their candidate moves are safe. This usually implies asking, "Does my opponent have a check, capture, or threat on the next move which I can't meet, allowing them to win material or checkmate?" It takes time to determine this for each candidate, so it's fairly guaranteed that anyone who is playing too quickly cannot be taking the time to ensure that the moves they are considering are safe. It only takes one bad move to lose a game, and it's possible that playing just one unsafe move can be enough to tilt the scales of the game against you.

I once had a student who played much too fast. I suggested he first try these two basic ideas for slowing down (look for a better move; ask if all candidates are safe). Alas, it did not work as he failed to do either one consistently. So he asked me to humor him and give him more things to help slow him down. Normally I would not do that, because if the basics weren't followed, why would anything more involved help? But since he was the customer and he asked me to humor him, I gladly tried by suggesting three other things he could do to slow down. The result was as expected: a bigger mess. So I learned what I suspected: if you play too fast and don't do these two basic ideas, then other "process" suggestions won't help. You have to learn to walk before you can run.

The main problem with play that is too slow is, ironically, that it usually leads the player into unnecessary time trouble where he is forced to play too fast! Thus the problems of playing too slow and too fast both result in needlessly hasty moves, with corresponding possibly dire consequences.

Although, as mentioned earlier, playing too slow is often a result of a psychological error, it can be caused by a variety of process errors. For example, a player might forget that his goal is not to figure out how good his best move is, but simply to identify that move. Once you figure out your best move or (more practically) that there can't be one that's clearly better, then your job is finished. Spending additional time trying to pinpoint exactly how much better your candidate move is than the other candidates may be interesting, but during a game it's a clear waste of time.

> Playing too slow can be caused by a variety of process errors. For example, a player might forget that his goal is not to figure out how good his best move is, but simply to identify that move. Once you figure out your best move or (more practically) that there can't be one that's clearly better, then your job is finished. Spending additional time trying to pinpoint exactly how much better your candidate move is than the other candidates may be interesting, but during a game it's a clear waste of time.

A second process error that might cause a player to play too slow is concentrating on one candidate move, often going into depth on that move before identifying other likely candidates. One reason that this "going deep before wide" procedure is a mistake is that there may clearly be superior candidates, so the time spent on the first one could easily turn out to be wasted, assuming (as should be the case) that the player does eventually wish to find a better move and is likely to recognize it, given the chance. Recall Dr. de Groot's discussion of "progressive deepening"— looking at a few candidate moves but only slowly deepening the search. That's a more efficient way of looking deeper than doing it all at once with one candidate.

A third process error that can cause unnecessary slowness is trying to decide between several candidates which are difficult to differentiate due to similar evaluations. The key lies in recognizing the similarity of the evaluations. Once you realize that none of the moves is that much more effective than the others, then trying to find the best among equals usually results in severely diminishing returns for your time. In other words, if the move is not that critical, picking a reasonable move is satisfactory. This process problem most often happens in the opening, when different orders of developing moves often are not that critical.

Another process error I have encountered which causes a player to play too slowly is spending too much time early in the thought process on "null-move" analysis ("passing") to determine threats. Null-move analysis assumes the player does not make a move but instead allows the opponent a second move in a row; determining what the opponent can do with this second move helps to identify threats that need to be met by the player's move. The problem occurs when the player starts analyzing these null moves "in depth" rather than just listing those threats. This is often a waste of time for two reasons: a) analyzing null-move sequences often involves positions which cannot occur since the player's move will affect the sequence (e.g., the player's move will often be a check, capture, or threat which forces different play); and/or b) it is only necessary to analyze these opponent threats in depth if the player chooses a candidate move which is passive enough to allow that threat. In that case, the player can analyze the threat in more depth without waste of time since it will be allowed, but to do so earlier at the "null move" stage would have possibly been a waste.

11.3 Playing "Hope Chess"

Along with Hand-waving (11.4), the most common thought process mistake of weaker players is to play Hope Chess. As we have described before, playing Hope Chess means making a move without consistently checking to see if the opponent has a forcing move (check, capture, or threat) in reply which you cannot safely meet. If they do make such a threat, then you are hoping that there is a defense, but it is entirely possible that your opponent has made a threat for which there is no answer. For example:

Black to play

Suppose Black plays **1...♕xb5??** here just because the pawn is *en prise*. Then after **2.♕h6** he asks, "How do I stop White from playing 3.♕g7# next move?" The answer is that the mate is unstoppable. Before playing 1...♕xb5??, Black needed to foresee that White had an unstoppable threat next move and instead had to make a move capable of parrying 2.♕h6, such as 1...♕d8 or 1...♔h8.

Note that making a threat and hoping that the opponent does not see it (thus allowing you to carry out the otherwise stoppable threat), or making a bad move and hoping the opponent will not see that either, is not (by my definition) Hope Chess – but it could have been. There are many situations where you might hope for something in chess; however, my original intention was for Hope Chess to cover only the situation where the opponent makes a forcing move that you did not attempt to anticipate, and then you hope you have a defense.

When you consistently ask if your candidate moves are safe and avoid Hope Chess, I call this "Real Chess."

Even when intermediate players (in this case USCF ~1300-1700) play very slowly, it is likely that they never ask themselves, "if I make move X, can my opponent then reply with a check, capture, or threat which I cannot meet?" Further, many players spend 10+ minutes on a move and never spend one second to consider what the opponent might do after that move! That's an important finding for anyone wondering why these players do not have a higher playing strength despite, in some cases, impressive chess knowledge. To avoid the possibility of a quick loss, a player has to expend some effort each move making sure that he can meet each check, capture, or threat after the move he plans to play.

Players are often inefficient in their thought processes or confused as to when, during that process, they should examine forcing moves: checks, captures, and threats. *One very effective way of improving a player's thought process is to advise them that there are three distinct points during the thought process when you should use the forcing-move selection:*

• During the "What are all the things my opponent's previous move does?" step (Step 1 in Section 9.2). By using the null-move process (assume you skip your move), ask "If I do nothing, what could he do to me next move?" and examine his checks, captures, and threats;

• During your candidate step (Step 3 in 9.2), it makes sense to at least consider all your checks, captures, and threats; and

• During your "Is my candidate move safe?" step (Step 4 in 9.2), check to see if any forcing move defeats that candidate. This is the Real Chess step.

On a note of efficiency, once a player does the "What are my opponent's threats?" step correctly, it makes it much easier to do the Real Chess step, since the forcing moves the opponent has in the first candidate are usually almost the same forcing moves he might do in the others. Of course, the difference is determined by how your candidate move affects the position, and this might make all the difference between safe and unsafe.

Let's return to an earlier example (see Section 11.1) involving Tactical Vision, but let the defender go first:

Black to play

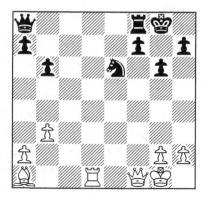

If Black is performing the threat step correctly, he will find that White is threatening 2.♕f6 with inevitable checkmate. Therefore, all his candidates should use 2.♕f6 as a killer move and not allow the mate.

So if Black chooses the candidate 1...h5, he can ask the Real Chess question, "Does White have any forcing move that can defeat 1...h5?" and he should examine first the killer move 2.♕f6 when afterwards he needs to see if the mate can still be stopped. Hopefully, he will then notice that 2...♔h7 allows the rook to guard h8, and that keeps 1...h5 alive as a possible final candidate. The difference in the position between the threat step and the Real Chess step was that 1...h5 allowed the king move, which in turn changed the safety possibilities after 2.♕f6.

If a player consistently plays Real Chess, then he has completed an important prerequisite toward becoming a good player.

11.4 Hand-waving – using principles instead of analysis

There are many quiet positions where careful analysis is not necessary. For example, if your opponent opens with 1.a4 and you don't know what to do, there are not many dangerous lines where you have to be careful not to lose material. However, later in the game, when the pieces clash, omitting the classic "If I go here and here goes there, what would I do?" analysis and choosing a move just on principle can be fatal. I call this mistake "Hand-waving." Many players think they can play chess entirely by Hand-waving and omit careful analysis even when it is required.

In the following position, after **1.fxg7+** my student admitted that he played quickly "on general principle" when some careful analysis was necessary. Black was ahead a ton of material, had only two legal moves, and enjoyed gobs of time on the clock. He only had to do a little calculation to finish the job.

Black to play after 1.fxg7+

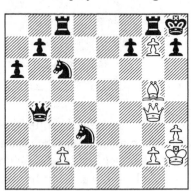

Here he reasoned, "Why expose my king unnecessarily? That would give White a dangerous discovered attack," about as good an example of middlegame Hand-waving as I could provide. So the game continued **1...♖xg7?? 2.♕xc8+ ♖g8** (other interpositions only delay the inevitable) **3.♗f6#**. Yet Black's previous play would have been completely justified after the "dangerous" 1...♔xg7:

- 2.♗h6+ ♔xh6 and White has nothing;
- 2.♗f6+ ♔xf6 ditto;
- 2.♗f4+ ♔h8 (2...♔f6 is fine also), when 3.♗e5+ is met by either knight capturing while the other guards the queen;
- Other bishop checks allow 2...♕xg4.

Yes, this takes a bit of analysis — which had to be done on the previous move to make sure that Black had a safe reply to 1.fxg7+ — but that's what it takes to become a good chessplayer. Hand-waving can only get you so far.

The endgame is an important place where careful analysis is usually required. Playing by principle can be either misleading or just downright criminal — I think you may find the following examples more on the criminal side...

235

Black to play

In this position, Black did not calculate, but remembered that, "When the king is on the seventh rank in a K+P vs. K endgame, it should go straight back," and played **1...♚f8??,** losing after **2.♔f6.** Of course, what he remembered was not a correct principle — it was what he should do when the *pawn reaches the sixth rank,* not just when the king is on the seventh, so that it would apply in positions like the following instead:

Black to play

Now 1...♚f8! is correct. *A little knowledge is a dangerous thing, but using knowledge without careful analysis can be even more dangerous.* Of course, in these easily-calculable positions you should not only rely on your knowledge, but double-check with careful analysis!

In the following position, White has 77 minutes on his clock and a 45-second increment:

White to play

White took three seconds (!) to throw away the win with **1.f5**. After **1...gxf5 2.♔xf5** the endgame is a basic draw. Instead White could have out-flanked Black's king and won easily after 1.♔d6, e.g. 1...♔f8 2.♔e6 ♔g7 3.♔e7 ♔g8 4.♔f6 ♔h7 5.♔f7 ♔h8 6.♔xg6. But obviously he was not interested in trying to calculate the best move (that's the fun of the game for me!). Want the amazing end of the story? After 1.f5? gxf5 2.♔xf5 **Black,** also with plenty of time, **resigned!** Apparently he wanted to rely on his own (faulty) knowledge as well, instead of calculating the easy draw after 2...♔g7 3.g6 ♔g8! as in the previous example.

I have given the following position, from a student's game, to several other students to see what they would do:

White to play

It would be easy to Hand-wave this position with, "White should play 1.♔xf6 because if he plays 1.exf6 he gets doubled, isolated pawns, so his winning chances are better if he keeps his pawn structure intact." It would be easy, but that's not how you play chess well — in positions like these, you should carefully analyze whether or not taking with the king or the pawn leads to the best result. As it turns out, this analysis shows the result exactly the opposite of what Hand-waving would expect:

1.♔xf6 draws: **1...♚e4** (to stop 2.f4 followed by 3.♔f6) **2.f3+** (if 2.♔xf7, then 2...♚xe5 draws easily) **2...♚f4!** and White has run out of constructive ideas.

On the other hand, the "bad" **1.exf6** wins: **1...♚d5 2.♔g5** (also winning is the cute and instructive 2.f4 ♚d6 3.♔g4! where White threatens ♔g4-h5-h6-g7 and, if at any point Black plays ...♚e6, then ♔g5 wins) **2...♚e5** (2...♚e6 3.f4 *Zugzwang*) **3.f3! ♚e6 4.f4 ♚d7 5.♔h6**, and Black cannot stop ♔h6-g7, winning the f-pawn and the game.

This is a great example of how Hand-waving in analytical positions often leads to very serious errors.

11.5 Making quiescence errors

A quiescence error is stopping too soon in analysis. The error is made when further forcing moves (checks, captures, or threats) on the following move — past the final one analyzed — can cause a meaningful difference in the evaluation.

The following is a trivial example:

White to play

White rejects 1.♕d8+ because it loses the queen to 1...♖xd8, stopping his analysis there. Of course, if he had asked if there were further checks, captures, or threats which would change this evaluation, the answer is that the simple recapture 2.♖xd8# would be quite acceptable.

From my experience in testing many players, I have concluded that the reason many inexperienced players would not allow this simple error is not due to a good thought process that minimizes quiescence, but rather their familiarity with this pattern. However, when faced with a less familiar pattern, this "mental database access" is not available and quiescence errors occur. In my *Novice Nook* column, "Classify Your Biggest Mistakes," I give the following example. The question I asked my students was, "Is 1...♗xb5 safe?":

Black to play after 1.♘e5

Many of my intermediate students said that 1...♗xb5 was safe. But if they had asked themselves after 2.♘xb5 ♕xb5, "Does White have any further checks, captures, or threats that might influence my evaluation?", then they might have noticed that the black queen was tied down to protecting the d7 square from ♕d1-d7#. That meant that any move that attacked the black queen had to be examined to see if it could continue to protect that square. Since moves like 3.c4 and even the pseudo-sacrifice 3.♖a5 win immediately, we can conclude that anyone thinking 1...♗xb5 is safe is making a quiescence error.

Note that, in the above position, other dangerous replies to 1...♗xb5 like 2.♕f3 and 2.♕h5 might be winning, so it's not all difficult to see that Black is in trouble. In fact, not only is 1...♗xb5 not safe, but Black has no good defense and is lost, e.g. 1...♖d8 2.♘c4 when the threats of 3.♘d6+ and 3.♘xb6 cannot both be met. If then 2...♗xb5 3.♘xb6 ♖xd1 4.♖xd1 axb6 5.♖a8+ is crushing. In those cases we can state, almost by definition, that it's too late for Black and no move is safe. He just has to find the best defense he can and hope that White misplays the attack.

An example of a quiescence error from de Groot "Ernie":

White to play

Suppose you think, "My queen and bishop are both attacked, so I need to move my queen and guard my bishop." So you examine 1.♕e4. To stop there and think the move is safe just because the queen is no longer attacked and the bishop is guarded would be a quiescence error because there are further forcing moves for Black which must be considered. Moreover, this thought process is also Hope Chess, since 1.♕e4 is a candidate and you did not even consider what Black might do to you after this move. After 1.♕e4? Black can play 1...d5!, hitting both the queen and the bishop at once and winning a piece.

Not all quiescence errors are also Hope Chess, although these two thought process errors are clearly related, especially at low ply (the first move and the possible reply).

The above is a "defensive" quiescence error since it misses that 1.♕e4 is not an adequate defense. Here is an example of an offensive quiescence error:

White to play

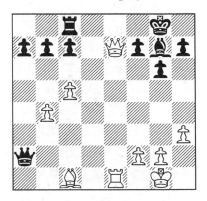

Suppose White rejects **1.♕e8+** because of **1...♖xe8 2.♖xe8+ ♗f8**. This would be a quiescence error because there are further lines to be analyzed, specifically **3.♗h6** setting up a mating net:

Black to play after 1.♕e8+ ♖xe8 2.♖xe8+ ♗f8 3.♗h6

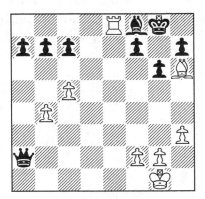

As it turns out, the best Black has is **3...♕a1+ 4.♔h2** and now either **4...♕e5+ 5.♖xe5 ♗xh6** or **4...♕g7 5.♗xg7 ♔xg7**. In either case White has a winning endgame as the rook can gobble up a queenside pawn or two.

11.6 Not asking what are *all* the things the opponent's move does

Many inexperienced players ask, "Why did my opponent make that move?", find an answer, and then stop. This in turn may be the critical mistake when it turns out that the move did multiple things and the ones they missed win the game.

As a simple example, take the following:

White to play

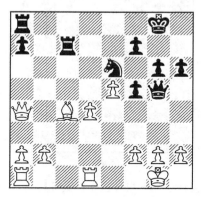

White aggressively pushes his central passed pawn with **1.d5,** attacking the knight and expecting Black to save it. When Black replies **1...♘f4,** White doesn't blink an eye, having expected the knight to move, then makes a move like **2.d6??** and finds that 1...♘f4 not only saved the knight, but also supported **2...♛xg2#.** Happens all the time! Earlier tonight (before writing this) I was giving a lesson and, in reviewing a student's game, it occurred once again:

White to play

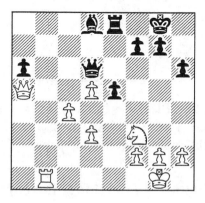

In this position White saved his attacked queen by moving **1.♛a4.** Black of course expected White to move the queen to avoid the threat from the bishop, and replied **1...a5??,** missing that in saving the queen White's move also threatened 2.♕xe8+. As I said, happens all the time...

For example:

White to play

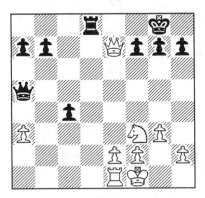

White is ahead a piece but Black's pawns can become menacing. White tries to counterattack and plays **1.♘e5**, threatening f7. Black replies with **1...♕d5:**

White to play after 1.♘e5 ♕d5

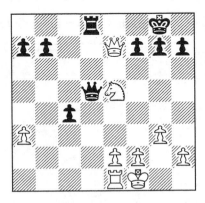

It would be easy for White to think, "I know why he made this move — Black had to defend f7," and then stop. If he did this, then he would miss the second, even more important reason for this move, which is that Black also threatens 2...♕h1#!

To White's credit, he did see the threat and decided to play 2.♘f3. Unfortunately, a few moves later after **2...c3 3.♕e5? c2:**

White to play after 2...c3 3.♕e5? c2

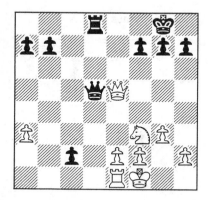

White played Hope Chess and quickly moved **4.♕xd5?** on general principles (Hand-waving), apparently believing that when ahead in material he should always trade queens. However, his sense of danger failed him; he did not look to the next move and realize that it would be very difficult to save the game after **4...♖xd5** because of the threat 5...♖d1. However, White has one final resource. Can you find it?

White to play and not lose immediately

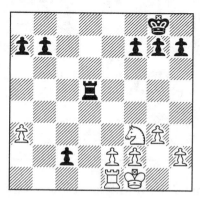

Thanks to *Rybka,* I found the correct plan: 5.♘e5! ♖xe5 (5...♖d1 6.♘d3) 6.♖c1 ♖c5 7.♔e1 and White will win the dangerous c-pawn with some chances to save the game. Unfortunately, White played **5.e3** and resigned after **5...♖d1.**

To read more about the idea of not asking what are all the things a move does, refer to the chapter "Just Because It is Forced" in my earlier work, *Everyone's Second Chess Book.*

11.7 Skipping the "Is it safe?" question

The main requisite for keeping a candidate move alive is passing the question "Is it safe?" – meaning, "Does my opponent have a forcing move (check, capture, or threat) in reply which wins material or checkmates?" If so, you either have to discard the candidate move or keep it as a purposeful sacrifice.

After **1.d4 d5 2.c4 ♘c6 3.♘f3 ♗f5 4.cxd5** a student, playing Black, had to decide on his fourth move:

Black to play

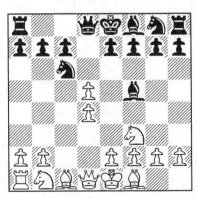

Here he decided to play aggressively and threaten a fork on c2, so he fairly quickly played **4...♘b4??.** When asked after the game if he checked to see whether the move was safe, he honestly admitted, "No, I wanted to play aggressively and go for the fork." Admirable, but hardly the stuff of legend as White calmly stopped the fork with **5.♕a4+**, winning the knight after either 5...♗d7 6.♕xb4 or 5...♘c6 6.dxc6. The best way to stop the threat was to win the threatening piece. Black should have asked himself, "If I play 4...♘b4, threatening the fork on c2, is that move safe?" and, "How can White best stop me?" The answer to both of those questions, by examining checks, captures, and threats in that order, should be to quickly determine that the only check in the position, 5.♕a4+, wins the knight and stops the threat.

An even more dramatic case was the only game I won in the second tournament I ever played in. We had already made the first time control and my opponent had plenty of time. However, he took almost twenty minutes on his move and I was quite surprised he did, for a reason that should be obvious:

Black to play after 45.g3+

After this long think, my opponent, much more experienced and highly rated than I was, played **45...♚e5??**. Instead of moving, I just stared at the board. My opponent then looked at the board as if for the first time, and his eyes grew wide when it dawned on him that I had 46.f4#! Instead of waiting for me to move, he took his fingers and flicked his plastic piece off the board with a loud "plink!", resigning.

If only my opponent had taken some of that thinking time to ask, "Is my proposed move 45...♚e5 safe? What are all his checks, captures, and threats in reply?" Had he done that and found 46.f4#, he could have played 45...♚g5 right away, instead of spending almost 20 minutes and then getting mated!

11.8 Not spending enough time on the move chosen

All chessplayers have at one time or another spent some time analyzing a critical line only to find it doesn't work, at which point another move has to be found. If the work on this rejected move has "overspent" the normal amount of time for the move, it is only natural to fall back to a safe move and play it quickly.

This is natural, but wrong. The only move that counts is the one you play, so not spending at least a reasonable amount of time on the move that will actually be played can be disastrous. I have seen a similar mistake many times in reviewing students' games (and in some of the protocols in this book): a player looks at several moves over a period of time, finally spots one he likes, and then plays it quickly. Of course, this "safe" move is often not as safe as you would like it to be.

Here's an example I made up for my online article, "Spend Time on the Move Chosen" (http://www.chesscafe.com/text/heisman107.pdf):

White to play

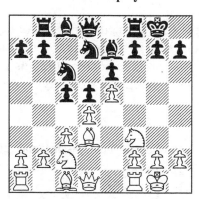

White spends time looking at the classical bishop sacrifice 1.♗xh7+ and finally concludes that it doesn't work. So instead he quickly plays the "safe" developing move **1.♕e2??**, only to find after **1...c4** that his bishop is trapped.

Therefore, a safer course is to set aside a minimum amount of time (say 15%, if possible) of the total time on the move that will be played, which should include the question, "Is it safe?" Sometimes, in time pressure, this

— like other desirable thought process habits— cannot be successfully performed, but it is a reasonable goal.

11.9 Stops selection after finding what he thinks is a reasonable move, but does not attempt to find the best move

There are many situations where finding the best move is not only difficult, but completely unnecessary. In many non-critical situations, finding "a good move" or "one of the many reasonable moves" can be perfectly acceptable. In endgame positions where three moves win, two draw, and the rest lose, it may be critical to find one of the three winners, but if they all win fairly easily then they are all equally best and trying to differentiate a #1 move is not necessary.

However, in many critical positions finding the best move (or at least moves that win, if some do) is necessary. Even strong players (such as the FM who did three protocols) fall under the influence of a good move and sometimes completely miss clearly better ones, even ones that are not that difficult.

Alas, for this example I am going to show one of my own games. I like to play an intermediate computer in a slow game "out loud" so my students can get an ongoing de Groot — they can hear my thought process throughout the game. Of course, this slightly detracts from my play, but hardly excuses the gaffe I made on this move:

Black to play: Betho(C)—Heisman 2013

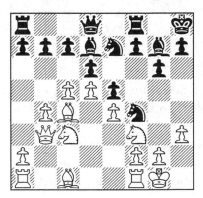

I had previously played ...♔g8-♔h8, anticipating ...f7-f5, but I still did not like it immediately due to ♘f3-g5 when ♘g5-e6 would be well protected by the battery ♕b3/♗c4/d5. So I contemplated playing 1...h6 first, but was worried about 2.c6?! bxc6 3.dxc6 (opening the battery) 3...♘xc6 4.♗f7, when I spotted 4...♕f6 with the multiple threats 4...♕xf7, 4...♖xf7, 4...♘xh3+ and possibly 4...♘xg2. Satisfied that this was at least adequate to justify **1...h6,** I played that move and sure enough the sequence followed **2.c6 bxc6 3.dxc6 ♘xc6 4.♗xf7.**

One of the things I preach is that if you calculate sequence ABC, where A is your first move, B is the opponent's move, and C is your next intended move, then if A and B do occur you don't just play C. Instead you re-analyze C and if it is as good as you originally thought, you still don't play it, but look for a better move (the theme of this section). So after 4.♗xf7 I first analyzed 4...♕f6 and was satisfied that it was as good as advertised, probably winning. Then I looked for a better move, but I could have done it more diligently. I think I looked at playing 4...♘xh3+ first and maybe one or two other ideas, but I only took 47 seconds on the move, too fast for the circumstances. So I played **4...♕f6** and won nicely in due course with a nice attack after **5.♗c4 ♘xh3+ 6.♔h1 ♘f4 7.♘b5 ♖ab8!.**

After the game, my student and I analyzed it with the strong engine *Houdini*. I was pretty embarrassed when it pointed out I could have easily won with 4...♖xf7!. The main line is 5.♕xf7 ♗e6, trapping the queen. If 5.♗xf4 first to remove the guard on e6, then of course 5...♖xf4 just wins a piece. What makes this all the more galling is that 4...♖xf7 is exactly the kind of move I normally pride myself in finding, so missing it is really aggravating, thinking out loud or not. I guess you could call this a combination of a quiescence error (11.5) and not looking diligently enough for a better move (11.9).

11.10 Uses bad deductive logic and erroneously thinks a particular sequence is likely to occur, when in fact it likely would not

I use many de Groot positions that are not in this book. One reason is that many of my students have the book and I need positions with which they are not familiar to do the exercise. In the following position, a student made an insufficient assumption during a de Groot exercise and came up with quite a bad conclusion:

Black to play: de Groot "Golden"

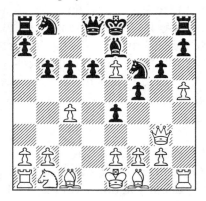

Two of Black's main candidate moves are 1...♞xh5 and 1...gxh5. After analyzing 1...♞xh5 and correctly seeing that the "sacrifice" 2.♖xh5 is the most dangerous move, my student turned his attention to 1...gxh5. But instead of analyzing a logical continuation like 1...gxh5 2.♕g7 or 2.♕f4, he started with 1...gxh5 2.♖xh5??! ♞xh5.

I expected him to quickly conclude that, unlike the promising exchange sacrifice after 1...♞xh5, the full rook sacrifice after 1...gxh5 could be ruled out. But instead he continued to assume that 1...gxh5 2.♖xh5 was the logical play, and he based his entire evaluation of the 1...gxh5 line on the consequences of 2.♖xh5. Assuming 2.♖xh5 as the move, if he had analyzed and evaluated this continuation correctly, he would have erroneously come to the conclusion that 1...gxh5 was a very good move because it basically won a rook! Of course, 1...gxh5 needed to be evaluated based on far better replies by White. All in all, a good example of mistakenly assuming a particular sequence when, in fact, the opponent would almost never play that way. When analyzing, you should assume the opponent's best and most dangerous moves; using a less-than-optimum move by the opponent will result in an evaluation that's better for you than it should be.

11.11 Overlooks an opponent's move, causing a tactical error

This is different from Hope Chess, where you don't "overlook" a move — you don't even attempt to find it (almost always one of the forcing moves: checks, captures, and threats).

Chess is a game of knowledge and skill, and if you miss a tactical pattern because you don't know it and you should, that reflects a lack of knowledge. But sometimes there are patterns that you just have to use your skill to figure out. If the move missed is a very subtle or clever one, that might not be a process error, but if the move missed is one that should have been analyzed but wasn't for some reason, that would be the cause of this error.

For example, I teach inexperienced players to ask whether their candidate move can be defeated in reply by a check, capture, or threat. If the player tries to do this, but in a haphazard manner, and overlooks a forcing move which he should have foreseen, that often may cause a tactical error.

For example, suppose in the following position that Black wishes to expand on the queenside, and his sense of danger is dulled because he doesn't see anything forcing his opponent might have — no immediate checks, captures, or threats worth parrying:

Black to play

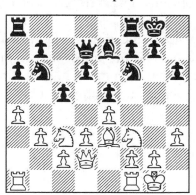

So he plays 1...♖fc8. Although White did not have a threat or tactic before this move, he does have one afterward, which makes this easier to miss. By taking away the knight's only retreat square, White can trap the unfortunate steed with 2.a5.

In the following position, White was ahead a rook and thought he had the opponent's passed pawn under control, so he thought the obvious thing to do was to force the trade of queens.

White to play

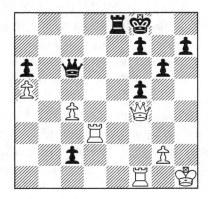

So the game innocently proceeded **1.♕d6+ ♕xd6 2.♖xd6** but when Black replied **2...♖b8!,** the move White missed, White's "easy win" ground to a halt since, amazingly, he had no good defense to 3...♖b1. The best White has is 3.♖b6 ♖d8! 4.♖bb1 cxb1♕ 5.♖xb1 ♖c8 and Black is much better. So, on the first move, White should have played 1.♕h6+ or 1.♖c1 rather than quickly going for the "obvious" queen trade 1.♕d6+?.

If you can identify which of the problems discussed in this chapter appear in your thought process and take the proper steps to minimize them, you are likely well on your way to having a much improved process. The first steps toward minimizing a problem are identifying it and being aware that it can occur.

Chapter 12

The Basics of Time Management

Next to winning, one of the most important goals of a chess game should be to use as much of your time as reasonable to maximize your thinking resource.

One of the controlling features of the thought process is *time management*. Because all serious chess games are played with a clock, managing your time wisely is an important skill. Time management is further divided into two main skills:

- *Micro Time Management* — The ability to allocate your time for each move, giving more time to moves which need it (i.e., critical moves where investing extra time is helpful) and less time to moves which don't; and

- *Macro Time Management* — The ability to pace yourself during a game to use almost all your time without getting into unnecessary time pressure.

12.1 Micro Time Management

Micro time management depends upon:

- The "normal" amount of time one should spend on a move (I call this *Trigger 2*);

- The possibility of being 100% sure you have found a "best" move before reaching Trigger 2 (I call this *Trigger 1*); and

- The awareness of how much time you have spent thinking about the move.

Breaking this down further, the normal amount of time one *should* spend on a move (Trigger 2) is based upon:

- The time control (the slower the time limit → more time can be spent per move);

- Your time remaining (more time remaining → more time per move);

- How many moves remain in the time control (more moves to play → less time per move); and

- *Criticality analysis:* the ability to identify critical moves, i.e., how important playing a best or near-best move can affect the outcome of the game (higher criticality → more time per move).

Finally, examples of what is meant by a *critical move:*

- The important strategic decisions: trading queens, where to place the king, whether to open the position, where and when to attack, trading into a king-and-pawn ending, whether the creation of an imbalance (such as a sacrifice) is worthwhile, etc.;

- Most moves in complicated positions;

- Moves that make key changes in the pawn structure, especially in the center;

- When the best move may be clearly better than the second-best move (excluding trivial recaptures); and

- The first move each game where you are no longer 100% certain you are in your opening "book" (as mentioned by both GM Alburt and GM Soltis).

The time control is a major factor. One could have the same decision on the same move number, but the proper amount of time could be vastly different based on the time control. For example, the same position on move 28 at 40 moves in 2 hours (40/2) would suggest much more time than it would on move 28 of a G/30 game.

A key point is that *reaching Trigger 1 or Trigger 2 should be the only two reasons for you to halt your thought process and make a move!* Either you have found a move which cannot be bettered or you have spent a reasonable amount of time to find a move. Once that reasonable amount of time is reached, further search will yield diminishing returns, and thus you should play the best move found up to that time (the King of the Hill — see Section 10.2). There is no other proper reason ever to stop your thinking process and make a move. If Trigger 2 is hit and the King of the Hill is completely unacceptable, then likely Trigger 2 was too short and it has to be extended.

What is the best way to know that one has reached Trigger 1? I call this the point where *you are willing to argue with a room full of grandmasters that they can't find a better move.* A couple of examples:

Example 1: A trivial recapture. Black has 1 hour and 57 minutes left on his clock to complete the game after **1.e4 e5 2.♘f3 d6 3.d4 f6 4.dxe5 dxe5 5.♕xd8+**:

Black to play after 5.♕xd8+
Arguing with a roomful of grandmasters (1)

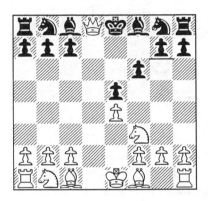

Here Black has plenty of time on his clock and thus Trigger 2 might be 30 seconds or more, but to take that much time is wasteful. Black should reach Trigger 1 quickly and play the trivial recapture **5...♔xd8** because the only alternative, 5...♔f7, is not worth further thought. I don't think anyone in that roomful of grandmasters would argue that 5...♔f7 is a better move.

This is also a great example of a non-critical move. While it *is* critical for Black to play **5...♔xd8** instead of the alternative, it is *trivially* critical since the alternative doesn't make sense. Therefore, *any time it is easy for players of all levels to see that there is only one reasonable move, by definition that is a non-critical move.* Taking more time than necessary to play such a move (e.g. to see what White will do after **5...♔xd8**) is counterproductive. Forced moves, once properly determined, should always be played as quickly as possible to preserve time for moves where there are choices.

Example 2: White has 1 minute remaining on his clock to complete the game:

White to play
Arguing with a roomful of grandmasters (2)

In this position, White has only a minute remaining to complete the game and spots the basic "stair-step" checkmate **1.♕c2+ ♔a3 2.♕b3#**. At this point it is reasonable to just play the forced mate using Trigger 1. However, suppose after the game someone steps forward and says, "Ah! But if you had just taken more time you would have found the better move **1.♗c1#** or **1.♕b3#**, since mate in one is better than mate in two."

Would it be reasonable to go in front of a roomful of grandmasters and argue that 1.♕c2+ cannot be bettered? Sure it would! There are two reasons for this:

- You can't do better than win a game, and a forced mate in two will not result in a worse result than mate in one; and

- Suppose you search for a mate in one and then, before you find it, your flag falls? That would be far worse!

So you have a strong argument that there can't be a better move than 1.♕c2+. A win is a win is a win. Is it possible some grandmasters may argue against you? Of course! But just as many might argue in your favor — the point is that you are willing to argue with the grandmasters because you have a good case.

With this arsenal in place, it is now easy to define what is meant by playing too fast and too slow!

- One plays *too fast* if making a move in less time than Trigger 2 without reaching Trigger 1; and

- One plays *too slow* if taking more time than Trigger 2.

For example, suppose you are playing a one-minute game, no increment or time delay, and have only five seconds left on your clock to make the last several moves. Then Trigger 2 becomes extremely small, so it is virtually impossible to play too fast in that situation.

Lasker's Rule: When you see a good move, look for a better one (and, if you see a better one, look for an even better one because you are trying to find the best one you can).

But *how long* should you look? How do you know when you are done?

Searching for better moves for a long period is often impractical. In many situations your clock will fall long before you can prove you have found the very best move. Instead, you should look for a better move until you have hit either Trigger 1 (the move about which you are willing to argue with grandmasters), or "t", the Trigger 2 time that is the reasonable amount to spend on that move. In time trouble Trigger 2 is always short, but the principle is the same, as in that situation thinking for only a short time is reasonable and necessary.

Average time per move

To calculate the average time to spend on a move for a game, do the following:

- Assume a conservative 40 moves to the game (the median number of moves in a game is less, but some games last *much* longer);

- Divide 40 into the number of minutes for the game;

- Add any time delay or increment.

During the game, adjust accordingly if the game looks like it will become much shorter or much longer than 40 moves.

257

Example: Suppose you are playing a 90-minute game (G/90) with a five-second time delay:

90/40 = 2¼, which is 2 minutes and 15 seconds. Add the five-second time delay, and you have 2 minutes and 20 seconds for each move in a 40-move game. Therefore, an optimum strategy is to take clearly less than 2 minutes 20 seconds for non-critical moves and to take more, sometimes much more, for critical moves.

When one examines the issue of the optimum time to analyze critical lines, one important question is, "How long should I analyze before I get diminishing returns and thus waste time?" Besides Trigger 2, there is a very helpful answer for this question with regard to sacrifices (whose consideration often requires a large amount of time!):

Continue to look at a sacrificial line so long as the reward remains greater than the possible risk, and adequate time is available.

For example, suppose you examine a line in which you sacrifice a bishop. If all you see is that you might later win a pawn, it is not worth spending time to see if that can be forced, since the reward is less than the risk. However, if you see you can possibly win a rook, then further analysis is worthwhile. Whenever the reward is checkmate, then any sequence of sacrifices is worth examining so long as there remains a reasonable chance for checkmate.

Finally, if the position remains unclear and forcing sequences cannot be resolved to quiescence (at least not in a reasonable amount of time), then your judgment becomes involved, but the overall time consequences remain the same. In this case you can probably save clock time, since – to paraphrase GM Rowson in *The Seven Deadly Chess Sins* – although your analysis gets better with additional thinking time, your judgment probably doesn't.

Here is another tip to help you decide in unclear situations:

If you are playing chess to improve, then always choose an unclear line over a clearly equal line.

There are several reasons to do this. One is that you are trying to improve your evaluation skills, and if you never play unclear lines they will always remain unclear to you. When you play unclear lines, you will start to develop a feel as to which "unclear" positions are good and which are not. Another reason is that, most non-titled players are much better on offense then they are on defense, so if you make an unclear sacrifice to get an attack (or some similar compensation), the defender often goes wrong and your practical results will improve.

Many players play too quickly, and one reason for this is that they consider few sacrifices because they think they are "losing" material. Those players tend to do well on tactical problems, but not so well on those same tactics when they occur in games! Section 9.5 has a discussion on this problem, which is usually due to quiescence errors.

12.2 Macro Time Management

Macro time management is the ability to use almost all your time every time a game goes "full course."

For example, if you are at the World Open and the first time control is 40/2, then you want to finish your first forty moves with at most a few minutes left on your clock. If you reach move 40 and have 37 minutes left, it is very likely you could have benefitted from some extra time thinking on some of your moves. On the other hand, if you reach move 21 and have only 9 seconds left on your clock (as one of my students once did!), then even with a five-second time delay you are in severe time trouble. You likely have taken much too long on some non-critical moves, when trusting your judgment sooner would have been much more effective.

How important is macro time management? Here is one way to look at this question: I estimate that if there is a typical middlegame position, and one side has only 5 minutes remaining and the other has 15 minutes (without a time delay or increment), that advantage is worth about 200 rating points. For example, suppose both players have the same rating and the position is even but the time is 15-5. Then the player with 15 minutes left is roughly a 3-1 (75%) favorite.

> If you are playing chess to improve,
> then always choose an unclear line over a clearly equal line.

It is possible to have excellent time management and have plenty of time left on your clock at the end *if* one of the players makes a gigantic mistake and resigns, thus greatly shortening the expected length of the game.

Interestingly, if one practices good micro time management then that usually results in good macro time management, but the reverse is not necessarily true. It is possible to pace yourself to use almost all of your time while misallocating more time to non-critical moves and less time to critical moves.

I once had a student who practiced exactly that reversal. He was too slow and thoughtful on close, but non-critical decisions: Where does the bishop go? Which rook to move to the middle first? Then, when the game finally got complicated and he had the extremely critical decision whether to capture a bishop with a pawn or a rook with a knight, he took the rook almost immediately, explaining, "That kind of calculation is too difficult for me, so I just used the principle, *Take the highest-valued piece.*" This "principle" does not exist, and taking the rook lost material, while taking the bishop would have won material. Thus, down material, he returned to slowly, but surely, losing his lost game, eventually using almost all his time. His macro time management was good, but his micro time management was abysmal.

However, if you allocate time correctly to each move, then your macro time management is likely good. It is also possible to practice good micro time management and run into reasonable time pressure: Suppose the game becomes critical early. Usually at some point the smoke clears and one side or the other emerges ahead, or the game becomes less complex. But sometimes, when two good players meet, the game stays critical and complex all the way through, as attack and defense both play equally well. Then it is entirely possible that the players will take more than the average amount of time on many early moves, and then have much less time than desirable to complete the game. In this case one or both players will get into time trouble, and this occurs even with strong, well-intentioned players.

Here are some tips to help your macro time management:

> Never agree to start a game at a certain time control
> unless you have the intention of using almost all your time.

- *Never agree to start a game at a certain time control unless you have the intention of using almost all your time* (assuming a "normal" game). If instead you feel like playing faster, then play a shorter time limit; playing the slower time limit when you don't have the intention of using it is simply giving your opponent an undesirable time handicap, since he/she can – and should – use that time.

- Periodically check your time when your opponent is thinking. Ask yourself, "Am I playing too fast or am I playing too slow?" and adjust accordingly. You should be consistently trying to adjust your playing pace toward the desired speed, and not, for example, "speeding up all at once" when you belatedly realize you have been playing too slow the entire game.

- Write down your time remaining (in minutes) after each move to make yourself more aware of your time situation. You can skip recording time for "book" opening moves you play quickly and, of course, for moves with less than five minutes remaining, when you generally should not be recording.

- Before the game, write "milestones" on your scoresheet for how much time you think you should have remaining at specific points in the game. This works best for time controls that aren't "sudden death," such as 40 moves in two hours. One major milestone to include is:

Botvinnik's Rule: World Champion Mikhail Botvinnik suggested that, for "normal" openings, one should not take more than 20% of the first time control to make the first 15 moves. At a 40/2 time control, 20% x 120 minutes = 24 minutes, so one should have about 1 hour and 36 minutes left on move 15.

For games with a large time increment, Botvinnik's Rule would imply that one would use less than 20% of the time control for the first 15 moves. For very short time-control games you would, on average, also use less than 20% for the first 15 moves, since in quick time controls setting aside additional time for the analytical moves which occur after move 15 is very helpful but additional time for judgment moves before move 15 is much less so.

Knowing the average time per move is not only helpful in micro time management, but also in macro time management. For example, suppose you are playing 40/2. Botvinnik's Rule would have you reach move 15 with 1 hour and 36 minutes left on your clock, leaving 96/25, or a little less than four minutes per move for the rest of the game, which should contain most of the critical moves. But if you have been playing the non-critical moves in the opening way too slowly, you will exceed Botvinnik's Rule limit by quite a bit. Let's assume you reach move 15 with only 65 minutes left. You have 25 moves remaining, so your average has decreased from the original 3 minutes per move to only a little over 2.5 minutes. If you don't adjust and speed up a little now, you will likely find yourself in time trouble.

I often get asked by slow players, "But if I play my non-critical moves more quickly, won't I either lose more games in fewer moves and/or have a worse position when I get to critical moves?" This is a good question, but it overlooks the fact that for every game you would lose more quickly, there should be many games where you win or draw later on instead of losing due to time trouble. No one is suggesting that you race through the non-critical moves. But taking 90 seconds instead of 5 minutes for moves that require judgment and not analysis should not have a strong detrimental effect on your play. Again, paraphrasing GM Rowson, your judgment does not necessarily get better as you take longer. So save the time for analytical moves, where the extra time is much more helpful!

A few years ago I was visiting the National Chess Congress, and all the sections were playing in one large room. The round started at 11 AM and was 40/2, so the first time control would be reached at 3 PM. At one point I stopped to rest next to a pillar in the middle of the room. To my left were all the high-rated sections; to my right were all the low-rated sections. I looked at my watch and it was 1 PM — exactly halfway through the first time control. One the left, almost every game was still in progress — the only seats unoccupied seemed to be players who were walking around and watching other games while their opponents were thinking. On the right, games were still being played on only about 25% of the tables! This was not a coincidence: the weaker players, on the average, had been playing much too fast.

The moral: following good macro time management is very important. *You don't want to beat yourself — you want to make your opponent beat you.* Players who play much too fast or much too slowly (these total about 80% of my intermediate students!) are at some point making unnecessarily quick decisions, and that has a very strong detrimental effect on their play. Correcting your macro time management will have a much better effect on your playing strength than learning more moves in the Caro-Kann.

Chapter 13

Beyond the Exercise

What the Researcher Learned

I have been administering the de Groot exercise for over forty years, a total of hundreds of exercises. What have I learned?

I often choose de Groot A as the exercise position and afterwards read Euwe's protocol (see Appendix A) to the student as a pristine example of how to process the position. Result: I can almost recite Dr. Euwe's 15-minute protocol by heart!

My principal findings:

Hope Chess is epidemic: Players rated below 1600 USCF/FIDE almost all practice Hope Chess — that is, they make moves without considering whether they can successfully deal with all the threats their opponents might make *next* move. To put it another way, they *often make a move without at all considering the consequences of what might happen when they do.* They even make analytical moves without a principal variation (PV) — not looking to see if their move allows an opponent a forcing reply (check, capture, or threat) that might win the game immediately. This was not a surprise; it is very difficult to have a rating that low if you have reasonable chess knowledge *and* play Real Chess.

One student e-mailed me:

I identified myself as a "Hope Chess" player when previously I had fooled myself into thinking I was largely past that phase. However, as with the weakest link, if I play Hope Chess on any move, the game is Hope Chess. Loosely analogous to 12-step programs, the first step to recovery is to admit that I am a Hope Chess player.

Yesterday's walk through my game where I had ignored many relatively simple responses (and only won because my opponent was equally lax) was a terrific eye-opener, as was the de Groot exercise.

For analytical positions, I advise students to first consider their most forcing moves as the first step in identifying candidate moves. However, many fail to realize how important this advice is, and don't systematically attempt to list these moves. Weaker players' analysis is sporadic and non-systematic, rarely covering *all* the pertinent lines, such as considering *all* their checks, captures, and threats, or possible opponent recaptures after a capture.

Lower-rated players often assume a particular recapture: After a capture that allows multiple recaptures, students often just *assume* a recapture without asking, "What are all the recaptures available, and which one would my opponent choose?"

Rarely did a weaker player consider all his captures, and rarer still did one list all the recaptures, e.g. the three recaptures (1...♞xd5, 1...♝xd5, 1...exd5) after **1.♞xd5** in de Groot A:

de Groot A
Black to play after 1.♞xd5

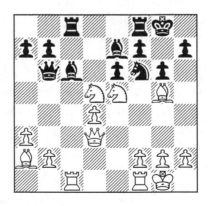

The mistaken assumption that the opponent will play the only recapture considered often leads to conclusions that prove very little. In mathematics there is a theorem that states, *Start with a false assumption and you can*

prove anything. A corollary would be, *Start with a false assumption and you are very likely to reach a false conclusion; if you reach a true conclusion, you are just lucky!* Making bad assumptions in chess analysis leads to similar failures. Strong players don't make this kind of mistake, especially in clear positions where, with a little effort, they can work out all the lines. Implementing a more systematic (but not rigid) approach would definitely benefit many weaker players.

Evaluation skills often help to identify strong players: While weak players analyze much worse than strong players, it is the *evaluation* skills that help to separate the 1900-2200 players from the international players. Grandmasters see immediately which positions are good or bad, and which are worth looking into more deeply. Players in the 1900-2200 range analyze fairly well, but arrive at much less accurate conclusions! For example, it was common that players in this range (including myself!) rejected **1.♗xd5** in de Groot A:

de Groot A
Black to play after 1.♗xd5

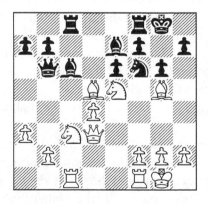

because Black can play **1...exd5** which, unlike the other recaptures, does not immediately lose material. However, to see that **1...exd5** is very good for White is much more difficult. Almost all the grandmasters evaluated this correctly:

265

de Groot A
White to play after 1.♗xd5 exd5
White is better

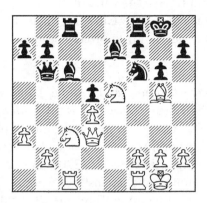

Players rated 1900-2200 typically used similar deductive logic as grandmasters to decide what is forced and what is not, and what is likely to happen. Their analysis results are not as consistently good, of course, but many times their logic is good and often they see the same lines as do the grandmasters. But when they get to the ends of the same lines, their evaluations are often faulty. For example, whereas a grandmaster might conclude, "That is good for me – if I don't find anything better I will certainly be happy with that!", the 1900-2200 player might look at the same position and say, "I am not winning any material and I don't see anything special, so I will probably play another move."

Players rated 2400+ are clearly better, but not extremely better, in analysis than the players in the 1900-2300 range. (Don't get me wrong; top players are more accurate *and* less error-prone!) *However, there is a relatively larger difference in evaluation abilities*, especially the evaluation of positions with even material. *Therefore, grandmasters and international masters are much more likely to be able to choose the best continuation among several alternatives when the most differentiating evaluation criteria of king safety and material are not big factors.* Moreover, weak players almost always value pawn structure above initiative and the entire army's activity, while strong players don't care nearly as much about the pawn structure if they can maintain a clear initiative.

Note: Although players in the 2200+ range evaluate much better, there is still a considerable difference – and thus much room for improvement – in analytical skills among lower-rated players, such that even Real Chess players in the 1600-2200 range can greatly improve their playing strength by improving their analysis skills as well. Some of the analysis mistakes in this rating range were quite striking — and that was on one single move. The cumulative effect of making this type of mistake on multiple critical moves can add up to several hundred rating points.

Rejecting trades just because they don't win material: Weaker players often evaluate "potential" tactical moves primarily on material, but non-tactical moves on positional grounds. This seemingly minor nuance often turns out to be a big mistake. For example, they will reject a capture because "it does not win material," but instead play a quiet move that often fails to force play, allowing the opponent to seize the initiative. Apparently they feel that when a capture fails to win material it fails in its primary purpose, and for that reason alone assign it a lower evaluation than a non-capture, even if the resulting material balance is the same in both cases. This is faulty logic. It is entirely possible that the capture leads to a better position than the non-capture. A part of chess skill is seeing how captures which *don't* change the material balance might prove favorable by trading your bad pieces for his good ones, eliminating key enemy defenders, improving the relative pawn structure, keeping the initiative, etc.

The percentage of players who make this "capture does not win material so it must be inadequate" mistake is very high. My conclusion is that at least some weaker players must confuse finding chess moves in games with doing chess problems. These players are always looking for forcing moves which win (as always happens in "play and win" problems). Many can't "switch gears" and realize that, in game situations, a forcing capture that doesn't win anything could be the best move, or at least a very good move worthy of their consideration.

Investigating irrelevant lines: Some players spend a ton of time looking at lines that are not forced and almost never could happen. They don't deduce, "Suppose I do this — would he really do that? And if so, what would I likely do?"

Analyzing de Groot A, one of my college chess teammates looked an astounding 40 ply (!!) or so ahead with perfect visualization, saying, "Suppose I do this and then he does that, then I will probably do this and suppose he does that and then I do this..." However, the ten minutes he took to do so were a complete waste of time because not only was the *initial* move he was contemplating not necessarily best, but none of the subsequent moves were, either. He made no attempt to show that the moves under consideration were best or forced, or why he or his opponent would play them. I would estimate the chances of that entire line occurring as less than one in a trillion – completely worthless! *It is much better to spend time analyzing moves and evaluating lines that occur early/shallow in the search and that might take place, than it is to spend time analyzing moves deep in the search that almost never could happen* – and even if such deep, non-forced lines did occur, you could always analyze them during later moves.

The de Groot exercise is intense and revealing: Most students love the de Groot exercise and consider it most revealing. A small minority find it hard to take for the exact same reason: because it so pointedly shows what they are doing wrong. As noted earlier, I once gave the de Groot exercise to a Class A player who made a clear thinking-process error that was easy for me spot due to its clear difference from what the grandmasters did. This serious error in his thought process may have been enough to prevent him from becoming an expert. However, after he was finished and I explained what he did and how that differed from grandmaster protocols, he became indignant and vociferously defended his process. Even when the exercise works and is *insightful,* unfortunately it is sometimes *inciteful!*

Evaluate and assess before analyzing new positions: Weaker players don't statically *evaluate* unfamiliar positions. I define evaluation as looking at a position and determining *who is better, by how much, and why,* and *static evaluation* as evaluation done before analysis. Many weaker players mention that one side has an isolated pawn or a weak square – one might call this an assessment – but don't conclude with *who is better, by how much, and why.* Players rated below 1800 rarely include anything similar to the following:

"The material is even, the kings are about equally safe. White has a better pawn structure, but Black seems to have more total piece activity. Since it is Black's move, I think he can take advantage of that activity, so I like Black much better."

When playing a real game, the knowledge of prior play removes the necessity of making an evaluation before each move. However, when starting a de Groot exercise, it is helpful to begin with an evaluation. Instead, weaker players often start by either making a general assessment with no conclusion or, worse, immediately searching for candidate moves. Many do not even count the material. That does not make much sense because, without an evaluation, how do you know what you might be looking for?

As a trivial example of how an evaluation is helpful, suppose you find a forced draw – would you take it? If you think that otherwise you are losing, you would probably be very happy with the forced draw. But if you thought you were winning, why would you settle for a move that forces a draw? So, *knowing which side you think is better provides meaningful goals for your analysis.*

Identify all threats before doing further analysis: Another thing weaker players should do, but don't always, is to assess the threats generated by the opponent's previous move. Since in a de Groot exercise you are *not* given the previous move, then one needs to look at *all* threats (in a real game you can often shortcut this process by primarily considering the new threats identified by the move played – see Section 10.8). The way to identify opponent threats is to ask, "Suppose it was not my turn, but again my opponent's, then what would he do?" Asking this also helps you to find all the opponent's "killer" moves, which are very strong threats that cannot be ignored (see Section 10.4). Killer moves can eliminate your candidate move from consideration if that candidate move does not meet the strong threat.

Getting fast players to slow down: Does a player who plays too quickly slow down because he:

- Acquires additional chess knowledge and has more to think about, or because he
- Knows he can play a lot better if he plays slower?

The de Groot exercises revealed that, for many, "A" is not the primary reason, although both usually apply. I rate the weight between these two as approximately 35%-65%, with reason "B" predominating. For example, suppose I teach someone "X" things they should think about every move, but they still play so fast that they could not possibly be thinking very much about those X. Then surely adding "Y" additional factors to consider so they now have "X+Y" will *not* slow them down – it might intimidate or confuse them so they are even less likely to think about the X! It is clear that, for players who do "X," Reason B is correct – they need to "buy" into the correct thinking process in order to slow down. For players who cannot do the basics (like, "When you see a good move, look for a better one"), teaching them additional things to consider during their moves gets severely diminishing, if not negative, returns.

A player's motivation to slow down often depends on how much fun the extra or correct thinking is, and how much he wants to improve and is willing to do the work. Once you are aware of what is involved, it is not magic to begin practicing a good thought process. Doing a minimal amount on every move religiously is required for high-level slow play.

Peer pressure is a strong motivating factor for players who play too quickly. Over-the-board players seem to learn to slow down better than Internet-only players because they go to strong tournaments and see all the good players taking their time! This sometimes works wonders, as most players don't want to be the first one done every round, and thus learn to "imitate" the time management of those around them.

Lower-rated players don't compare moves: Even intermediate-level tournament adults don't always follow the advice, "If you see a good move, look for a better one – you are trying to find the best move." Even in critical, analytical situations, often they just calculate briefly to see if their intended move is reasonable and, if so, then immediately make that move. This is a big mistake. *On most moves that require analysis, the goal of your thought process is to prove that you have found the best move, not to show that a move that attracts you is reasonable!* Proving that a move is reasonable is only an efficient way to find a good move in non-analytical positions, and doing so in analytical positions is a primary reason why some players play too fast.

In *Thought and Choice in Chess,* de Groot identifies four phases of the thought process of stronger players and labels them 1) Orientation to Possibilities, 2) Phase of Exploration, 3) Phase of Investigation, and 4) Striving for Proof (see Section 9.3). Weak players rarely go through all – or sometimes any – of these phases. And intermediate and weaker players almost never strive for proof. ("Proof" in this sense means that they have systematically gone through the process of showing that the move they are about to play is at least as good as any of the other candidates – that is, that *it leads by force to a position that is equivalent to or better than the other candidate moves*).

The relationship between playing strength and time management: As one would expect, as one gets stronger, the average length of time per move also increases, but this has to stop at the optimum time limit. In other words, very weak players generally – but not always – play much too fast, while almost all stronger players take roughly the same amount of time, which is all the time allowed. However, how the time is spent is not always the same. Not all levels of players spend the same percentage of their time doing analysis.

Word choice affects move choice: The words that players think to themselves often make a big difference! In Protocol E-2 the subject sacrificed a piece to win "a rook" when all he was winning was the exchange. Weaker players often make bad, aggressive moves instead of "retreating" when the retreat is simply moving back to the only safe square. Many weaker players don't want to trade queens because they don't want to "lose" their queen! Another misconception is that trades lead to drawish or uncomplicated games when, in many cases, trades might lead to much *less* drawish positions. Some of the most complicated positions are simple-looking endgames where the right sequence is buried amidst a minefield of danger.

Determining when to stop analyzing and make a move: The weaker the player, the less they understand how to end their thought process. Rather than going through de Groot's fourth stage of *Proof,* which is indicative of a strong player's process (see Section 9.3) or because of Trigger 2 (see Section 12.1), the weaker players often ended their analysis in seemingly random ways. While I could usually tell when a strong player was nearing the finish (by his/her "closing in" on the proof), weaker players often surprised me by making their move "out of the blue" for no apparent reason. On occasion, very weak players would choose moves they had not previously mentioned!

Delaying safety determination can waste time: Over the years, I have found that many players who *do* determine whether their candidate moves are safe (Step 4 in Section 9.2) do so much too late. For example, suppose a player goes through an entire thought process and then, during a sanity check just before making the move, first asks, "Is my move safe?" and then discovers it is not.

The good news is that he has caught himself in time and avoided a blunder. The bad news is that he wasted quite a bit of time and is now back to "square one" (actually Step 4).

Therefore, it is a major finding that one way to improve the thought process is to teach players to first determine the safety of their move before trying to compare safe (final) candidate moves to see which one is best. Doing it in any other order is very inefficient. In other words, don't combine Step 4 and Step 5 – as well as you can, perform Step 4 in its entirety before moving to Step 5.

Thinking out loud can affect performance: I learned the differences between a player thinking quietly during a tournament game and having to "perform" by thinking out loud:

* Some players are naturally verbal and can perform almost as well during a de Groot exercise. For others it is like pulling teeth to try to convince them to say something. Take each protocol in this book and calculate the number of lines per minute; the average will vary greatly from quite low to quite high.

* Some players could not help "showing off" for the exercise by clearly taking longer (i.e., doing more analysis) on this exercise than they do in actual play. Very few took less. Many of my students who consistently play too fast used remarkable patience when put under the microscope! Moreover, this phenomenon is not limited to de Groot exercises. During lessons, students who normally play too fast often take considerably more time to do a puzzle or find a move when it doesn't count than they do when it counts! When that happens, I usually ask, "Should you spend more time calculating a move in a lesson than you would in a tournament game?" The implication is that they *can* take their time, so doing it when it counts should be the norm.

What Players Learn from the Exercise

In addition to the lessons I learned from administering de Groot exercises, what should the average player learn? The obvious answer is all the "lessons" discussion given throughout this book that is specific to each student's protocol. Therefore, let's address the more generic learning that takes place with each exercise.

After doing a de Groot A exercise, students who listen to Dr. Euwe analyze the same position – and even subjects who used other positions for their exercise — always get an eye-opener! But, despite the imposing depth of Dr. Euwe's thorough analysis (see Appendix A), it is not terribly difficult to emulate his *process*. Thus everyone who hears this process can, and should, strive to do something similar. The harder part lies not in emulating the process, but in picking up all the extra knowledge and skills that allow one to analyze and evaluate well. It takes years of good practice and judgment refinement to be able to evaluate a position well, and more years to be able to do so with anywhere near the sophistication of a grandmaster, even if you have the capability. It does not take nearly as long to learn how to *analyze* well, but even dramatic improvement in that skill is almost always measured in years and not weeks or months, as so many players would wish.

The amount of work it takes to analyze well is much higher than most players realize, or possibly even find fun. After students listen to all the work Dr. Euwe did to find the best move, some of them wonder, "Do I really want to do all that?!" That is a reasonable reaction: *If you do not enjoy performing extensive analysis and delicate evaluation in positions that demand it, then you probably won't do it now or ever.* However, unless you change your preference, your chances of ever becoming a very strong player are likely nonexistent.

Listening to Dr. Euwe also causes many average players to realize that the gap between them and the top players is larger than previously imagined. Many players fool themselves into thinking that if they studied more openings and endgames for a few years that they could or should or would eventually move up 1000 rating points or so. I think doing the de Groot exercise is an epiphany that shows that there are more important things to do to get really proficient than just learning some new moves in the Caro-Kann or rook-and-pawn endgames. Not to say that studying openings and endgames isn't important, but how many players do you know that have played 10+ years, read 100+ books, can quote chapter and verse on book knowledge, and yet are still rated 1500 or not much higher? Without testing them, I can tell that these players have poor thinking processes, and will never get much better until they correct these deficiencies.

Finding Positions to Use for de Groot Exercises

I sometimes get asked how I find positions suitable for de Groot exercises. There are not many restrictions and the range of possible types of positions is wide, but I would suggest the following criteria make for the best de Groot exercises:

- The position has some richness, either analytical/tactical, strategic, or both.

- The range of possible initial candidate moves is fairly great. Even though it may be possible to narrow this down to a very few, the narrowing process should not be trivial.

- When giving multiple positions to a student, they should range in expectations. For example, giving all positions where a player has a winning move, or even a clearly best one leading to a good position, is counterproductive as the student will then always treat a de Groot as almost a "play and win" exercise. Instead, provide some positions where the evaluation is equal or the player stands worse and must defend.

- As per the above, a mixture of defensive problems, especially ones requiring careful analysis, is very helpful.

- Avoid too many "trick" positions where the outcome, or best move, would be surprising to a strong player. Students learning through the exercise have a tough enough time with regular, "nitty-gritty analysis" positions, and don't need ones where normal hard work will not be rewarded because the position is exceptional and the exceptions are difficult to spot.

- Present a range of positions from the opening through the endgame. Sometimes a position with a tough choice on the best way to finish development can be just as challenging and instructive as critical, complicated positions.

- Include positions with both Black and White to move. It may seem obvious that both sides should be included, but some students naturally "ally" with White in problems so it's good to "promote" both sides.

- Include positions where computers find that there are several moves that are almost equally best, as well as positions where there is one clearly best move. The latter is often expected in exercises, but including the former is more realistic and instructive – it keeps the students "honest."

With these criteria in mind, and based on actual lesson experience, I have chosen the following half-dozen positions as valuable additions to the ones given in Chapter 1:

1. Black to play

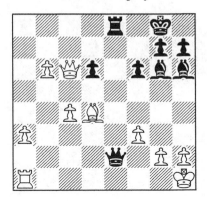

2. White to play

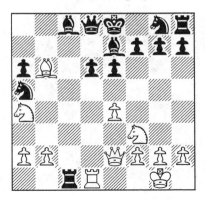

3. White to play

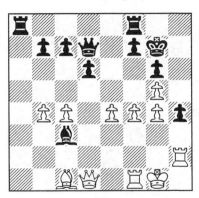

4. Black to play

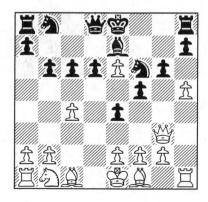

5. White to play

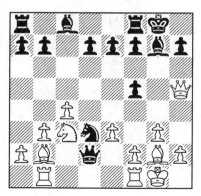

6. White to play

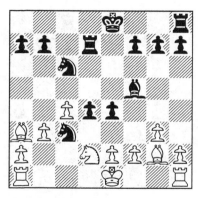

I am sure that with a little research you can generate many more positions of interest, even from your own games!

How Instructors Can Use the Exercise

I highly recommend that all serious chess instructors consider helping their students' thought processes via the de Groot exercise. Any tools which are designed to diagnose and aid the thinking process and/or time management have a powerful impact on improvement, as these two non-traditional areas are often overlooked by many instructors.

To teach the exercise, an instructor needs the following:

- A series of positions. The best positions are those with frequently occurring analytical or strategic decisions which are not easy — but not impossible — for average players;

- The ability to hear the student via live or phone lessons. Doing the exercise via email or typing on a server would be far less efficient;

- The ability to record or quickly copy down the student's thoughts;

- Some samples (such as Euwe's in Appendix A) of a good thought process.

I recommend administering the exercise no earlier than the third or fourth lesson, except possibly with very strong students, when it may be used sooner. The reason for doing the exercise at that time is because an instructor wants to spend the first few lessons trying to diagnose a student's needs and weaknesses, to make sure they have the fundamental background which would make the positions chosen meaningful, and to make them comfortable with his teaching style. The de Groot exercise is not the most interactive and is fairly intense, so performing it within the first two lessons may be doing too much too fast. On the other hand, the lessons from the de Groot exercise are so diagnostically helpful that waiting until well past the third or fourth lesson is probably putting off a good thing for too long! Therefore, doing it in about that time frame seems best.

Before administering the de Groot exercise, be careful to give the instructions as stated in Chapter 1. Failure to include even one of the instructions can be quite detrimental. For example:

- Suppose you forget to tell your student to use algebraic notation and he says, "Suppose I move the knight over there" or "I could take the pawn" – these could mean any of many possible moves, and later it will be quite confusing to try to sort out what they meant;

- Suppose you are giving a phone lesson and forget to tell the student to say "Push clock" at the end. The student says, "I think I will play ♗e4" and then the instructor initiates the post-exercise review. Later the student might say, "Yes, but I really was not finished – I was just verbalizing that I *might* play ♗e4 and then you interceded."

After these problems arose, I adjusted my instructions to include items that would preclude them from recurring. Future instructors can learn from my mistakes!

At the end of the exercise, I recommend that an instructor comment on the time taken for the verbalization, in comparison to the time control and the criticality of the position. Since roughly 80% of students at intermediate level and below play either too fast or too slowly, the time taken (roughly twice as long as it would take to do silently) should help indicate how well the student is using his time. For example, if a student took 20 minutes to make his move, that would equate to about 10 minutes in a real event, and that may be too slow or too fast.

Players who move too quickly have a tendency to slow down for de Groot exercises. This is both bad and good. But I do tell everyone to not "show off" for the exercise by doing more – or less – analysis than they would in a real World Open 40/2 game.

I recommend repeating the de Groot exercise – with different positions – every few months with each student. That way one can track progress in the areas of weakness exposed in the earlier exercises.

Between de Groot exercises, I often perform what I call a "DATSCAN" with students. This is a similar exercise, but it is "Dan-assisted thinking" where the student and I find a move *together*. That way the student has the benefit of not just hearing Euwe analyze, but doing it "live" with my help. In order to facilitate a DATSCAN, I find a recent position from a game which neither my student nor I have seen. For this purpose I often use the "finger live" command on the Internet Chess Club (ICC) to get a list of recently played grandmaster games, and then my student randomly picks a game and chooses a move number.

For example, we may pick "Linares09" and, if there are 30 games on the ICC library list, my student picks a number in that range. Once the game is selected, he may want to find White's move 23. Therefore, I forward 43 ply to Black's move 22. We reveal Black's move 22 and together try to find White's 23rd. At the finish — after we have methodically chosen our move — we see what White actually played, play over the rest of the game and, finally, give White's move 23 to a strong chess engine to compare how we — and the grandmaster — did.

Both the de Groot and DATSCAN thought process exercises are very popular with my students and get great feedback "ratings" as instructional tools.

Another View of the Thought Process

After administering a de Groot exercise, I am often asked, "What is a minimally correct thought process that can be applied to a typical slow game 'analytical' position?" The student is usually looking for something less imposing than the detailed process I presented in a Chess Café (http://www.chesscafe. com/text/heisman14.pdf) *Novice Nook* titled "A Generic Thinking Process." The following reflects my answer and will hopefully not conflict, but rather augment, the basic thought process discussion in Chapter 9.

1. After your opponent's move, ask yourself, "What are all the things that move does?" and, "What are all the moves he can do now which he could not do before?" Concentrate on your opponent's moves and ideas that can really hurt you. Obviously, if he made a check you need to get out of it, and if he made a capture you likely need to recapture, possibly next move after a *Zwischenzug* (in-between move). However, if his move is not a check or a capture, look for the *threats* it created. Threats can be found by asking, "Suppose I pass and my opponent just moves again. What could he do to me that I would not like?"

2. To begin looking for *your* move, consider moves that meet your opponent's threats and also forcing moves: checks, captures, and threats. If there

are none of consequence, plan to make your army more active, e.g. identifying your piece which is doing the least and finding a move or plan which makes it do more or, conversely, moves that restrict your opponent's activity. Another approach is to find moves that take advantage of the opponent's weaknesses or your strengths. Don't waste time on grandiose plans that are not, to paraphrase IM Jeremy Silman, both feasible and effective. Discard potential threatening moves that are easily met and leave your position worse than before. The reasonable moves you generate are called *candidates*.

3. Find the checks, captures, and threats that your opponent could reply with *after* each candidate. If he can make even one reply that you cannot survive, then your candidate should likely be discarded and is not a final candidate.

4. For each of the remaining candidates, assume that your opponent will make *his* best reply and try to figure out what (short) sequence is likely to occur. Visualize the position at the end of that sequence and evaluate it. In order to evaluate a position, it usually should be a quiet one and not in the middle of a checking or capturing sequence. For unclear sacrifices, you just have to use your experience and judgment. Do *not* make the common mistake of evaluating the position immediately after the candidate move, ignoring your opponent's possible replies, and failing to anticipate threats! If your sequence is reasonable (for both sides), the evaluation of the position at the end of the sequence will reflect how much you like that candidate move.

5. *If you see a good move, look for a better one!* After performing #4 for each candidate, compare the evaluation of the resulting position with the evaluation of the best position you have found so far, the "King of the Hill." If the new move's position is even better, it becomes the new King of the Hill.

6. Once you have finished evaluating all your candidates (or as many as possible within reasonable time constraints), your move of choice is the final King of the Hill! The sequence of moves you found for that "best" move is called the Principal Variation (PV). A PV is the sequence that *Chessmaster, Fritz, Rybka,* and other chess engines display as their top analysis line. If you see that the PV wins by force, then your current position must be winning!

7. Do a sanity check. When playing over the board, write down your move, close your eyes, and/or take a deep breath. Re-examine your move with fresh

eyes. Is it just crazy? Does it leave a piece *en prise?* Miss a mate for you or allow one for your opponent? You should not try to redo your entire analysis of the move. If the move *is* crazy, then erase it and reconsider, starting with the "second-best King of the Hill." If it is not crazy, make the move, hit the clock, and record your move and your time remaining.

Conclusion

Chess is a thinking game; however, although there are thousands of books written about chess knowledge such as openings and endgames, there are very few about the thinking process itself. The de Groot exercise provides excellent insight into a chess player's thought process. The results of the exercise not only provide a roadmap into that process, but can help to pinpoint areas of improvement for players at all levels. I hope that *The Improving Chess Thinker* not only helps to illuminate the processes used by typical players, but also provides a representative selection of my many recordings of these exercises.

Chapter 14

Additional Exercise and Lesson Tales

After all the seriousness in this book, I thought we would finish with something short and light. In Chapter 1, I provided a couple of fun and interesting stories that occurred during de Groots. Here I thought I would widen the scope and provide additional stories that happened during de Groots or other exercises and puzzles.

⬦⬦⬦

For many years, my instructions for a de Groot exercise were exactly as given in Chapter 1. They always ended, "When you are finished, say 'Push Clock!' which indicates you are finished." This worked fine for the first 1,000 or so students, well past the publication of the first edition of this book, but not for #1,001. He was rolling along in his de Groot when suddenly he said "Push Clock!"

"But sir," I protested, you pushed your clock but you didn't make a move. In a real game you can't push your clock until after you make a move."

His reply was brief but logical: "You said to say 'Push Clock' when you were done. You did not specify that I had to indicate a move before you were done, so I didn't!"

So now I have added to my instructions, "Indicate the move that you would play and then say 'Push Clock'"!

⬦⬦⬦

The following discussion took place while reviewing a game with a student. He had played White's side of a French Defense and we were in a queenless middlegame featuring an open c-file:

Me: There is only one open file, so you should now double your rooks on it.

Student: I know. (But his move is not putting his rooks on the open file.)

Me: Hmm. Why didn't you double your rooks on the open file?

Student: I wanted to do X first.

Me: Well, if you don't double your rooks on the open file, your opponent will do so first and you won't be able to oppose him.

Student: I know; that's how I lost. (!)

This story is yet another example of why some intermediate players often don't improve: they don't apply the things they already know because they are too busy doing things that are clearly less important (to stronger players).

My new student had a position in the opening where he had pawns on d4 and e4 and his opponent had pawns on e5 and d6. In this position he was ahead in development, so I suggested he play dxe5 to open lines.

However, my student protested, "But I took lessons from a grandmaster and he said that in general when you have pawns on d4 and e4 and your opponent has pawns on e5 and d6 you have a space advantage, so you should not play dxe5 because after ...dxe5 in response the pawn position is symmetric and you have lost your space advantage."

I replied, "Well, that is true *in general* but in this position you are ahead in development and need to open up the position, so that guideline, 'When ahead in development, open the position' takes precedence over the general guideline given by the grandmaster about capturing on e5."

At the end of the lesson, I asked this new student if he wanted another lesson and he said "Yes." So I suggested Saturday at 2 PM, but he replied,

"I can't do that — I have another lesson with the grandmaster." (!)

Uh-oh! I thought. I didn't realize he was *still* taking lessons from the grandmaster! Oh well, at least we can clear up one thing:

"OK, when you see the grandmaster, show him that game and see if he agrees that you should capture on e5."

Then my student made a remark I will always remember, one that left me dumbfounded:

"Oh, I *already* showed the game to the grandmaster and he also said I should have captured on e5. (!!)

I was shocked — and confused. "Then why did you tell me the grandmaster said that in general you should not capture on e5 when I said to capture?"

"Oh, well he had also said to capture and that doing so was more important than the general rule, but I was not entirely clear why, so I thought I would ask you and I thought your explanation was better." (!!)

So I felt a lot better after that...

Sometimes the student is me...

Although Penn State professor (and international master) Donald Byrne was never my full-time instructor, as an undergraduate I had the honor of going over many games with him and getting the benefit of his sage advice.

Except on one occasion.

I was showing Professor Byrne a game where I had reached around move 10 and had three candidate moves: 10.♖e1, 10.♗g5, and 10.0-0. I told Professor Byrne I was not sure which of the three was correct.

"Oh, that's easy," he said. "Play 10.♗g5!"

Now we were getting somewhere — I could learn why to play this move at this time. "So why 10.♗g5?"

"I don't know."

"You don't know? But you're a professor! Surely there must be a reason why 10.♗g5 is played in this type of situation first. How would I know if I were in a similar enough position to apply this advice?"

"All I know is that in this position you play 10.♗g5 – I can't explain it!"

So much for learning how to play those positions...

Appendix A

Dr. Max Euwe's Protocol of 'de Groot A'

The following is excerpted from *Thought and Choice in Chess* by Adriaan D. de Groot, published by Basic Books, Inc., in 1965. It has been translated from descriptive notation into algebraic notation, with a couple of explanatory parenthetical notes added:

de Groot A: White to play

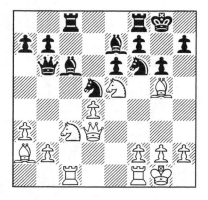

GM Dr. Max Euwe's Protocol of de Groot A
Time: 15 minutes. Date: December 15, 1938

"First impression: an isolated pawn; White has more freedom of movement.

"Black threatens ...♛xb2; is it worthwhile to parry that? It probably is. If he takes, then a3 is also attacked. Can White then take advantage of the open file? Does not look like it. Still again 2.♘xd5 and then by exchange the pawn at a3 is defended by the queen, indirectly in connection with the hanging position of the knight at f6 and possibly because of the overburdening of the bishop at e7.

"But wait a moment. No, ...♛xb2 is rather unpleasant after all because the bishop at a2 is undefended. Can I do something myself? Investigate that first: the pieces at f6 and d5 are both somewhat tied down. Let us look at the consequences of some specific moves:

"1. ♘xd5, possibly preceded by 1.♘xc6. Then (after 1.♘xc6) 1...♖xc6 is probably impossible because of taking on d5. Black has a number of forced moves; there may be a possibility to take advantage of that. It is not yet quite clear.

"Let us look at other attacks:

"1. ♗h6 in connection with f7 – but I don't really see how to get at it.

"1. b4 in order to parry the threat. But then exchanging at c3 will give some difficulties in connection with 2...♗b5 – oh, no! that is not correct, one can take back with the queen.

"So far a somewhat disorderly preliminary investigation. Now, let's look in some more detail at the possibilities for exchange: 1.♘xc6 or 1.♘xd5 or maybe 1.♗xd5 or maybe first 1.♗xf6.

"1. ♘xc6 ♖xc6 2.capture on d5; for instance 2.♘xd5 exd5 wins a pawn, but there may be compensation for Black on b2. But better is 2...♘xd5, then 3.♗xd5 ♖xc1 is nearly forced...no, it is not, he can play 3...♗xg5 as well. I see no immediate advantage. 1...bxc6 is not forced therefore, and even if it were forced you couldn't be quite certain to win. It's happened before that such a position proved less favorable than it seemed to be. The point d5 is re-inforced by it; that is a disadvantage. (Let's look at) taking on d5. 1.♘xc6 at any rate gives the pair of bishops; if I don't find anything better, I can always do this.

"1.♘xd5 ♗xd5, is that possible? d7 is free then. 2.♗xf6 ♗xf6 3.♘d7 ♛d8 can then be done. 1.♘xd5 ♗xd5 2.♗xf6 ♗xf6 will probably yield something. 1...♘xd5 is also possible, maybe better. Then 2.♗xd5 ♗xg5 and now there are the possibilities to take on c6 or to play something like f4; once again:

"1. ♘xd5 ♘xd5 2.♗xd5 ♗xg5 — no, nothing then, 3.♖xc6 is a cute move but at the end of it all everything remains hanging. Something else: 2.♗xe7 — he just takes back. 1...exd5 is very favorable (for me); he won't do that; it needn't be investigated.

"1. ♘xd5 ♘xd5 remains. 2.♗xd5 ♗xg5 3.♗xc6 ♗xc1 is then possible. No, (I) can find no way to make anything out of this. 1...♘xd5 2.♗h6 ♖fd8 3.♕f3 with some threats; if Black now has to play his bishop back to e8, then one gets a good position.

"1.♗xd5: this must be looked into. Does that make any difference? 1.♗xd5 ♗xd5 is again impossible because of ♘d7. That is to say, we will have to look out for ...♗c4, but that we can possibly cope with; the worst that can happen to me is that he regains the exchange, but then I have in any case some gain of time. 1.♗xd5 ♘xd5 ... same difficulty as before. No! That is now impossible. 2.♘xd5 wins a piece!

"1.♗xd5 ♗xd5 2.♗xf6 ♗xf6 3.♘d7 ♕d8. Let's have a closer look at that: 4.♘xd5 exd5 and I'm an exchange to the good — very strong. 1.♗xd5 exd5 is therefore forced. But that's good for White. The knight on f6 is weak and the bishop at e7 hangs — and the bishop on c6 stands badly. On positional grounds, one could already decide on 1.♗xd5.

"Is there some immediate gain? 1.♗xd5 exd5 looks bad for Black. Probably some more accidents will happen. Much is still up in the air. One plays, for instance, 2.♕f3. Defending the knight on f6 is not so easy; 2...♔g7 looks very unpleasant. Yes, I play 1.♗xd5."

Comments

Dr. Max Euwe was the World Chess Champion from 1935 through 1937. In *Thought and Choice in Chess,* thanks to the proximity of the famous AVRO tournament in 1938, de Groot was able to obtain and study the protocols of several leading grandmasters, including Alexander Alekhine, Reuben Fine, and Paul Keres, mostly on this position A. But Dr. Euwe, the math professor, has the most logical and instructive protocol. For that reason I have used his assessment as a shining example of how to think in analytical positions. Some highlights:

- Dr. Euwe's order is classic: evaluate the position, evaluate the opponent's threats, and then start figuring out if there are any forcing lines in his favor.

- He clearly uses the "King of the Hill" device, as per his statement, "...if I don't find anything better I can always do this."

- His choice of the order to examine the forcing moves is systematic and logical. 1.♘xc6 wins the bishop pair, 1.♘xd5 is a fair trade of knights, 1.♗xd5 gives up the bishop pair, and lastly 1.♗xf6 not only gives up the bishop pair, but also trades off the bishop of the color on which his opponent is weak. So the chances are that the first one he examines will be the best, and that is usually the most efficient order to analyze.

- Not only does Dr. Euwe consider 1.♘xc6 as his first capture, but he also makes a point to conclude that it is favorable to win the bishop pair and that the move is worthy of strong consideration. Although I am careful to ensure that almost all my students understand the value of the bishop pair before they do a de Groot exercise, most don't even mention winning the bishop pair, and no one has begun the "candidate" portion of his analysis with something like, "I can always start by playing 1.♘xc6 to win the bishop pair, which is worth about a half-pawn on the average. Now let's see if we can find something better..." (For IM Larry Kaufman's article about his scientific experiment to compute the average value of the pieces, see http://danheisman.home.comcast.net/~danheisman/Articles/evaluation_of_material_imbalance.htm.)

- After finding a forcing move that is better than any other, he does not need to consider non-forcing moves. Euwe understands that it is virtually impossible that a non-forcing move can be better than a move which successfully forces the opponent to make a major concession.

- At the end, Dr. Euwe makes his move even though several of his statements indicate uncertainty as to how good that move is. This shows that Dr. Euwe understands that he is trying to find the best move, not to determine (i.e., waste time figuring out) how much better that best move is than the next-best move. Dr. Euwe has calculated that 1.♗xd5 is best, but does not take the time to figure out if it is actually winning, saying, "Probably some more accidents will happen. Much is up in the air..."

Appendix B

Computer Analysis of the de Groot Positions

Most of the following analysis is provided by *Rybka* 3 multiprocessor 32-bit, at the time of the first edition the top-rated program in the world.

de Groot A: White to play

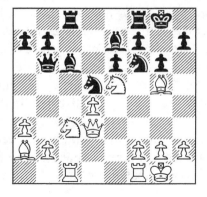

1.♗xd5

According to a deep search by *Rybka,* the second-best move — believe it or not — is 1.♕e2, e.g. 1...♕xd4 2.♗xd5 ♘xd5 3.♖fd1 with a slight advantage.

Let's consider the more common candidate 1.♘xd5. It is amazing that almost no player (among hundreds!) rated below 2000 reached the critical position that is necessary to show that 1.♘xd5 is not best: 1...♘xd5! 2.♗xd5 (attempting to remove the guard) 2...♗xg5!. For some reason it was very difficult for intermediate players to deduce that this line was forced for Black after 1.♘xd5 — perhaps they missed the discovery idea on g5 after the attempted removal of the guard on d5.

In the hundreds of de Groot A exercises performed, no one has ever noticed that if White does not move and Black plays 1...♕xb2, then 2.♘c4 might trap the queen! For example, 1...♕xb2 2.♗xf6 (the immediate 2.♘c4 ♗b5! is good for Black, as pointed out by Al Lawrence in his review of the first edition in *Chess Life* magazine) 2...♘xf6 (2...♘xc3 is also equal) 3.♘c4 ♗b5 4.♘xb2 ♗xd3 5.♘xd3 ♗xa3 5.♖c2 ♘e4 6.♘c5=. So 1...♕xb2 is not a strong threat. Even the grandmasters in de Groot's book failed to mention 2.♘c4 – not that it was all that relevant.

1...exd5

After 1.♗xd5, this pawn capture is pretty much forced: 1...♘xd5? 2.♘xd5 wins a piece as the queen and e7-bishop are both attacked, while 1...♗xd5 2.♗xf6 ♗xf6 3.♘d7 picks up the exchange.

2.♖fe1

Apparently equally effective (and preferred by *Houdini* in 2013) is 2.♕f3, with play against the dark squares f6 and e7, e.g. 2...♕d8 3.♖ce1 ♘e4 4.♗h6 removing the guard on f7 and White is pretty much winning. Also winning is 2...♔g7 3.♘g4, e.g. 3...♘xg4 4.♗xe7 and, if 4...♖fe8, then 5.♕xg4 and Black cannot regain his piece with 5...♖xe7 due to 6.♕xc8.

2...♕d8 3.♕e2 ♖e8 4.♕f3 with a winning position, though not an easy win, for White, e.g. 4...a6 5.h3 ♔g7 6.♖e3 ♖f8 7.♖ce1.

Against many of the passive defenses of b2 preferred by weaker players (1.b4, 1.♖c2, 1.♕d2), the capturing sequences started by 1...♘xc3 are at least even and sometimes even better for Black. For example, 1.b4 ♘xc3 2.♖xc3 ♗b5 3.♗c4 ♗xc4 4.♘xc4 ♕a6 with queenside play for Black. This again shows that it is better to punch first than to wait until your opponent punches you!

de Groot B: Black to play

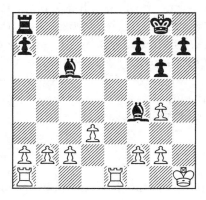

Without computers, de Groot was handicapped in his analysis of most positions. He wrote about position B, "An objective solution to this position cannot be given." In both B and C there were important errors in his possible "truth" of the position. For example, here he presented a main line of play as **1...♖b8 2.b3 ♖b5 3.c4 ♖g5 4.f3 h5 5.gxh5 ♖xh5+ 6.♔g1 ♗e5 7.♖ad1 ♗d4+ 8.♔f1 ♖h1+ 9.♔e2 ♖h2.** But White has a couple of important improvements retaining a winning advantage. For example, White can play 4.d4 instead of guarding g4 with 4.f3?!, with the idea that 4.d4 ♗xg4 5.d5 is worth a pawn as it protects against the kingside attack, blocks the bishop out of the game, and gets the pawns rolling. Even after the less effective 4.f3 h5 5.gxh5 ♖xh5+ 6.♔g1 ♗e5, White can sacrifice with 7.♖xe5 ♖xe5 8.♔f2, although this line is less clear.

de Groot C: Black to play

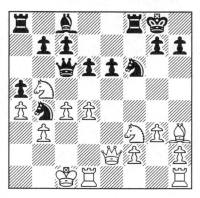

In position C, de Groot suggests Black should play **1...e5 2.♗xc8 ♖axc8** with the two main lines of continuation **3.♘a7** and **3.dxe5.** *Rybka* suggests that Black has at best a fight for equality with 1...♘e4 or possibly the passive 1...h6 or 1...♖e8. The key contention occurs in the long forcing line after **1...e5 2.♗xc8 ♖axc8 3.dxe5 ♕e4 4.♖he1 ♕xe2 5.♖xe2 ♘g4 6.exd6 ♖xf3 7.d7 ♖d8 8.♖e8+ ♖f8 9.♘xc7 ♘xf2.** Here de Groot bases his defense on White's playing **10.♖xf8+** but the computers greatly prefer 10.♖d4 with a nice edge for White, and so 1...e5 is not as good as he thought.

de Groot Shafritz: White to play

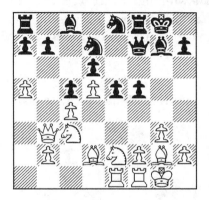

Unlike most of the other exercises in this book, de Groot Shafritz does not feature much friction between the forces, and thus is more strategic than analytical in nature. I played Black and had fallen behind in development. During the game I realized that White would be better if he found the only dangerous continuation, **1.f4 e4 2.g4!,** taking advantage of the rooks' excellent position on the kingside. No other plan would do, as waiting even one move would allow Black to guard g4 with a move like 1...♘df6 and the danger would pass. Interestingly, it seems like *this problem is a good one to separate experts from masters,* as in my small sample the experts did not see that 1.f4 followed by 2.g4 was the panacea, while some masters did. In the game, White played the cautious 1.♘d1(?), and after 1...♘df6, Black was almost equal and went on to win in fine style:

Shafritz, Arnold (1900) – Heisman, Dan (2285)
Main Line CC Champ G/75 (rd.3), Oct 22, 2002

1.d4 ♘f6 2.c4 g6 3.♘c3 ♗g7 4.e3 0-0 5.g3 d6 6.♗g2 ♘bd7 7.♘ge2 e5 8.0-0 c6 9.♕b3 ♕e7 10.♗d2 ♘b6 11.d5 c5 12.a4 ♘e8 13.e4 f5 14.a5 ♘d7 15.exf5 gxf5 16.♖ae1 ♕f7 (de Groot Shafritz occurs here) **17.♘d1** (17.f4! e4 18.g4! and White is much better, e.g. 18...♗d4+ 19.♔h1 ♕g7 20.♗c1 ♕xg4 21.♗xe4) **17...♘df6 18.♔h1** (18.f4! is still best but not as powerful as before) **18...♕h5 19.♗f3** (White is still a little better after 19.♘e3 or 19.f3) **19...♘g4 20.♗xg4 fxg4 21.♘g1?** (White can maintain equality with 21.♘ec3 ♕f5) **21...♘f6 22.♕e3 ♗f5 23.♘c3 ♖f7 24.♕g5?** (preferable is 24.♘ge2 when Black is better but not winning) **24...♕xg5 25.♗xg5 ♗d3 26.♗xf6 ♗xf6 27.♘e4 ♗e7 White resigns.** One possible continuation would be 28.b3 ♖b8 29.f4 b5 30.axb6 ♖xb6 31.♘d2 ♗xf1 32.♖xf1 exf4 33.♖xf4 ♖xf4 34.gxf4 ♖a6, etc.

de Groot Zyme: White to play

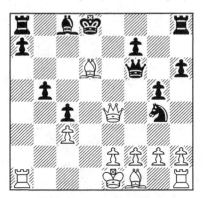

Here Black has strong threats, e.g. 1.♕xa8?? ♕xc3+ 2.♔d1 ♘xf2# (a move often missed by weaker players who instead spot 1...♕xa1+ first and never look for a better move). Whenever the opponent has a threat of a forced mate, one must either mate the other player first or stop the mate, which sharply narrows White's possibilities. Passive defenses of both c3 and f2 are possible, e.g. 1.♕d4 or 1.♕f3. However, the proper defense is the forcing deflection **1.♗e7+!** ♕xe7 when White can now safely capture the rook with 2.♕xa8 or, even better, throw in the *Zwischenzug* **2.♖d1+ ♔e8 3.♕xa8** with a much better game. In order to play 1.♗e7+ it is *not* necessary to figure out whether 2.♖d1+ or 2.♕xa8 is better, since either one leads to a game far superior to White's alternatives on move 1. Therefore, the proper thought process strategy is to determine that 1.♗e7+ is the correct move and, at that point, play it, and then next move decide on the best way to take advantage of the situation.

In 2011 the strong engine *Houdini* found the amazing resource **1.♗b4!?**, which it considered slightly stronger than 1.♗e7+. *Houdini*'s best play for both sides runs **1...♕xf2+ 2.♔d1 ♔c7** (2...♘e3+ 3.♔d2 is even worse for Black) **3.♕e7+** (3.♕xa8?? ♖d8+ mates in 8 for Black) **3...♗d7 4.♕d6+ ♔c8 5.♕a6+ ♔d8 6.♕b7 ♖c8 7.♖xa7 ♕f5 8.e4 ♕e6 9.♔c1 ♕c6 10.♕xc6 ♖xc6 11.♗e2 ♘e5 12.♖d1,** with continued pressure and the bishop pair more than making up for the one-pawn deficit.

de Groot Ernie: White to play

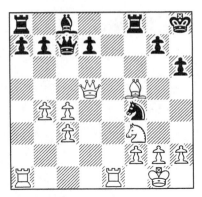

According to a *Rybka* deep search, the best line for both sides is **1.♕d4! ♖xf5 2.♖e8+ ♔h7 3.♖e7!** (3.♕e4?! d5! with counterplay) **3... ♖f7! 4.♖ae1** (4.♖xf7?? ♘e2+ wins the queen) **4...♖xe7** (also insufficient is 4...♘h3+!?, a computer desperation move to clear f4 for the queen: 5.gxh3 ♕f4 6.♖xf7 ♕xf7 7.♘h4 with a big initiative for White) **5.♖xe7 ♘e6 6.♕e4+! ♔g8 7.♕xe6 fxe6 8.♖xc7,** which leads to a clearly winning endgame for White.

Other reasonable tries are 1.♕e5 ♕xe5 2.♖xe5 d6 3.♗xc8 (forced) 3... dxe5 4.♗xb7 with a nice advantage for White, and 1.♕a5 ♕xa5 2.♖xa5 b6 3.♗e4 (the move I missed when presented with this interesting position), and again White retains a nice advantage. One common error was 1.♕e4?? to save the queen and guard the bishop, but then 1...d5! and Black wins a piece.

The tricky and attractive 1.♕f7? fails to 1...♕d8 2.♘e5 d6 3.♗xc8 dxe5 and, due to the attack on the white queen, the bishop on c8 falls.

Glossary

Activity
The amount of beneficial things that a piece (or pieces) can do in a given position.

Amateur
In chess, a non-master. At the U.S. Amateur, masters may not play. At the U.S. Amateur Team tournaments, the average rating of the team members must be below master. (Note: in chess, amateurs can win money, sometimes quite a bit at tournaments like the World Open.)

Analysis
The part of the thought process where you generate the move tree, e.g., "If I go there, what would he do?"

Analytical position
A position where analysis is required to figure out which move to play. This would include all positions with potential tactics, dangerous forcing moves, etc. See "Non-analytical position."

Back rank
The rank where a player sets up his major pieces (first for White; eighth for Black)

Bishop pair
(The advantage of the...) This is possessed when one player has two bishops and the other does not.

Book
Besides the kind with a spine, a "book" move is one that a player has learned to make in a particular position in the opening (from a "book" or other media) without the need to "calculate." The set of book moves in a certain opening before a major deviation forms a *tabiya*.

Blunder
A bad move; primarily a move that turns a win into a loss or draw, or a draw into loss. Note that *any* bad mistake

is a blunder — not just a counting mistake, or falling into another tactic.

Break move
A pawn move attacking an opponent's fixed pawn (thus forcing the possible "breakup" of his pawn structure). Also known as a "pawn break."

Calculation
The part of analysis involving forced sequences.

Candidate (move)
A move under consideration (during the thought process). Here are some special types of candidates:

- King of the Hill — the best candidate found so far
- Initial Candidate — any move which does something positive
- Final Candidate — a candidate which is safe (cannot be easily defeated by a forcing move)

Closed file
A file with pawns belonging to both sides.

Closed position
A position without any open or semi-open files.

CM
Candidate Master — A FIDE title for those with FIDE ratings between 2200 and 2299.

Coordination
The ability of various pieces to work together harmoniously to achieve a goal.

Counting
Determining if pieces are safe from capturing sequences; analyzing to see if any forced sequence of captures on any square or squares will gain or lose material.

Critical move
A move in a position where the best move (or moves) is (are) better enough than the second best to make a difference (win to draw or loss; draw to loss; easy win to difficult win). The exceptions are "only" recaptures where only one piece can recapture; these are, by definition, non-critical. Critical moves often include complicated decisions, trading pieces, or inflexible plans that cannot

be changed. Critical moves should be played carefully and slowly.

Criticality assessment The ability to determine from a position how crucial it is to determine the best move(s) (i.e., their effect on the possible outcome).

De Groot exercise A "think out loud" exercise where a player is given a position and asked to find a move as if he were playing a normal slow game, except he is verbalizing his thoughts. De Groot positions are not "problems" with a defined goal, but rather just normal chess positions from games where there may be no clear "solution."

Discovered attack An attack by a piece that was opened up as the result of another piece's move (also called a "discovery").

Discovered check A discovered attack where the discovered piece also gives check.

Discovery See "Discovered attack."

Double attack An attack on two (or more) pieces by a single move.

Double check A discovered check where the discovering and the discovered piece both deliver check. In that case, the opposing king must move.

Doubled pawns Two pawns of the same color on the same file as a result of a capture.

En passant The capture of a pawn that moved two squares by a pawn that could have captured it had the advancing pawn moved only one square. This may occur on the next turn only.

En prise "In take" — able to be captured for free. A piece is *en prise* if it can be captured but is not guarded. Pronounced "aan-preez."

Evaluation   The part of the thought process performed at analysis nodes (moves that generate positions) which asks, "Who stands better, by how much, and why?"

Exchange (the) Trading a bishop or a knight for a rook is *winning the exchange*. Losing a rook for a bishop or a knight is *losing the exchange*. This is *not* the same as trading pieces. For example, losing a queen for a rook is not losing the exchange; the exchange refers only to trading a bishop or knight for a rook.

Expert   A player with a U.S. Chess Federation rating between 2000 and 2199.

Fianchetto   To develop a bishop on a long diagonal behind a knight's pawn (b2 or g2 for White; b7 or g7 for Black).

FIDE   Acronym for the *Fédération internationale des échecs,* the French name for the World Chess Federation.

FIDE Master (FM) A player with an international chess title below International Master but above the lowest title, Candidate Master. It requires a minimum FIDE rating of 2300.

File   The rows of a chessboard going up and down, lettered a-h (lower case), with "a" always on White's left (and Black's right).

Flexibility   The capability of a piece or entire army to do multiple good things. A lack of flexibility is rigid and generally very bad.

Flip-Coin Chess A type of thought process used by beginners in which they make their move without even checking the threats made possible by the opponent's previous moves. The results of games between flip-coin players are somewhat random, like flipping a coin.

Forcing moves   Checks, captures, and threats.

Fork   A double attack, usually by a knight or a pawn (thus form-ing a pattern like a "fork" in the road).

Grandmaster (GM) A player with the highest title in international chess.

Hand-waving   Using general principles to find a move in an analytical position. This is often a serious error since careful analysis is usually required in such positions.

Hole   An opponent's weak square on his side of the board which can be occupied by an attacking piece.

Hope Chess   Making a move without considering whether a possi-ble reply by the opponent involving a check, capture, or threat can be met.

                     Hope Chess is *not* these other "Hope" possibilities:

                     •   When you make a threat and hope your opponent does not see it
                     •   When you make a bad move on purpose but hope your opponent makes a worse one
                     •   When you make an unanalyzed move quickly and hope that the move/idea/maneuver works anyway

Houdini   The highest-rated computer chess engine at the time of this second edition.

Increment   Time (in seconds) added to a player's clock for each move. For example, in the Team 45 45 League the time control is 45 45, meaning that each player gets 45 minutes for the game plus 45 seconds added for each move. Compare to "time delay" (see definition below).

Initiative   When your opponent is constantly responding to your forcing moves (checks, captures, and threats).

International Master (IM) The second highest FIDE title, just below grand-master.

Internet Chess Club (ICC) A leading chess server and owner of the ICC Chess. FM radio station.

Isolated pawns   Pawns that have no other pawns of the same color on ad-jacent files.

Judgment position   See "Non-analytical position."

King of the Hill   The best candidate move found so far during analysis. The move which creates the position for which you are trying to find another move that creates a better position.

Lasker's Rule   If you see a good move, look for a better one (because you are trying to find the best move you can in a reasonable amount of time).

Master   A player with a U.S. Chess Federation rating between 2200 and 2399 is a national master (NM).

Material   **Piece value** – when you win a pawn, a piece, or the ex-change, you are winning "material." On the average, the knight and bishop are worth 3.25 pawns, the rook 5 pawns, and the queen 9.75 pawns, with the king having a fighting value of about 4 pawns. Give yourself a bonus of 0.5 pawns if you have the advantage of the bishop pair.

Mobility   The number of moves a piece has. Sub-types:

- potential mobility – the number of moves a piece could make from a given square if the board were empty
- actual mobility – the number of moves a piece can make in any given position
- global mobility – the number of future squares a piece can land upon in any given position, given multiple moves.

Non-analytical position A position in which judgment, rather than analysis or calculation, can be used to select a move. These are "quiet" positions, such as those arising early in the game where the opponent has no dangerous forcing moves to consider in reply. Also known as a "judgment position."

Notation   The recorded moves of a game. Not used as a verb: you don't "notate" a game — you record it.

Null move   An analysis technique which assumes a player "passes" (makes no move) for the purpose of determining the threat of the previous move.

Open file   A file where there are no pawns of either color.

Outpost   A piece occupying a hole (see "Hole" above) and guarded by a pawn.

Pawn chain   A series of pawns on contiguous files, usually where most of the pawns are protecting each other.

Pawn structure   How the pawns for each side are currently arranged on the board.

Pin   An attack by a rook, bishop, or queen on a piece that cannot/should not move because a piece behind the attacked piece along the line of attack is worth even more. If the piece behind is a king, this is called an "absolute" pin and the piece is not allowed to move, lest it put the king into check, which is illegal.

Ply   A half-move, or the move of one player. When both players move, that is "two ply," or one full move.

Promote   What a pawn does when it reaches the other side of the board. The moving player replaces it with a queen, rook, bishop, or knight on the promotion square. Therefore, a player can have a maximum of nine queens.

Protocol   The transcript of a "think out loud" exercise, containing the entire thought process used to find a move.

Quiescence error   The error of stopping analysis too soon (thinking that the resultant position is "quiet") when there are further forcing moves which may possibly affect the evaluation of the sequence.

Rank   The rows of a chessboard going sideways, numbered first to eighth starting from the rank closest to White as the first rank. White's pieces start out on the first rank; Black's, on the eighth.

Rating   A quantitative measure of skill. USCF ratings range from roughly 0 (basically impossible to get this low — no one ever has) up to 3000; most scholastic beginners start around 400. Even if you lose all your games in your first few tournaments you are still usually rated about 200. "Rating" is different from *ranking,* which places players in some sort of top-bottom order. For example, a rating of 2800 would usually have a player ranked first.

Real Chess   The highest generic type of thought process: for every move, you consider whether a possible reply by the opponent involving a check, capture, or threat can be met. Compare to the lower Hope Chess and the lowest Flip-Coin Chess.

Removal of the guard   A chess tactic where the defender of a piece or square is captured or forced to move so that it is no longer defending it. The two main types are "deflection" and "overworked piece."

Round robin   A system for pairing players where everyone in the same (small) section plays everyone else. Unlike a Swiss system, this type of tournament calls for some level of commitment on the part of the players to attempt to complete all of their games. The number of rounds in a single round robin is the number of players minus one.

Rybka	The best PC-based chess playing program in 2006-09.
Semi-open file	A file on which only one side has pawns. Also known as a "half-open file."
Skewer/X-ray	Tactical Motif: sort of an inside-out pin. A move that attacks a piece of value, and behind it along the line of attack there is a piece (of equal or lesser value) that will be attacked anyway if the attacked piece moves.
Slow chess	Chess played at long enough time controls such that good moves are generally more important than the time remaining.
Tactics	A forcing sequence of moves that involves piece safety and checkmating. In increasing level of complexity, this includes:

- *En prise* (can take a piece for free)
- Counting (is each piece safe for potential captures on its current square?)
- Motifs (pins, double attacks, removal of the guard, etc.)
- Non-sacrificial combinations of motifs
- Sacrificial combinations

Tempo	Italian word, used to indicate the "time" it takes for one of the players to make one move. For example, moving a knight from g1 to e5 might take two tempi (♘f3-g5).
Threat	A move which can win material, deliver checkmate, or make progress *next move* if the opponent does not stop it. Attacks on under-defended pieces are an example of a threat.
Time control	How much time one has for a whole game. "G" means all the moves and "SD" is sudden death, meaning that the time control requires that all the remaining moves must be played within a certain amount of time (on each player's clock).

In USCF over-the-board notation, one uses a slash for moves/time: "40/2; SD/1" is 40 moves in 2 hrs (hours) followed by the remaining moves in 1 more hr; "G/30" means all moves in 30 min.

Online, the two numbers are minutes per game and seconds incremented. Thus, "60 5" is one hour for the game plus 5 additional seconds per move.

Time delay The preferred way of using a chess clock at a USCF tournament; a digital clock is set to *not* run for the first N (usually 5) seconds on each move. Time is not added, as it is with a time increment.

Time increment See "Increment."

Time management The skill where, when done correctly, you aim for two goals:

- To spend almost all of your time allotted for the game ("macro time management"), and
- To spend more time on moves that require it (critical, complicated, etc. – "micro time management"). See the two move "Triggers" below.

Trade To exchange one piece for another of the same or similar value. *Not* the same as "the exchange."

Trigger 1 Finding a move such that there can't be a better one (thus triggering a player to make that move).

Trigger 2 A reasonable amount of time to make a move, given the position, the time control, the time left on the clock, and possibly the move number.

Two bishops Short for "The advantage of the two bishops." (See "Bishop pair.")

USCF United States Chess Federation

Weak square   A square which can no longer be guarded by a pawn.

Zugzwang   German word indicating a situation when you have to
                make a move, but any move is bad for you. Note: Some
                contend it is not true *Zugzwang* unless your opponent
                could not win without this compulsion (in other words, if
                you could pass but your opponent can still win, then al-
                though any move is bad for you it is not a true *Zugzwang)*.

Bibliography

Books

Aagaard, Jacob. *Inside the Chess Mind*. Everyman Chess (London), 2004.

Alburt, Lev and Lawrence, Al. *Chess Rules of Thumb*. Chess Information and Research Center (New York), 2003.

Bain, John. *Chess Tactics for Students*. Learning Plus, Inc. (Corvallis, OR), 1993.

de Groot, A.D. *Thought and Choice in Chess*. Basic Books, Inc. (New York), 1965.

Heisman, Dan. *Elements of Positional Evaluation* (3rd ed.). Chess Enterprises (Moon Township, PA), 1999.

Heisman, Dan. *Everyone's Second Chess Book*. Thinker's Press, Inc. (Davenport, IA), 2005.

Heisman, Dan. *Looking for Trouble*. Russell Enterprises, Inc. (Milford, CT), 2003.

Heisman, Dan. *The Improving Annotator: From Beginner to Master*. Mongoose Press (Newton Highlands, MA), 2010.

Kotov, Alexander. *Think Like a Grandmaster*. Chess Digest, Inc. (Dallas), 1971.

Krogius, Nikolai. *Chess Psychology*. Alfred Kalnajs (Chicago), 1972.

Lasker, Emanuel. *Common Sense in Chess*. Dover Publications (New York), 1965.

Meyer, Claus Dieter and Müller, Karsten. *The Magic of Chess Tactics*. Russell Enterprises, Inc. (Milford, CT), 2002.

Nunn, John. *John Nunn's Chess Puzzle Book.* Gambit Publications Ltd. (London), 1999.

Rowson, Jonathan. *The Seven Deadly Chess Sins.* Gambit Publications Ltd. (London), 2000.

Rowson, Jonathan. *Chess For Zebras.* Gambit Publications Ltd. (London), 2005.

Silman, Jeremy. *Silman's Complete Endgame Course.* Siles Press (Los Angeles), 2007.

Soltis, Andrew. *Catalog of Chess Mistakes.* David McKay Company, Inc. (New York), 1979.

Soltis, Andrew. *Finding a Good Chess Move.* B.T. Batsford Ltd. (London), 2004.

Soltis, Andrew. *The Wisest Things Ever Said About Chess.* B.T. Batsford Ltd. (London), 2008.

Articles/Columns

Heisman, Dan. "Novice Nook," www.chesscafe.com.

Heisman, Dan. "The Thinking Cap," www.jeremysilman.com.

Kaufman, Larry. "The Evaluation of Material Imbalances," *Chess Life,* March 1999.

About the Author

Dan Heisman attended Caltech and Penn State, receiving a Master's degree in Engineering Science. In 1972, his team won the U.S. Amateur Team Championship. He won the Philadelphia Closed Invitational Championship in 1971 and the Philadelphia Open Championships in 1971 and 1976. Mr. Heisman holds the titles of National Master from the U.S. Chess Federation and Candidate Master from FIDE, the international chess federation. He is also a USCF Senior Tournament Director.

Since 1996, Mr. Heisman has been a full-time chess instructor and author. His other 10 chess books include *Elements of Positional Evaluation, Everyone's 2ⁿᵈ Chess Book, A Parent's Guide to Chess, Looking for Trouble, Back to Basics: Tactics, The World's Most Instructive Amateur Game Book, A Guide to Chess Improvement,* and *The Improving Annotator.*

Mr. Heisman's *Novice Nook* column at Chess Café has won the Chess Journalists of America's award for Outstanding Column in any Media three times, and has been selected six times by that organization for Best Instruction. In 2010 the CJA voted him Chess Journalist of the Year. Mr. Heisman's question-and-answer show aired weekly on the Internet Chess Club's (ICC) Chess.FM radio station from 2001 through 2008. A similar web television show, "Q&A with Coach Heisman," began in 2012 on Chess.com TV. Mr. Heisman has recorded over 220 instructional videos for the ICC.

Radio personality Howard Stern was one of his many students. Mr. Heisman currently lives with his wife Shelly in Wynnewood, Pennsylvania, and can be contacted via his website, www.danheisman.com.